MW01680153

## TABLE OF CONTENTS

## Secret Key #1 - Time is Your Greatest Enemy

### Pace Yourself

Wear a watch. At the beginning of the test, check the time (or start a chronometer on your watch to count the minutes), and check the time after every few questions to make sure you are "on schedule."

If you are forced to speed up, do it efficiently. Usually one or more answer choices can be eliminated without too much difficulty. Above all, don't panic. Don't speed up and just begin guessing at random choices. By pacing yourself, and continually monitoring your progress against your watch, you will always know exactly how far ahead or behind you are with your available time. If you find that you are one minute behind on the test, don't skip one question without spending any time on it, just to catch back up. Take 15 fewer seconds on the next four questions, and after four questions you'll have caught back up. Once you catch back up, you can continue working each problem at your normal pace.

Furthermore, don't dwell on the problems that you were rushed on. If a problem was taking up too much time and you made a hurried guess, it must be difficult. The difficult questions are the ones you are most likely to miss anyway, so it isn't a big loss. It is better to end with more time than you need than to run out of time.

Lastly, sometimes it is beneficial to slow down if you are constantly getting ahead of time. You are always more likely to catch a careless mistake by working more slowly than quickly, and among very high-scoring test takers (those who are likely to have lots of time left over), careless errors affect the score more than mastery of material.

## Secret Key #2 - Guessing is not Guesswork

You probably know that guessing is a good idea - unlike other standardized tests, there is no penalty for getting a wrong answer. Even if you have no idea about a question, you still have a 20-25% chance of getting it right.

Most test takers do not understand the impact that proper guessing can have on their score. Unless you score extremely high, guessing will significantly contribute to your final score.

### Monkeys Take the Test

What most test takers don't realize is that to insure that 20-25% chance, you have to guess randomly. If you put 20 monkeys in a room to take this test, assuming they answered once per question and behaved themselves, on average they would get 20-25% of the questions correct. Put 20 test takers in the room, and the average will be much lower among guessed questions. Why?

1. The test writers intentionally write deceptive answer choices that "look" right. A test taker has no idea about a question, so picks the "best looking" answer, which is often wrong. The monkey has no idea what looks good and what doesn't, so will consistently be lucky about 20-25% of the time.
2. Test takers will eliminate answer choices from the guessing pool based on a hunch or intuition. Simple but correct answers often get excluded, leaving a 0% chance of being correct. The monkey has no clue, and often gets lucky with the best choice.

This is why the process of elimination endorsed by most test courses is flawed and detrimental to your performance- test takers don't guess, they make an ignorant stab in the dark that is usually worse than random.

### $5 Challenge

Let me introduce one of the most valuable ideas of this course- the $5 challenge:

*You only mark your "best guess" if you are willing to bet $5 on it.*
*You only eliminate choices from guessing if you are willing to bet $5 on it.*

Why $5? Five dollars is an amount of money that is small yet not insignificant, and can really add up fast (20 questions could cost you $100). Likewise, each answer choice on one question of the test will have a small impact on your overall score, but it can really add up to a lot of points in the end.

The process of elimination IS valuable. The following shows your chance of guessing it right:

| If you eliminate wrong answer choices until only this many remain: | Chance of getting it correct: |
|---|---|
| 1 | 100% |
| 2 | 50% |
| 3 | 33% |

However, if you accidentally eliminate the right answer or go on a hunch for an incorrect answer, your chances drop dramatically: to 0%. By guessing among all the answer choices, you are GUARANTEED to have a shot at the right answer.

That's why the $5 test is so valuable- if you give up the advantage and safety of a pure guess, it had better be worth the risk.

What we still haven't covered is how to be sure that whatever guess you make is truly random. Here's the easiest way:

*Always pick the first answer choice among those remaining.*

Such a technique means that you have decided, **before you see a single test question**, exactly how you are going to guess- and since the order of choices tells you nothing about which one is correct, this guessing technique is perfectly random.

This section is not meant to scare you away from making educated guesses or eliminating choices- you just need to define when a choice is worth eliminating. The $5 test, along with a pre-defined random guessing strategy, is the best way to make sure you reap all of the benefits of guessing.

# Secret Key #3 - Practice Smarter, Not Harder

Many test takers delay the test preparation process because they dread the awful amounts of practice time they think necessary to succeed on the test. We have refined an effective method that will take you only a fraction of the time.

There are a number of "obstacles" in your way to succeed. Among these are answering questions, finishing in time, and mastering test-taking strategies. All must be executed on the day of the test at peak performance, or your score will suffer. The test is a mental marathon that has a large impact on your future.
Just like a marathon runner, it is important to work your way up to the full challenge. So first you just worry about questions, and then time, and finally strategy:

### Success Strategy

1. Find a good source for practice tests.
2. If you are willing to make a larger time investment, consider using more than one study guide- often the different approaches of multiple authors will help you "get" difficult concepts.
3. Take a practice test with no time constraints, with all study helps "open

book." Take your time with questions and focus on applying strategies.
4. Take a practice test with time constraints, with all guides "open book."
5. Take a final practice test with no open material and time limits

If you have time to take more practice tests, just repeat step 5. By gradually exposing yourself to the full rigors of the test environment, you will condition your mind to the stress of test day and maximize your success.

## Secret Key #4 - Prepare, Don't Procrastinate

Let me state an obvious fact: if you take the test three times, you will get three different scores. This is due to the way you feel on test day, the level of preparedness you have, and, despite the test writers' claims to the contrary, some tests WILL be easier for you than others.

Since your future depends so much on your score, you should maximize your chances of success. In order to maximize the likelihood of success, you've got to prepare in advance. This means taking practice tests and spending time learning the information and test taking strategies you will need to succeed.

Never take the test as a "practice" test, expecting that you can just take it again if you need to. Feel free to take sample tests on your own, but when you go to take the official test, be prepared, be focused, and do your best the first time!

## Secret Key #5 - Test Yourself

Everyone knows that time is money. There is no need to spend too much of your time or too little of your time preparing for the test. You should only spend as much of your precious time preparing as is necessary for you to get the score you need.

Once you have taken a practice test under real conditions of time constraints, then you will know if you are ready for the test or not.

If you have scored extremely high the first time that you take the practice test, then there is not much point in spending countless hours studying. You are already there.

Benchmark your abilities by retaking practice tests and seeing how much you have improved. Once you score high enough to guarantee success, then you are ready.

If you have scored well below where you need, then knuckle down and begin studying in earnest. Check your improvement regularly through the use of practice tests under real conditions. Above all, don't worry, panic, or give up. The key is perseverance!

Then, when you go to take the test, remain confident and remember how well you did on the practice tests. If you can score high enough on a practice test, then you can do the same on the real thing.

## General Strategies

The most important thing you can do is to ignore your fears and jump into the test immediately- do not be overwhelmed by any strange-sounding terms. You have to jump into the test like jumping into a pool- all at once is the easiest way.

**Make Predictions**
As you read and understand the question, try to guess what the answer will be. Remember that several of the answer choices are wrong, and once you begin reading them, your mind will immediately become cluttered with

answer choices designed to throw you off. Your mind is typically the most focused immediately after you have read the question and digested its contents. If you can, try to predict what the correct answer will be. You may be surprised at what you can predict.

Quickly scan the choices and see if your prediction is in the listed answer choices. If it is, then you can be quite confident that you have the right answer. It still won't hurt to check the other answer choices, but most of the time, you've got it!

**Answer the Question**
It may seem obvious to only pick answer choices that answer the question, but the test writers can create some excellent answer choices that are wrong. Don't pick an answer just because it sounds right, or you believe it to be true. It MUST answer the question. Once you've made your selection, always go back and check it against the question and make sure that you didn't misread the question, and the answer choice does answer the question posed.

**Benchmark**
After you read the first answer choice, decide if you think it sounds correct or not. If it doesn't, move on to the next answer choice. If it does, mentally mark that answer choice. This doesn't mean that you've definitely selected it as your answer choice, it just means that it's the best you've seen thus far. Go ahead and read the next choice. If the next choice is worse than the one you've already selected, keep going to the next answer choice. If the next choice is better than the choice you've already selected, mentally mark the new answer choice as your best guess.

The first answer choice that you select becomes your standard. Every other answer choice must be benchmarked against that standard. That choice is correct until proven otherwise by another answer choice beating it out. Once you've decided that no other answer choice seems as good, do one final check to ensure that your answer choice answers the question posed.

**Valid Information**
Don't discount any of the information provided in the question. Every piece of information may be necessary to determine the correct answer. None of the information in the question is there to throw you off (while the answer choices will certainly have information to throw you off). If two seemingly unrelated topics are discussed, don't ignore either. You can be confident there is a relationship, or it wouldn't be included in the question, and you are probably going to have to determine what is that relationship to find the answer.

**Avoid "Fact Traps"**
Don't get distracted by a choice that is factually true. Your search is for the answer that answers the question. Stay focused and don't fall for an answer that is true but incorrect. Always go back to the question and make sure you're choosing an answer that actually answers the question and is not just a true statement. An answer can be factually correct, but it MUST answer the question asked. Additionally, two answers can both be seemingly correct, so be sure to read all of the answer choices, and make sure that you get the one that BEST answers the question.

**Milk the Question**
Some of the questions may throw you completely off. They might deal with a subject you have not been exposed to, or one that you haven't reviewed in years. While your lack of knowledge about the subject will be a hindrance, the question itself can give you many clues that will help you find the correct answer. Read the question carefully and look for clues. Watch particularly for adjectives and nouns describing difficult terms or words that you don't recognize. Regardless of if you completely understand a word or not, replacing it with a synonym either provided or one you more familiar with may help you to understand what the questions are asking. Rather than wracking your mind about specific detailed information

concerning a difficult term or word, try to use mental substitutes that are easier to understand.

**The Trap of Familiarity**

Don't just choose a word because you recognize it. On difficult questions, you may not recognize a number of words in the answer choices. The test writers don't put "make-believe" words on the test; so don't think that just because you only recognize all the words in one answer choice means that answer choice must be correct. If you only recognize words in one answer choice, then focus on that one. Is it correct? Try your best to determine if it is correct. If it is, that is great, but if it doesn't, eliminate it. Each word and answer choice you eliminate increases your chances of getting the question correct, even if you then have to guess among the unfamiliar choices.

**Eliminate Answers**

Eliminate choices as soon as you realize they are wrong. But be careful! Make sure you consider all of the possible answer choices. Just because one appears right, doesn't mean that the next one won't be even better! The test writers will usually put more than one good answer choice for every question, so read all of them. Don't worry if you are stuck between two that seem right. By getting down to just two remaining possible choices, your odds are now 50/50. Rather than wasting too much time, play the odds. You are guessing, but guessing wisely, because you've been able to knock out some of the answer choices that you know are wrong. If you are eliminating choices and realize that the last answer choice you are left with is also obviously wrong, don't panic. Start over and consider each choice again. There may easily be something that you missed the first time and will realize on the second pass.

**Tough Questions**

If you are stumped on a problem or it appears too hard or too difficult, don't waste time. Move on! Remember though, if you can quickly check for obviously incorrect answer choices, your chances of guessing correctly are greatly improved. Before you completely give up, at least try to knock out a couple of possible answers. Eliminate what you can and then guess at the remaining answer choices before moving on.

**Brainstorm**

If you get stuck on a difficult question, spend a few seconds quickly brainstorming. Run through the complete list of possible answer choices. Look at each choice and ask yourself, "Could this answer the question satisfactorily?" Go through each answer choice and consider it independently of the other. By systematically going through all possibilities, you may find something that you would otherwise overlook. Remember that when you get stuck, it's important to try to keep moving.

**Read Carefully**

Understand the problem. Read the question and answer choices carefully. Don't miss the question because you misread the terms. You have plenty of time to read each question thoroughly and make sure you understand what is being asked. Yet a happy medium must be attained, so don't waste too much time. You must read carefully, but efficiently.

**Face Value**

When in doubt, use common sense. Always accept the situation in the problem at face value. Don't read too much into it. These problems will not require you to make huge leaps of logic. The test writers aren't trying to throw you off with a cheap trick. If you have to go beyond creativity and make a leap of logic in order to have an answer choice answer the question, then you should look at the other answer choices. Don't overcomplicate the problem by creating theoretical relationships or explanations that will warp time or space. These are normal problems rooted in reality. It's just that the applicable relationship or explanation may not be readily apparent and you have to figure things out. Use your common sense to interpret anything that isn't clear.

**Prefixes**
If you're having trouble with a word in the question or answer choices, try dissecting it. Take advantage of every clue that the word might include. Prefixes and suffixes can be a huge help. Usually they allow you to determine a basic meaning. Pre- means before, post- means after, pro - is positive, de- is negative. From these prefixes and suffixes, you can get an idea of the general meaning of the word and try to put it into context. Beware though of any traps. Just because con is the opposite of pro, doesn't necessarily mean congress is the opposite of progress!

**Hedge Phrases**
Watch out for critical "hedge" phrases, such as likely, may, can, will often, sometimes, often, almost, mostly, usually, generally, rarely, sometimes. Question writers insert these hedge phrases to cover every possibility. Often an answer choice will be wrong simply because it leaves no room for exception. Avoid answer choices that have definitive words like "exactly," and "always".

**Switchback Words**
Stay alert for "switchbacks". These are the words and phrases frequently used to alert you to shifts in thought. The most common switchback word is "but". Others include although, however, nevertheless, on the other hand, even though, while, in spite of, despite, regardless of.

**New Information**
Correct answer choices will rarely have completely new information included. Answer choices typically are straightforward reflections of the material asked about and will directly relate to the question. If a new piece of information is included in an answer choice that doesn't even seem to relate to the topic being asked about, then that answer choice is likely incorrect. All of the information needed to answer the question is usually provided for you, and so you should not have to make guesses that are unsupported or choose answer choices that require unknown information that cannot be reasoned on its own.

**Time Management**
On technical questions, don't get lost on the technical terms. Don't spend too much time on any one question. If you don't know what a term means, then since you don't have a dictionary, odds are you aren't going to get much further. You should immediately recognize terms as whether or not you know them. If you don't, work with the other clues that you have, the other answer choices and terms provided, but don't waste too much time trying to figure out a difficult term.

**Contextual Clues**
Look for contextual clues. An answer can be right but not correct. The contextual clues will help you find the answer that is most right and is correct. Understand the context in which a phrase or statement is made. This will help you make important distinctions.

**Don't Panic**
Panicking will not answer any questions for you. Therefore, it isn't helpful. When you first see the question, if your mind goes blank, take a deep breath. Force yourself to mechanically go through the steps of solving the problem and using the strategies you've learned.

**Pace Yourself**
Don't get clock fever. It's easy to be overwhelmed when you're looking at a page full of questions, your mind is full of random thoughts and feeling confused, and the clock is ticking down faster than you would like. Calm down and maintain the pace that you have set for yourself. As long as you are on track by monitoring your pace, you are guaranteed to have enough time for yourself. When you get to the last few minutes of the test, it may seem like you won't have enough time left, but if you only have as many questions as you should have left at that point, then you're right on track!

**Answer Selection**
The best way to pick an answer choice is to eliminate all of those that are wrong, until

only one is left and confirm that is the correct answer. Sometimes though, an answer choice may immediately look right. Be careful! Take a second to make sure that the other choices are not equally obvious. Don't make a hasty mistake. There are only two times that you should stop before checking other answers. First is when you are positive that the answer choice you have selected is correct. Second is when time is almost out and you have to make a quick guess!

**Check Your Work**

Since you will probably not know every term listed and the answer to every question, it is important that you get credit for the ones that you do know. Don't miss any questions through careless mistakes. If at all possible, try to take a second to look back over your answer selection and make sure you've selected the correct answer choice and haven't made a costly careless mistake (such as marking an answer choice that you didn't mean to mark). This quick double check should more than pay for itself in caught mistakes for the time it costs.

**Beware of Directly Quoted Answers**

Sometimes an answer choice will repeat word for word a portion of the question or reference section. However, beware of such exact duplication – it may be a trap! More than likely, the correct choice will paraphrase or summarize a point, rather than being exactly the same wording.

**Slang**

Scientific sounding answers are better than slang ones. An answer choice that begins "To compare the outcomes..." is much more likely to be correct than one that begins "Because some people insisted..."

**Extreme Statements**

Avoid wild answers that throw out highly controversial ideas that are proclaimed as established fact. An answer choice that states the "process should used in certain situations, if..." is much more likely to be correct than one that states the "process should be discontinued completely." The first is a calm rational statement and doesn't even make a definitive, uncompromising stance, using a hedge word "if" to provide wiggle room, whereas the second choice is a radical idea and far more extreme.

**Answer Choice Families**

When you have two or more answer choices that are direct opposites or parallels, one of them is usually the correct answer. For instance, if one answer choice states "x increases" and another answer choice states "x decreases" or "y increases," then those two or three answer choices are very similar in construction and fall into the same family of answer choices. A family of answer choices is when two or three answer choices are very similar in construction, and yet often have a directly opposite meaning. Usually the correct answer choice will be in that family of answer choices. The "odd man out" or answer choice that doesn't seem to fit the parallel construction of the other answer choices is more likely to be incorrect.

# Top 20 Test Taking Tips

1. Carefully follow all the test registration procedures
2. Know the test directions, duration, topics, question types, how many questions
3. Setup a flexible study schedule at least 3-4 weeks before test day
4. Study during the time of day you are most alert, relaxed, and stress free
5. Maximize your learning style; visual learner use visual study aids, auditory learner use auditory study aids
6. Focus on your weakest knowledge base
7. Find a study partner to review with and help clarify questions
8. Practice, practice, practice
9. Get a good night's sleep; don't try to cram the night before the test
10. Eat a well balanced meal
11. Know the exact physical location of the testing site; drive the route to the site prior to test day
12. Bring a set of ear plugs; the testing center could be noisy
13. Wear comfortable, loose fitting, layered clothing to the testing center; prepare for it to be either cold or hot during the test
14. Bring at least 2 current forms of ID to the testing center
15. Arrive to the test early; be prepared to wait and be patient
16. Eliminate the obviously wrong answer choices, then guess the first remaining choice
17. Pace yourself; don't rush, but keep working and move on if you get stuck
18. Maintain a positive attitude even if the test is going poorly
19. Keep your first answer unless you are positive it is wrong
20. Check your work, don't make a careless mistake

# Language Concepts and Language Acquisition

**Stages of first-language acquisition**

Children go through five recognizable stages in the development of their primary language skills. The first stage occurs when the child is between six and eight months old, and is known as the babbling stage. During this period, the child begins making repetitive patterns of sound with his mouth. During the one-word (also known as one-morpheme, one-unit, or holophrastic) stage, which extends from nine to eighteen months of age, the child begins to make basic word stems and single open-class words. During the two-word stage, which extends from eighteen to twenty-four months, the child begins making miniature sentences with simple semantic relations. During the telegraphic stage (also known as the early multiword or multimorpheme stage), which extends from twenty-four to thirty months, the child begins to express sentence structures with lexical rather than functional or grammatical morphemes. Finally, during the later multiword stage, which typically occurs after thirty months, the characteristic grammatical or functional structures of the primary language emerge and are incorporated.

**Behaviorist model**

The behaviorist view of language acquisition, developed by B.F. Skinner, asserts that individuals learn language as a direct response to stimuli. Certain words or patterns of language produce certain activities or events in the external world, and then the individual over time develops a mental response to those stimuli. Correct responses to stimuli are reinforced and therefore perpetuated. There are a few problems with this theory as it applies to language acquisition. For one thing, the creation of language is a somewhat improvisatory act and is therefore difficult to see as a response to stimuli in many cases. Also, many scientists feel that the behaviorist interpretation of language acquisition is overly simplistic and does not take into account the extreme complexity of language. Finally, linguistic response does not always elicit clear and recognizable rewards or punishments, which suggests that it would be difficult for a child to have his responses reinforced.

**Nativist model**

The nativist model of language acquisition, pioneered by Noam Chomsky, is an attempt to explain how people are able to understand and produce a seemingly infinite number of linguistic expressions. According to this model, individuals are born with a universal grammar wired into their brains, which they use as a template for language acquisition. According to this theory, all a child needs to learn is the specific ways in which his native language utilizes the rules of universal grammar. In other words, the principles of language are innate, and the specific parameters of each language are acquired in the first few years of life. The human mind has a "language acquisition device" that enables the acquisition of the linguistic principles of other languages. This theory remains present in much contemporary thought, though researchers continue to explore the relationship between an innate capacity for language and environmental factors.

**Vygotsky and Bronfenbrenner**

Vygotsky's sociocultural theory states that learning begins as a result of interpersonal communication and is then internalized as intrapersonal. Vygotsky studied incremental gains in learning and came up with the phrase "zone of proximal development" to describe the difference between what a person knows and what he could know if given a bit of assistance from someone else. The process of giving temporary aid to facilitate learning is called scaffolding, and includes modeling, providing cues, and encouraging the person. Bronfenbrenner's ecological model described development in terms of four nested levels: microsystem (child's immediate environment); mesosystem (interactions between components of the microsystem); exosystem (more general elements of the child's environment); and macrosystem (overarching environmental influences, like cultural beliefs).

**Steven Pinker and Jim Cummins**

Steven Pinker and Jim Cummins are two of the most prominent living theorists on human language acquisition. Steven Pinker agreed with Noam Chomsky that human beings are born with an innate capacity for learning and understanding language. However, he added the idea that this capacity is the result of millions of years of evolution. According to Pinker, people developed a predisposition towards language because communication increased their odds of survival. Jim Cummins, meanwhile, coined the terms Basic Interpersonal Communicative Skills (BICS) and Cognitive Academic Language Proficiency (CALP), which are distinct types of fluency. In general, BICS is the use of language in informal and social settings, and CALP is the use of language in the classroom. The use of these terms has made it easier for educators to assess linguistic ability.

**Social interactionist model**

The social interactionist interpretation of language acquisition emphasizes the relationship of the newborn with his caregivers. According to this model, the child will learn to speak in the manner and syntax of those people who speak to him. The child's ever-expanding knowledge of the world and linguistic context will give him tools for understanding language. According to the social interactionists, the child will begin to establish goals in the world and will need to devise linguistic strategies for achieving them. The child will draw on the linguistic and nonlinguistic utterances that he has heard, and will use this information in combination with other knowledge to achieve his ends. The social interactionist model is useful but, like the nativist approach, it does not provide an explanation for the startling ability to improvise language exhibited by even very young children.

**Cognitive model**

The cognitive model of language acquisition, developed by Piaget, asserts that individuals develop linguistic skills in order to control their environment. Piaget outlined four basic stages of cognitive development: sensorimotor intelligence (zero to two years of age), in which the child learns to physically handle the objects of the external world; preoperational thought (two to seven years), in which the child improves physically and begins to think conceptually; concrete operations (seven to eleven years), in which the child develops logical thinking skills; and formal operations (eleven to fifteen years), in which the child begins to think abstractly and can develop mental hypotheses. As the child moves through these stages, he will work through various strategies of language use. In the assimilation phase, the child uses a known word to describe a new object or concept until he is corrected. In the accommodation phase, the child learns to correct his own errors of linguistic identification. In the equilibrium phase, the child uses the right word to describe the object.

**Acquisition-learning model**

One model of second-language learning, known as the acquisition-learning hypothesis, posits two ways in which an individual develops proficiency in a second language. The first way is called acquisition, and is the subconscious process by which vocabulary and the basic rules of grammar are slowly and steadily absorbed. Acquisition is the way that small children learn their native language. The second way in which people develop language is called learning: a conscious study and knowledge of vocabulary and the rules of grammar. In general, this theory emphasizes the superiority of acquisition as a means of acquiring fluency. Although learning can be helpful in speeding the process of acquisition, it is ultimately long-term exposure to a language that allows the individual to develop an unconscious sense of its rules and idiom.

**Input hypothesis**

The input hypothesis is one of Stephen Krashen's models of second-language acquisition. According to this model, individuals need to be given information slightly above their ability level in a given language. As the individual acquires the ability to understand the given material, the level should be raised. In order for acquisition to be possible at all, the learner needs to understand the majority of what he is hearing. However, the addition of a small amount of incomprehensible information will encourage the listener to continue expanding his vocabulary and overall sense of grammatical structures. The input hypothesis can be difficult to apply in a classroom setting, because it is very difficult to set the instruction level at the appropriate point for each child. It is for this reason that self-instruction techniques like reciprocal teaching and scaffolding are essential parts of practice as an ESL teacher.

**Monitor hypothesis**

The monitor hypothesis explains how learning grammatical rules affects language acquisition. According to this hypothesis, when an individual learns rules of grammar, he is able to monitor consciously the discourse he hears in the future. Over time, learning these rules of grammar encourages the individual to refine and polish his speech. Individuals will use grammatical rules to monitor their speech to a greater or lesser degree depending on temperament. Krashen found that extroverted individuals tend to ignore the rules of grammar and simply plunge ahead, while introverted individuals strive for perfection in their speech. Most language experts agree that the basic rules of grammar will be unconsciously acquired over time regardless of whether they are ever explicitly learned. However, the monitor hypothesis indicates that it can be helpful to learn these rules as a part of second-language training.

**Sociocognitive approach**

According to the sociocognitive approach to language development, true competence is demonstrated in the ability to express oneself in different social contexts. Unlike the other approaches to language development, the sociocognitive approach emphasizes conversation in social contexts. The sociocognitive school admits that certain semantic, cognitive, and syntactical achievements must be made before language can be produced, but nevertheless asserts that social necessity is the primary motivator of language development. In other words, according to the sociocognitivists, children develop their linguistic ability by engaging with different people. A student must learn to converse with teachers, parents, siblings, other students, and strangers. True language development is evident when a student can modify his expression in these different contexts.

**Natural order hypothesis**

The natural order hypothesis asserts that the acquisition of a second language will follow predictable patterns. For any given language, certain grammatical structures will almost always be acquired before others, regardless of the age of the learner. This supports the idea that bilingual programs should follow a specific order of instruction. There are occasional exceptions to the natural order of language acquisition, but they are so few as to not merit consideration. Interestingly, Krashen felt that the appropriate specific order of instruction will not be exactly the same as the natural order. He felt that in order to achieve the most rapid and comprehensive acquisition of a second language, a rigid sequence of grammatical instruction should be avoided in favor of immersion and interactive performance.

### Affective filter hypothesis

According to the affective filter hypothesis, a number of emotional factors contribute to the acquisition of a second language. Specifically, self-confidence, anxiety, and motivation exert a significant influence on the ability to internalize vocabulary and grammatical rules. The presence of significant anxiety or low self-esteem can make it almost impossible for a student to incorporate comprehensible input in the formation of a new language. This is known as raising the affective filter. It should be noted that the presence of relaxation and high self-esteem does not in and of itself guarantee success in language acquisition; these qualities merely make it possible for the individual to succeed with hard work and aptitude. This hypothesis has been used to stress the importance of establishing a positive and welcoming environment in the bilingual classroom.

### BICS

In their consideration of second-language acquisition, experts distinguish between social and academic discourse. The language skills required in social situations are known as Basic Interpersonal Communication Skills (BICS). These are the basic expressions and linguistic formations that an individual will need to conduct himself in normal situations. Students will be using these skills in interactions with their fellow students in the cafeteria, on the playground, and on the school bus. While these interactions are not necessarily demanding in a cognitive sense, they do require a subtle understanding of context. Most students are able to acquire BICS within six to twenty-four months of beginning language study. Teachers are often mistaken when they declare that a student has achieved fluency because the student has developed excellent social language skills. Until a student has also acquired a mastery of formal discourse, he cannot be said to have achieved total fluency.

### CALP

The ability to participate in formal and grammatically correct discourse is known as Cognitive Academic Language Proficiency (CALP). Students with adequate CALP are able to listen, speak, read, and write about content material at their grade level. Students are not considered to have achieved total language proficiency until they can do so. Some recent research indicates that achieving CALP takes between five and seven years. This is because academic language acquisition requires not only learning new vocabulary, but also developing academic skills such as comparing, synthesizing, summarizing, and inferring. There is also much less context in academic language than there is in social interaction, so students are constantly forced to utilize their own contextualization skills to understand new information. There is some evidence to suggest that students can use what is known as a common underlying proficiency (CUP) to incorporate ideas and skills learned in their first language.

### Relationship between primary language academic success and English

Research suggests that for ESL students, the development of high proficiency in cognitive academic language in the primary language is often the basis for a similar proficiency in English. Once a student has achieved a high level of cognitive academic language proficiency in the primary language, he should be able to make normal academic progress. This is because such a student can receive content information in his primary language even when it is impossible to deliver it in English. The increase in cognitive academic language proficiency in the primary language allows the student to acquire similar skills in English by increasing the range of comprehensible input. Indeed, research suggests that for language minority students, the development of high cognitive academic language proficiency in the primary language directly contributes to a positive adjustment to both minority and majority cultures.

**Verbal/linguistic and logical/mathematical students**

Beginning teachers will need to develop instructional strategies that are appropriate for students of every learning type. Students who are predominantly verbal/linguistic will enjoy reading, learning about language, speaking, writing, and manipulating words in puzzles. These students are often best served by a "traditional" approach to language instruction. They will enjoy reading stories in the new language, writing letters, and participating in role-play exercises. Logical/mathematical students, on the other hand, will enjoy solving problems with numbers, performing experiments and calculations, and coming up with hypothetical questions. These students will enjoy collecting and evaluating data about the new language and culture.

**Kinesthetic and visual/spatial students**

Beginning teachers will need to develop instructional strategies that are appropriate for students of every learning type. Kinesthetic students are often poorly served by a traditional instructional approach. They typically enjoy exercise and need to move around the classroom frequently in order to maintain concentration and absorb new material. These students should manipulate new objects whose names they are learning, and they should participate in activities in which they are required to follow directions in English. Visual/spatial students, meanwhile, learn best with their eyes, and will enjoy making maps, charts, drawings, and illustrations of new material.

**Musical and interpersonal students**

Beginning teachers will need to develop instructional strategies that are appropriate for students of every learning type. Musical students have a knack for singing and playing instruments, and they also enjoy rhythmic games and listening to music. Helping these students acquire English might be ameliorated by teaching them songs and musical mnemonics. Interpersonal students thrive in a group, are able to mediate disputes between other students, and are excellent judges of the moods of others. These students will perform best in activities that allow them to communicate with their peers and interpret the social cues and gestures of English speakers.

**Intrapersonal and naturalistic students**

Beginning teachers will need to develop instructional strategies that are appropriate for students of every learning type. Intrapersonal students are introverted; they prefer to work by themselves and set their own goals. These students are often capable of thinking deeply on a particular subject, but may not be as good at thinking on their feet. Students of this type often enjoy pen-pal relationships with students from other schools. Naturalistic students, on the other hand, enjoy the outdoors and are sensitive to small differences and details among living things. These students will especially enjoy exploration of the language for natural phenomena, and would benefit from being encouraged to maintain a journal in English.

**Language variation**

Many people who study language assume that there is a standard, correct version of a language that can serve as a reference point for other versions. This is only partially correct. While there are general rules that can be used to systematize the currently accepted version of a language, there is no such thing as a permanent, infallible standard language. Instead, every language undergoes constant variation, as denotations, connotations, phonology, and pragmatics vary. Many critics suggest that standard language is simply the version of language preferred by the group in power. They cite examples from history in which a dominant religious or ethnic group attempted to formalize the language used by the people. It should be noted that all of these attempts met with failure. At this point, most scholars agree that languages are constantly evolving to meet the needs of the speakers.

**Dialect**

A dialect is the version of a language that is used by a particular group of people. This may be a group of people of a certain region, socioeconomic background, or ethnicity. Dialects are usually indicated by idiosyncratic vocabulary. Dialects that are common to individuals of a certain social class are occasionally referred to as sociolects. Many social critics suggest that upward mobility in many countries is hindered by the stigmatization of certain dialects. The particular speech of an individual may be referred to as an idiolect. Each person's idiolect is created from the influence of regional and class dialects. As a teacher, one must be careful not to prejudge students based on their dialects.

**Register**

The register of a language is the form of that language that is appropriate to a given situation. The register appropriate to the situation may vary depending on setting, the relationship between the two parties, and the intention of the linguistic interaction. Attaining the proper register is often one of the most difficult lessons for an individual learning a new language. Teachers need to keep the concept of register in mind when instructing students in a second language and assessing language proficiency. Often, students will learn a "classroom" form of a language and will be unable to speak the language in an informal setting. Comprehensive language instruction should include opportunities for both formal and informal communication.

**Slang**

Slang is a general term used to describe any nonstandard form of a language. Slang is typically used in a derogative sense, to indicate words and phrases that are not considered proper for social interaction. Slang is also known for being ephemeral, meaning it does not last for very long. Particular socioeconomic and ethnic groups often have their own slang, which gives them a sense of community and excludes nonmembers from participating in discourse. The distinction between what is standard and what is lacking is increasingly being seen as an arbitrary one made by whichever group happens to be in power. Often, slang terms obtain a more universal usage and enter the lexicon.

**Development of phonics knowledge**

Logographic phase

There are three phases in the development of phonics knowledge: the logographic phase, the analytic phase, and the orthographic phase. In the logographic (literally, "word-picture") phase, the child will be able to identify familiar words by sight. Interestingly, most children can identify common words before they can name the individual component letters in those words. They see words as shapes. Many pre-literate children can recognize their own names and the names of their friends, and almost all children will be familiar with the fonts and color schemes of well-known logos and product names. People may bemoan the ubiquity of advertising in our culture, but one advantage is that it establishes an early link between the shapes of words and the way they sound. Teachers often augment this process by labeling classroom objects such as plants, doors, windows, etc. This is an excellent method of passive instruction: simply being around the labeled objects will encourage children to make the connection between printed words and the names of things.

### Analytic phase

In the analytic phase of phonics knowledge, children begin to take a closer look at the components of words. They begin to notice that words that sound alike often have a similar appearance as well. For instance, students may see the resemblance between the words *boy* and *toy*. In this phase, children are receptive to instruction about the reasons for the differences between sounds; for instance, why *boy* sounds different than *toy* because of the initial letter. Many teachers exploit this curiosity by creating "word families," or collections of printed words that resemble one another. Students should be asked to brainstorm possible additions to these families. The analytic phase of phonics development is also a good time to focus on rhyming words, which will be almost identical except for the beginning letter. The analytic phase is the most intense period of phonics development.

### Orthographic phase

The third phase of phonics knowledge is called the orthographic phase. In the orthographic phase, students have acquired almost all of the tools required to sound out familiar and unfamiliar words. They know all of the sounds of the letters and read most common words automatically. Indeed, the development of a large sight vocabulary indicates the shift into the orthographic phase. A word is in sight vocabulary when the student no longer has to break it down or sound it out one syllable at a time. In large part, sight vocabulary emerges from frequent and prolonged exposure to simple texts. However, many teachers take extra effort to help students memorize common words and words with irregular spellings. Once students have a sufficient sight vocabulary, they can begin to understand unfamiliar words from context and thus move on to more sophisticated texts. Most education experts believe that it is only in the orthographic phase of phonics knowledge that students can truly begin to obtain knowledge and pleasure from reading.

## Spelling development

There are four stages in the development of spelling. In order, they are the pre-phonetic, phonetic, transitional, and conventional stages. The pre-phonetic stage of spelling is characterized by incomplete understanding of the relationship between sounds and letters. At this stage, children will not understand that every sound in a word must be represented by at least one letter. So, children will often leave out syllables in their attempts at spelling. Also, children in the pre-phonetic stage may still be in the logographic stage of phonics development, meaning that they may identify words simply as pictures and not as sequences of individual letters. In other words, pre-phonetic children may not yet have acquired the alphabetic principle. Students may attempt to spell words with a jumble of letter-like forms rather than with a series of discrete letters. Such students are sometimes referred to as pre-communicative spellers, because their work does not yet demonstrate understanding of the correspondence between sounds and symbols.

### Pre-phonetic to phonetic

The transition out of the pre-phonetic stage is marked by steady progress rather than sudden enlightenment. Gradually, students will begin to use the appropriate letters for the sounds of a word, and over time students will attempt, however imperfectly, to represent all of the sounds in a word. Indeed, once students demonstrate these skills, they are considered to be in the phonetic stage of spelling development. In this stage, students are likely to use one letter to represent a complex sound that requires two or more letters. Students in the phonetic stage understand how to write all of the letters, though occasionally they will write letters upside down or backwards. By this stage, it should be possible to make out what the student intends to communicate with his writing. However, students will have a limited sight vocabulary at this point, and therefore will always misspell words with silent vowels or unusual consonant patterns.

Transitional stage

Once the student has developed a small sight vocabulary and a solid understanding of the correspondence between English letters and sounds, he is in the transitional stage of spelling development. In this stage, it should be easy to understand a written message composed by the student. Indeed, students may be capable of writing short sentences with no spelling mistakes at all. The development of a basic sight vocabulary means that the student will spell some difficult words correctly, but is still likely to misspell words with long vowel sounds, which in English tend to be represented in different ways.

Conventional stage

The final stage of spelling development, known as the conventional stage, is characterized by near-perfect spelling and a massive sight vocabulary. Students in the conventional stage of spelling will spell irregularly written but common words correctly almost all of the time. Spelling errors will mainly be confined to especially large and unusual words. Also, students in the conventional stage will have developed an intuitive sense of spelling, such that they will often detect a spelling error even before precisely locating it in the sentence. Of course, in order to attain this degree of spelling competence, a student will have to be a fluent reader with excellent comprehension skills as well. In the conventional stage of spelling development, students are ready to learn content-specific words. In particular, spelling instruction should focus on words from the sciences and mathematics. Also, spelling instruction should focus on words with extremely unusual spellings. It can be assumed by this stage that students will be able to improvise the correct spelling of a regular but unfamiliar word.

**Phonology**

The way a language sounds is known as its phonological system. The smallest distinguishable unit of sound that can hold meaning in a given language is known as a phoneme. Each human language has a different set of phonemes. Each of these sets is relatively small compared to the entire set of possible sounds that can be made by the human voice. For instance, many languages do not distinguish between the plosive *p* and *b*, as we do in English. Individuals who speak these languages are incapable of telling the word *pan* from the word *ban* because they are not used to differentiating the voiced *b* from the unvoiced *p*.

**Morphology**

The morphology of a language is the system by which words are constructed out of letters. The smallest meaningful unit of a morphological system is known as a morpheme. Morphemes may appear by themselves as coherent words, but also may be combined with other morphemes to form words that are more complex. For instance, the morpheme *boy* can stand by itself, but it can also be combined with the morpheme *-s* to form *boys*. Every language has a distinct morphology, but there may be many exceptions to the basic rules of the system. English in particular is notorious for its morphological exceptions. Students of language should be aware that words are constructed in a systematic way, just as sentences and paragraphs are.

**Syntax**

The syntax of a language is the basic structure of the sentences. Syntax is distinguished from grammar by the fact that grammar offers recommendations for proper syntax, whereas syntax is the entire collection of proper and improper formulations. Utterances that appear crude and ungrammatical will still be understandable if they are placed into a standard acceptable syntax. Syntax, then, is the basic set of linguistic rules that must be followed in order for linguistic expressions to be understood. Grammar, on the other hand, is the set of rules that must be followed in order to attain a certain, somewhat arbitrary standard of acceptable expression. The concept of a standard of language has been frequently debated in education.

**Phonetics**

Phonetics is the study of sounds made during human speech. These sounds, known in the discipline as "phones," have distinct properties with respect to their production, audition, and perception. Phonetics is distinct from phonology in that it deals with real, measurable sounds, rather than abstract or arbitrary sound units like phonemes. In other words, phonetics focuses on specific sounds and does not concern itself with the context in which these sounds are used. There is no consideration of semantics in the field of phonetics. There are three main areas of research in phonetics. Articulatory phonetics focuses on the precise positions and movements of the speech organs. Acoustic phonetics focuses on the properties of sound waves and their reception by the inner ear. Auditory phonetics focuses on the process by which the brain forms a perceptual representation of phonetic input.

**Semantics**

The semantics of a language are the meanings of its words. Basic semantics studies explore the denotations and connotations of words. The denotation of a word is the thing or set of things to which it refers. The word *table*, for instance, denotes a four-legged, flat-topped piece of furniture. Of course, this word may have other denotations, such as a chart of data or an underground collection of water. The connotation of a word is the set of judgments and references that accompany it. For example, the word *idealist* denotes someone loyal to a particular idea, but it connotes a person out of touch with mundane matters. Every language is a mass of ambiguous denotations and connotations.

**Pragmatics**

The pragmatics of a language is the system by which it is used in social interactions. The ways in which people use language with one another are determined by the type of expression required as well as by the relationship of the speaker with his audience. Similar linguistic utterances can have vastly different pragmatic utility depending on their context. For example, the words *will you go out with me* have a different meaning when they are uttered by a young man to a young woman than when they are uttered by someone wanting to go outside to throw the Frisbee! People who speak a given language fluently will have an intuitive understanding of the pragmatics systems in that language. Indeed, this type of understanding often only comes with long experience.

**Phonemic awareness**

Perhaps the most basic prerequisite for literacy is phonemic awareness: that is, the understanding that words are made up of individual speech sounds. Phonemes are any speech sounds that can be distinguished from one another. For instance, if a teacher said the words *ball* and *fall*, the class would be able to distinguish the words because they would hear a difference between the /b/ and /f/ sounds. These sounds, then, are phonemes, though of course they are not the only phonemes in the words *ball* and *fall*. Phonemic awareness does not require written language, because it is entirely based on speech. At its core, phonemic awareness is the understanding that language is made up of sounds.

**Phonemic awareness vs. phonics**

Phonemic awareness should not be confused with phonics, which is the direct correspondence between letters and sounds (and which therefore requires the presence of print). Phonemic awareness precedes phonics instruction. Phonics depends on the alphabetic principle, which is that letters or other characters represent sounds. Phonemic awareness is much more basic. It has been said that literacy cannot develop without phonemic awareness and phonemic awareness cannot grow without the advance of literacy. In any case, it is recommended that all kindergartners develop phonemic awareness as part of their preparation for learning to read.

**Phonemes and graphemes**

As mentioned above, the core of phonemic awareness is the perception of distinguishing sounds, otherwise known as phonemes. Phonemes can be represented in two different ways. Some teachers use a phonetic alphabet, in which each phoneme is always represented with the same symbol. A hard *c* or *k* sound, for instance, is represented by /k/. Another way to represent phonemes is with an illustrative series of letters called graphemes. According to this method, the hard *c* or *k* could be represented as the *c* in *cold* or the *k* in *kilogram*. The vowel sounds permit a number of grapheme depictions: for example, a long *i* could be represented as the *y* in *fly* or the *igh* in *sigh*. Both the phonetic alphabet and the grapheme are acceptable modes of depicting phonemes.

**Consonants and vowels**

Phonemes can be either consonants or vowels, depending on how they are formed by the mouth. Consonants are formed by a motion that somehow blocks the flow of air. This is one reason why it is hard to hold a consonant sound while singing. Vowels, on the other hand, are formed by the vibration of air moving through the voice box and mouth. The English vowels are *a*, *e*, *i*, *o*, and *u*. The letter *y* is considered a vowel in words like *fly* and *rhythm*, and the letter *w* is considered a vowel in words like *now* and *brown*. All of the other letters in the English language are consonants exclusively.

**Consonant blends, diphthongs, and digraphs**

A consonant blend is a combination of two or more consonants into a single sound. Some examples of consonant blends are the initial sounds in *stay*, *drive*, and *gloat*. A diphthong is a single but shifting sound made by the combination of two or more vowels. Developing an ear for diphthongs takes a little work. One example is the word *boil*, in which the *oi* combination is pronounced first as *oy*, and then as a short *u*, such that the pronunciation is essentially *boy-ull*. This gliding vowel sound is characteristic of the diphthong. Finally, a digraph is a group of two or more letters that create a sound different from the individual sounds of the letters. Some common English digraphs are *sh*, *ph*, and *ch*, respectively. Note that none of these combinations produces a sound like the component sounds of the letters.

**Onsets and rimes**

English phonemes may be distinguished by their placement in a syllable or a word. The sound that initiates a syllable is known as the onset, while the vowel and any consonants after the vowel are referred to as the rime. For instance, in the one-syllable word *boy*, *b* is the onset and *oy* is the rime. It is not necessary for a syllable to have an onset, but every syllable has a rime. *I*, *of*, and *at* are all examples of words without an onset. Every syllable has a rime because every syllable has some sort of vowel sound.

**Beginning, end, and medial phonemes**

Another way in which phonemes are distinguished is by their placement in a word. The initial phoneme in a word is called the beginning phoneme, the final phoneme in a word is called the end phoneme, and all of the phonemes in between the beginning and end are called the medial phonemes. In the word bully, then, /b/ is the beginning phoneme, /u/ and /l/ are the medial phonemes, and /e/ is the end phoneme. Of course, a word may have numerous medial phonemes, though there may only be one initial and end phoneme. It is not necessary for students to understand the distinctions between these phoneme positions.

**Skills associated with phonemic awareness**

As a concept, phonemic awareness seems almost too vague and abstract to teach. For this reason, education experts have invented a program for testing and improving phonemic awareness. Phonemic awareness is demonstrated by the performance of six tasks. A student is not considered to have phonemic awareness unless he can perform all six. The tasks are sound matching, sound isolation, sound blending, sound substitution, sound deletion, and sound segmentation. Of these, sound segmentation is considered the most difficult and is therefore the last to be taught. There are specific exercises and assessments for each of the six components of phonemic awareness.

**Transfer of literacy competence**

According to the most current research, students are able to make positive transfers of knowledge between a first language and English in several areas: phonemic awareness, reading phonics, word recognition strategies, and cognates. In particular, the research has suggested that there are reading strategies common to English and languages like Spanish. However, there are some aspects of the graphic and phonetic systems particular to each of languages. In these areas, teachers will need to provide explicit instruction. For most students, the biggest obstacle to the transfer of literacy is the lack of vocabulary in English. Also, students need to possess a certain amount of background knowledge in order to understand specific texts. After students have developed adequate translation skills and acquired a satisfactory set of cognates, their ability to transfer literacy skills from their first language to English will be greatly improved.

Research focusing on the transfer of literacy from a first language to English has emphasized that transitions will occur at different points of English development for different students. Teachers should be aware of the potential for rapid gains and long plateaus in this development. A transition point is loosely defined as a shift in the relationship of the two languages to one another. It is a point at which the teacher will shift his expectations for the student. The first point of transition in literacy instruction occurs when students who have received formal instruction in their first language begin formal reading and content-area instruction in English. A second point of transition, known as redesignation, occurs when students receive all their instruction in English, without language support in their first language. In order to accurately ascertain that a student has reached one of these transition points, a teacher needs to be skilled in language assessment and evaluation of test data. Students will need to demonstrate competence in phonemic awareness, structural analysis, word recognition, comprehension skills, writing skills, and overall reading fluency in order to be considered literate.

**Microprocesses**

The most basic reading functions in English as a second language are called microprocesses. At this level, students are working to group the words and ideas within sentences into units of meaning. Essentially, the student will be unconsciously deciding what is important about the sentence and storing that information in short-term memory. For English language learners, lack of proficiency in grammar and syntax may force them to read word by word and miss the overall concept described by the sentence. The students may also be confused by idiomatic expressions and unfamiliar grammatical constructions. Some activities that can be useful at improving microprocesses are choral reading (in which students read aloud) and marking sentences to identify units of meaning. Students may also write sentences out on paper and cut them into meaningful units. In order to accelerate microprocesses, teachers may need to describe explicitly unfamiliar grammatical and syntactic forms. Also, teachers will need to explain the meaning of common idiomatic expressions.

**Integrative processes**

In order to be successful in learning English as a second language, students will need to improve their integrative processes: that is, their ability to identify relationships between clauses and sentences at the multiple-sentence and paragraph level of complexity. In order to do this, readers will have to notice pronoun substitutions, infer cause and effect, identify synonym substitutions, and recognize conjunctions. English language learners will probably have more difficulty with complex and compound sentences. They are more likely to lose the meaning of references when there is a frequent use of pronouns. The use of pronouns often varies from language to language. One way to improve integrative processes is to perform a close reading of sentences and paragraphs. Students may also perform sentence transformation activities to gain a better understanding of the construction of complex sentences. One helpful activity can be to go through a sample of text and replace antecedents and referents with nouns. Teachers can isolate a paragraph and have students diagram or draw relationships using circles and arrows.

**Macroprocesses**

The macroprocesses of learning English as a second language are relating small chunks of text to the whole text and organizing sections of text. In order to develop these skills, students will need to understand elements of story structure, expository text structure, poetic formulas, and the various literary genres. Often, English language learners have a hard time varying their reading strategy to align with the intent of the author. Students may not be familiar with the particular structures of genres in another language. One way to improve macroprocesses is by outlining and summarizing paragraphs, with an emphasis on the ways in which the main idea is supported by details. Students might be asked to identify the problem and solution in an expository text. Through the use of guided questions, teachers can encourage students to think critically about the structure and content of the text. Finally, more advanced students can benefit from going through a text paragraph by paragraph and identifying the function of each section.

**Elaborative processes**

The elaborative process of reading is extending literal comprehension to an understanding of the author's intent and themes. In order to exercise this skill, readers need to make personal connections with what they read, using prior knowledge and making predictions. Readers also need to identify with characters and understand their emotional responses. Sometimes, English language learners have a hard time identifying themes within a literary work if those themes are particular to the culture. Differing expectations and cultural norms may cause students to miss the intent of a literary work. The chains of cause and effect may be unfamiliar to students from another culture, and therefore the consequences or emotional reactions in the story may be incomprehensible. In order to develop the elaborative processes of English language learners, teachers can provide background knowledge and encourage students to connect literary material to their own lives. Teachers can use graphic organizers, maps, and other visual representations to familiarize students with characters, setting, and plot. Whenever necessary, teachers must explicitly describe the cultural values and beliefs that inform a piece of literature.

## Metacognitive processes

The metacognitive process of reading is the ability to self-critique comprehension and analysis. In order to develop metacognitive processes, students need to be able to predict, organize, and relate the information in a text to their own lives. Students who achieve excellent fluency in English will be able to recognize cognates and translate/paraphrase ideas from a literary text in English into their primary language. However, one of the obstacles to metacognitive development is the tendency to apply the grammatical and syntactic patterns of the native language to English. Unfamiliar vocabulary can hinder metacognitive development, especially when students lack the strategies to discover meaning from context. In order to develop metacognitive skill, teachers can model self-monitoring through read-and-retell lessons, in which students read independently and then report on what they have learned. Also, students may be able to improve their metacognitive skills by working with a partner or in a small group.

## William Labov and Joshua Fishman

William Labov and Joshua Fishman are sociolinguists responsible for popularizing and providing academic backing for marginalized dialects and languages. William Labov is responsible for establishing African-American Vernacular English as a legitimate dialect. He did this by demonstrating that AAVE has its own internal grammatical and syntactical rules. One result of Labov's research is that speakers of AAVE are now instructed in a manner similar to English language learners. Joshua Fishman, meanwhile, concentrated on the evolution of languages. Fishman's work concentrated on Gaelic, Yiddish, and Welsh, but it has been used to describe the societal forces that cause all languages to thrive or disappear. Fishman is a strong advocate for the survival of obscure languages, which he describes as the most important artifacts of a culture.

## Dell Hymes and Basil Bernstein

Dell Hymes was a sociolinguist primarily concerned with the interactions between language, society, and cultural context. He came up with the SPEAKING mnemonic for the essential characteristics of discourse: Setting and Scene; Participants; Ends (as in goals or intentions); Act sequence (that is, the structure of the linguistic interaction); Key (gestures or inflections that influence tone and mood); Instrumentalities (methods or conventions of speech); Norms; and Genre. Basil Bernstein, meanwhile, is famous for distinguishing between the restricted code, which is used by people who have a similar cultural background or know each other well, and the elaborated code, which is used by people who are unfamiliar with one another or with one another's culture. Expression in the elaborated code requires more explicit context and verbiage.

## Sheltered English approach

The sheltered English approach to content-area instruction is similar to language immersion. Sheltered English instruction is characterized by comprehensible input, meaning that all the information disseminated in the class should be understandable to the students. The teacher will strive to encourage student interaction, including frequent small-group and cooperative learning. There will be more hands-on activities in a sheltered English classroom, with students encouraged to become active participants in the lesson. In order for sheltered instruction to work, a teacher should engage in careful and comprehensive planning, and should develop a warm environment for students. Teachers should use student background knowledge and experience to determine activities. Teachers should also incorporate a variety of instructional strategies and frequent formal and informal assessment. Teachers should always explicitly state the lesson objectives.

Components
A sheltered English instructor will have to use a variety of instructional strategies and materials to be effective. Specifically, sheltered English instruction requires frequent hands-on activities. Modeling and demonstrations are common activities in the classroom. The teacher will also want to incorporate maps and globes for social studies or geography lessons. Many teachers find computers with interactive software to be especially helpful in sheltered English instruction. Teachers will also want to use other graphical displays, such as timelines, bulletin boards, pictures, and graphs. In order to ensure that all content in the classroom is comprehensible to students (as mandated by the terms of sheltered English instruction), the teacher will want to incorporate objects with which the students are already familiar.

Language and conceptual development
In order to provide effective sheltered English instruction, a teacher will need to understand certain theoretical principles. Specifically, teachers will need to understand the relationship between language development and conceptual development. Language gives us the labels and categories for certain familiar concepts. It also provides a means of describing or expressing insights about concepts that have already been learned. In other words, a student's mastery of language must increase along with his mastery of concepts. Teachers need to take into account both the linguistic and conceptual complexity of content-area instruction. It is essential that all input be comprehensible to students and that students receive adequate linguistic support. So, when a teacher is describing an unknown concept, he should use known language; when the teacher is describing linguistic principles that are unknown to students, he should use known concepts as illustration.

Making input comprehensible
In order to help students remain at grade level in their conceptual understanding, a teacher needs to ensure that all content-area instruction is comprehensible. To that end, the teacher should explicitly define any tricky vocabulary associated with the lesson. Manipulatives and graphical depictions can be especially useful in making some material comprehensible. The teacher should create a context in which students can solve problems, and should design activities that can be performed cooperatively to foster group understanding. If necessary, the teacher should provide content-area instruction in the primary language of students. In order to provide this kind of instruction, teachers need to receive explicit training in sheltered English and SDAIE (specially designed academic instruction in English) methods and strategies.

Mathematics instruction
Of all the content areas, mathematics is the one that ESL teachers often have the most trouble determining how to teach. This is due in part to the large amount of vocabulary unique to the discipline. The essential accomplishment that a teacher needs to make is to help develop a conceptual understanding of mathematics, and to help the student make connections between concrete, semi-concrete, and abstract expressions of new concepts. In mathematics, a single symbol can often represent several different words or an entire conceptual relationship. Often, a word may have a different meaning in mathematics than it does when used in ordinary conversation. In order to surmount the challenges of mathematics instruction, a teacher needs to pay special attention to issues of terminology. Manipulatives and group work can be especially helpful for students whose first language is not English. Above all, teachers and students need to remain patient as students work to achieve the linguistic understanding that will enable conceptual mastery in mathematics.

Sheltered instruction vs. ESL
In sheltered instruction, the focus of instruction is mastery of the content area, whereas in ESL, the focus is on development

of English skills. So, a sheltered instruction program will follow the mainstream scope and sequence, whereas an ESL program may follow some other prescription. In order to provide sheltered instruction, a teacher should be certified in the content area and must have some ESL training, whereas an ESL teacher need only be endorsed in ESL. Both sheltered instruction and ESL focus on the terminology of content areas. Finally, both sheltered English instruction and ESL instruction emphasize the need to teach metacognitive strategies; that is, both sheltered English and ESL instruction encourage students to self-monitor and think about their performance.

**Submersion programs**

One of the more extreme versions of an ESL program is known as a submersion program. The image conjured up by this name, of a student literally drowning in new information, is supported by the motto of this kind of program: sink or swim. Submersion programs provide very little structured support for the acquisition of English, with students being thrust directly into content-area instruction at their grade level. The advocates of submersion programs usually insist that most students in them will fall hopelessly behind unless they learn English almost immediately. Instruction is given almost exclusively in English, and students are not provided with very much opportunity to ask questions and receive scaffolding. As one might suspect, submersion programs have a high rate of failure. Unfortunately, however, it is very common for school administrations to blame the students for their failure to acquire English rapidly. In general, submersion programs are currently thought to be inappropriate.

**Transitional ESL education**

One of the more common models of ESL education is known as transitional education. In this model of instruction, the methodology of teaching a second language is incorporated. Students will receive content-area instruction in both their primary and secondary language according to their proficiency. Over time, the teacher will attempt to raise the level of English use in the classroom. To begin with, however, students will be assessed in their first language and will be given direct instruction to help them master the cognitive academic language required for each content area. Transitional education is considered one of the more beneficial forms of education for non-English-speaking students. It also aligns nicely with Krashen's input hypothesis, which declares that students should receive gradually increasing levels of difficulty in language.

**Primary language instruction**

In some ESL programs, a great deal of the content-area material is covered in the native language of the students. This is especially common in classes where the overwhelming majority of the students are native Spanish speakers. The goal of this method of instruction is to prevent students from falling far behind their grade level during the process of English acquisition. Over time, the teacher will gradually increase the amount of English used in content-area instruction. A classroom that incorporates primary language instruction will typically have a slightly expanded amount of time every day devoted to mastering the fundamentals of cognitive academic language in English, with the ultimate goal being instruction in every content area in English.

**English language development**

One of the more common methods used in ESL programs is English language development, which simply means a graduated program of improvement in English language proficiency. This model of education requires summative assessment at its beginning, so that the teacher can differentiate levels of proficiency among students. One of the things that separate English language development programs from other programs is the focus on incorporating a wide variety of methods and approaches to address various learning styles. English language development programs also endeavor to provide a large amount of practice time and ungraded opportunities for students to apply their burgeoning knowledge of English to specific content areas. In order to adequately provide an English language development program, all teachers must be fluent in both languages and well versed in the full spectrum of instructional methods in all content areas.

**SDAIE**

One of the methods used for teaching academic content to non-English-speaking students is called specially designed academic instruction in English, or SDAIE. In order for this method to be used, the student must have at least intermediate fluency in English. The student is given all course material in his native language, but is provided with access to English language versions of all content as well. Students are encouraged to use the English language versions of the content material as much as possible. This approach puts great demands for motivation on each student, and is therefore not appropriate for students who are not prepared to work. The teacher will set out goals for both content and language acquisition for each student. In the best SDAIE classes, students acquire language skills almost involuntarily as they are going through the normal process of learning course content. Of course, in order to be successful at this method, a teacher will need to be well organized and fluent in both languages.

**Characteristics of an ESL program**

In an ESL program, content is taught in the students' primary language and separate instruction is provided in English language skills. The methodology used to teach English does not necessarily involve making connections with other content areas. ESL programs work best when they are intensive, taking up the majority of the school day. One of the dangers of these programs, of course, is that they can prevent students from learning other content material. Also, students who participate in ESL programs may have a difficult time transferring their knowledge of English language skills to the core curriculum. For this reason, many schools at present avoid ESL courses except in those cases where students need intense English training in order to survive in other areas.

**Dual immersion programs**

One of the newer models of ESL program is known as dual immersion. In this kind of program, groups of students with different first languages are placed together and encouraged to learn each other's native tongue. Research has suggested a number of excellent benefits to this instruction model. In many cases, it has been found to promote true bilingualism and a healthy respect for another culture. Many students have seen their skills in their native language improve as a result of explaining themselves to their peers. In other words, dual immersion programs force students to consider and analyze their original language, which improves their skill in that language as well as their ability to learn English. Also, of course, schools that feature dual immersion programs typically have fewer problems integrating non-English speakers into the student body. At present, dual immersion programs are uncommon but increasing in number.

**Basic orientations for teaching ESL**

There are four basic orientations to teaching English as a second language: structural/linguistic; cognitive; affective/motivational; and functional/communicative. The structural/linguistic approach is based on comparisons between the structures of different languages. Teachers who use this method isolate grammatical and syntactic elements in each language and teach their students in a prescribed sequence. A cognitive approach entails objectives that enable the student to make generalizations about the rules of English. There is an emphasis on individual learning style with this approach. The affective/motivational approach emphasizes the predispositions of the student that can enhance or inhibit learning. Teachers who use this approach try to diminish the anxiety associated with learning by increasing identification with native English speakers. The functional/communicative approach involves selecting language structures on the basis of their utility in achieving a communicative purpose. The focus of this instruction is on transmission and reception of speech.

### Audiolingual method

The audiolingual method of teaching English as a second language relies on repetition of structural patterns. Material is supposed to be overlearned, so students can easily incorporate it in future lessons. Instruction tries to prevent student errors and immediately reinforces correct expression. Grammar is typically taught inductively, meaning that students are informed of the rules of grammar after they have intuitively learned proper expression. New material is typically presented in a dialogue format and essential linguistic structures and skills are placed in a set sequence. Exposure to new vocabulary is rigidly controlled and linguistic patterns are taught using rote memorization and repetitive drills. The audiolingual method has somewhat fallen out of favor in recent years, though it is still a major component of traditional programs.

### Total physical response approach

The total physical response method of teaching English as a second language incorporates psychomotor systems to inculcate vocabulary and syntactic forms. Students are not required to produce language, either orally or in written form, until they are ready. Command forms are typically used to convey information, and the teacher must gradually increase the complexity of his linguistic expressions in English. This type of instruction is especially suited to students with a kinesthetic learning style. The sequence of instruction in total physical response is as follows: the teacher gives the command and performs the accompanying action; the teacher then says the command and both the teacher and the students perform the action; the teacher then says the command as students perform the action; the teacher tells one student to perform the action; and finally the students give one another commands or command the teacher to perform the action.

### Communicative strategy

The communicative approach to teaching English as a second language assumes the comprehension of linguistic principles always comes before production of speech or writing. The overarching goal of this approach is for students to create meaningful communication. Because this method relies heavily on goodwill among the students, it is important for the teacher to create a positive learning environment to lower the affective filters of the students. When this method is used, the language is gradually acquired through interaction with fellow students at the same time that it is being learned from the teacher. In order to create a successful lesson, the teacher will need to ensure that students have the specific vocabulary and expressions they will need in order to accomplish the communicative intent. In some cases, it may be useful to prepare dialogue before practicing an actual verbal exchange. Teachers may also use graphs and displays.

### Grammar-translation approach

For most of American history, second languages were taught according to the grammar-translation approach. This method of instruction still persists in some ESL classrooms. In this format, lessons are taught almost exclusively in the primary language of the students. There is very little active use of English. Vocabulary is taught in list format, and students are provided with detailed explanation of grammatical rules. From close to the beginning of a course of study, students will be required to read complex and advanced texts. These texts, however, are primarily studied for their grammatical structures rather than for their specific content. There is very little attention given to spoken forms of the language, and almost no instruction in pronunciation is given. Almost all work in the class involves translating sentences from one language to the other.

Direct approach

The direct approach to teaching English as a second language came after the grammar-translation approach and attempted to incorporate the secondary language in instruction a bit more. When this approach is used, lessons begin with a dialogue incorporating a modern conversational style in English. There is a translation at this point, as students are given a series of questions in English based on the dialogue that was just presented. Students learn the rules of grammar through induction; that is, they generalize rules from practice and experience with English. Students will not read advanced literature until they are well along in their mastery of cognitive academic language. When they do read literature in English, they will consider it in terms of its own content rather than its grammatical structures. There is some attempt to teach the English-speaking culture in the direct approach method.

Reading approach

The reading approach to teaching English as a second language has both practical and academic benefits, but is only appropriate for certain individuals. Specifically, the reading approach is appropriate for those individuals who will not be living in an English-speaking community and for whom reading is the most important skill to master. The two primary emphases of the reading approach are improving reading ability and establishing current events and historical knowledge of English-speaking countries. Grammar instruction is limited to what is necessary for reading comprehension and fluency. There is almost no attention paid to pronunciation or the development of conversational skills. As one would expect, the majority of time is spent on reading passages. There is a constant emphasis on the acquisition of vocabulary. Teachers who use this approach will rely almost exclusively on translation from English into the native language of the student.

Community language learning approach

According to the community language learning approach, the most important thing is to lower the affective filter of the student and gradually introduce him to a linguistic community in English. The student is considered more as a client, and the teacher is trained in counseling skills. At first, the teacher/counselor tries to make the student comfortable by getting a sense of his anxieties about language acquisition. The student and teacher work closely to develop linguistic independence for the student. There are five basic stages of language acquisition in community language learning. At first, the student is completely dependent on the teacher. In the second stage, the student begins to have contact with other members of the target linguistic group (i.e., English speakers). In the third stage, the student begins to speak directly to the members of the target linguistic group. In the fourth stage, the client can speak freely and assume that the members of the target linguistic group understand him. In the final stage, the student refines his linguistic skills.

Functional-notional approach

Among the communicative approaches to teaching English as a second language is the functional-notional approach, which emphasizes a strictly organized syllabus of language. Teachers who take the functional-notional approach divide a language into discrete units of analysis, usually by social context. In other words, the specific units of instruction are situations in which the student will be forced to express himself in English. The term *notion* refers to meaningful expressions of language. The intent of the functional-notional approach is to equip students with appropriate notions for every common social situation. This may involve variations of dialect, formality, and mode of expression. A special set of terminology is used in this approach to ESL instruction. An *exponent* is the statement that is appropriate to a given function, situation, and topic. A *code* is the shared language of a community of speakers. *Code-switching* is the process by which individuals shift the tone or formality of their speech in order to convey hierarchy, bonding, or some other interpersonal relation.

### Categories of discourse

The functional-notional approach to teaching English as a second language asserts that there are five major functional categories of discourse: personal, interpersonal, directive, referential, and imaginative. The personal function involves expressing and elaborating one's own thoughts, ideas, or feelings. The interpersonal function is used to establish and maintain positive social and professional relationships, whether by exchanging basic pleasantries or organizing social relations. Examples of speech used in an interpersonal function are apologies or invitations. Language that is used in a directive function attempts to change the actions of others. This may include giving instructions, requesting permission, or asking for directions. Language that is used in a referential function describes things, actions, events, or people. Referential language can also be used to discuss abstract concepts. Finally, imaginative language expresses creativity and artistic expression. The most obvious example of imaginative language is fictional dialogue, but this category can also include creative solutions to concrete problems.

### Marie M. Clay, Sharon Taberski, Priscilla Vail, and Marilyn Jager Adams

Marie M. Clay is credited as the originator of the Reading Recovery movement, which is an effective method of accelerating the progress of struggling readers. The foundation of the program is continuous and specific assessment, which enables teachers to diagnose reading problems early on. The program usually lasts twelve to twenty weeks, after which the student ought to be ready to rejoin the class. Sharon Taberski has written a number of popular books about the personal relationships between teachers and new readers. Priscilla Vail is an expert on dyslexia, and in particular on the assessment of dyslexic children. She advocates a whole-language approach to teaching dyslexics and other students with special needs. Marilyn Jager Adams established basic criteria for early reading success and helped to create voice recognition software for developing readers.

### Listening for comprehension

There are five basic kinds of intentional listening: appreciative, therapeutic, discriminative, comprehensive, and critical. Listening for comprehension is probably the most familiar form of listening. Students in a classroom are engaged in listening for comprehension when they take notes during a lecture. Whenever we listen to an informative or persuasive speech in order to obtain information about a subject, we are engaged in listening for comprehension. The validity and accuracy of other forms of listening, such as critical listening and discriminative listening, depend on effective listening for comprehension. If an individual is unable to understand the message that is being presented, he will not be able to critique it insightfully. Listening comprehension depends on attention to the organization and structure of the message.

### Detached, intentional listening

An ideal listener is often described as detaching or decentering, meaning that he is considering the speaker's message on its own terms rather than in the context of the listener's experience and emotions. In other words, the listener is giving a speaker a fair hearing before applying critical thinking to his message. It is inappropriate to pre-judge a message based on past experience or existing opinions. This not only prevents the listener from acquiring a better understanding, but it also significantly handicaps the listener's ability to listen for comprehension. Even when a speech is being delivered on a subject with which the listener is quite familiar, he should try to keep an open mind in order to gain as much as possible from the speech.

**RRA technique**

Active listening may be based on the RRA (review, relate, anticipate) technique. This technique breaks the process of active listening down into three easy steps. To begin with, an active listener is constantly reviewing what has been said and placing new information into the evolving model of the message. As the listener considers the speaker's argument or idea, he relates it to his foundational knowledge. In other words, the listener tries to compare and contrast the speaker's message with his own knowledge of the subject. Finally, an active listener tries to anticipate the rest of the speaker's message. Not only is this a good way to stay engaged with a speech, but it also provides an excellent measure of attention. When a listener is able to predict confidently the direction of a spoken message, he can be certain that his understanding of what has been said so far is sound.

**Spoken message**

When considering the content of a spoken message or speech, audience members should pay special attention to three basic areas: main ideas, organization, and supporting evidence. The main ideas of the speech are the fundamental arguments or concepts the speaker is trying to convey. If the speech is effective, the main ideas will be obvious. Listeners should be paying the most attention to the articulation and elaboration of these main ideas. The way in which the main ideas are expressed and supported is referred to as the organization of the speech. In order for a speech to be effective, the speaker needs to organize his ideas clearly and avoid long digressions that obscure the main points. Finally, the listener needs to consider what supporting materials the speaker is using to provide evidence for his ideas or arguments. The listener needs to consider whether these supporting materials are appropriate and credible.

**Listener assessment**

In order to get the most out of a spoken message or speech, a listener needs to consider all of the various factors that contribute to the speaker's message. One of the factors that do not receive a great deal of attention is the situation in which the speech is delivered. Many times, the physical and interpersonal setting in which a speech is delivered has a great deal of influence on the message. For instance, a listener might consider whether the speaker has been required to make his address more or less formal for the occasion. The listener also might consider whether the occasion on which the speech is being delivered has influenced the quality of the speaker's message. Finally, the listener should consider whether the physical environment in which the speech is delivered has been more or less conducive to his understanding and appreciation of the speaker's message.

As part of the overall critique of a speech, a listener should consider the personal characteristics of the speaker. For instance, the listener might consider what he knew about the speaker before the speech, and then decide whether this information had any influence on his interpretation of the speaker's message. The listener might also consider whether the speaker's personal presentation indicated credibility or made his message difficult to believe. Many times, a speaker with a good message and solid supporting materials comes across as vague and disorganized because of his physical appearance and vocal mannerisms. Listeners should try to distinguish between weaknesses in the speaker's message and weaknesses in the speaker's personal presentation.

**Listener analysis**

When a member of an audience (formal or informal) listens to a speech, he should be attending to three fundamental factors: ideas, organization, and support. The most important thing to consider is whether the speaker's main ideas are logical and clearly expressed. If the ideas are comprehensible, the listener can then consider whether they have been expressed in a logical order or whether the speaker has presented them in a disorganized fashion. Finally, the listener needs to consider whether the speaker's main ideas have been adequately supported by argument or factual evidence. Does the speaker provide enough support for his arguments to remain credible? Is the evidence provided relevant to the main ideas of the speech?

**Critical listening**

Critical listening is the most active form of audience behavior. It entails organizing and interpreting the information contained in a speech. As a speech is given, the critical listener will be evaluating the arguments or ideas presented by the speaker, weighing the evidence given, and thinking of possible problems with the speech. As consumers, we are engaged in a form of critical listening every time we hear an advertisement. During a speech, however, many people sympathize with the speaker rather than evaluate the message of the speaker critically. A critical listener will guard against this sympathy, not out of hard-heartedness, but out of a determination to assess the content of the spoken message on its own merits. Detachment is an essential prerequisite for critical listening.

**Discriminative listening**

Discriminative listening focuses on the aspects of a speaker's message that are implied rather than spoken directly. A discriminative listener is paying attention to the sound of voice, body language, and implicit argument of the speaker. To a certain extent, we are all always involved in discriminative listening, though some of us focus on it more than others. A sophisticated listener obtains information not only from the message but from the medium in which it is delivered. Often, the information obtained through discriminative listening is more important than the bare facts expressed in the message. For instance, a discriminative listener might perceive if a speaker does not fully believe what he is saying. Similarly, an excessive zeal on the part of the speaker might lead the discriminative listener to question the impartiality of the message.

**Speech topic**

A listener needs to be constantly asking himself whether each point and piece of supporting material in a speech is essential. There needs to be a clear and explicit reason to include everything that is in the speech, or else it must be considered superfluous. The listener must also ascertain that all of the evidence clearly and directly supports the points it is intended to support. Finally, the listener needs to make sure that the points made in the speech are made in the proper order, that they progress in an orderly fashion, and that they climax with the appropriate conclusion. It is possible for a speaker to present sufficient information to make her case, but to present it in the wrong order and thereby confuse the listener. The listener must decide whether disorganization has invalidated the claims of the speaker.

**Faulty attribution of causation**

One of the most common errors of logic made in a speech is a faulty analysis of causation. This occurs when the speaker erroneously assumes that just because one thing followed another, the second thing was caused by the first. For instance, I may grab my umbrella on the way out the door before it starts raining, but if I later use my umbrella, I cannot say that bringing my umbrella made it rain. When the speaker is describing large historical or social events, it is usually a faulty attribution of causation to suggest that there is only one cause. Major social and historical movements are simply too complex to be attributed to only one cause. At the very least, a speaker will need to provide detailed substantiation for any assertions of causation.

**Circular reasoning**

A common logical error in speeches is circular reasoning. A chain of logic is described as circular when the assumptions made at the beginning of the argument depend on the conclusion of the argument being true. For instance, imagine a speaker declaring that the Tigers baseball team will certainly lose their playoff series. As evidence for this claim, the speaker declares that the Tigers always lose their playoff series. As you can see, this reasoning does not hold up: in order to believe that the Tigers will lose their playoff series, we have to assume that they always lose their playoff series, which we do not really know yet and which depends on their performance in the upcoming playoff series. In other words, the claims made by the speaker depend for their support on the assumptions made by the speaker.

**Contradictory argument**

Occasionally, a speaker will fall victim to the logical error known as the contradictory argument. A contradictory argument is one in which the speaker introduces information that directly contradicts his main argument. For the most part, this error should be easy to avoid. After all, a speaker will be careful not to include information that undermines his main point. However, the inclusion of inconsistent arguments in a speech does happen and can be highly detrimental. Contradictory argument is especially problematic in a persuasive speech, in which the speaker is attempting to alienate the audience from its pre-existing opinions and sell it on the merits of an alternative view.

**Social context**

When speakers consider the characteristics of the environment in which their speech will be delivered, they sometimes neglect to consider the social context. The social context is the set of relationships between the listener and the speaker, and between the members of the audience themselves. The speaker should know beforehand how he stands in relation to the audience. For instance, a speaker may be recognized as an expert, an entertainer, or an intriguing fraud. Also, the speaker should understand how the members of the audience stand in relation to one another—for instance, whether they are friends, colleagues, or strangers. The information obtained from this consideration of social context should inform the construction and delivery of the speech.

**Communication rules**

Sometimes, a speech will be delivered in a particular environment or to a particular group that is governed by specific communication rules. For instance, a speech delivered in church is unlikely to be followed by a question-and-answer period. As another example, some debating societies have strict rules for the presentation and critique of a speech. More informally, some groups will have different expectations for speaker behavior. For instance, a gathering of senior citizens is unlikely to respond well to coarse humor. So, communication rules may be explicit or implicit. During the preparation of a speech, the speaker needs to consider the formal considerations that will influence his message.

# ESL Instruction and Assessment

### Recommended sequence for phonics skills instruction

Having outlined the three phases of phonics knowledge, let us now examine the instructional techniques for nurturing this development. There is a prescribed sequence for the teaching of phonics skills. Teachers should begin by naming the letters, both uppercase and lowercase. Once students have mastered the names of all twenty-six letters, the teacher should move on to the sounds of the letters. It is not necessary at this point to explore the various sounds a letter can make, such as long and short vowel sounds. It is at this point that many teachers discuss the differences between consonants and vowels. One easy way of doing so is to show how vowels can be spoken indefinitely, while consonants can only be spoken in staccato bursts.

### Three-letter words, basic digraphs, and consonant blends

Having covered the letters and their sounds, the teacher can begin to discuss very short words. The simplest words for young students to understand are three-letter words with a consonant-vowel-consonant (known as CVC) structure: for example, *boy*, *cat*, *dog*, and *hat*. To begin with, the teacher should only discuss CVC words with short vowel sounds. Next, the teacher can introduce simple words that have initial digraphs: that is, two consonants that produce a sound unlike either of the component letters (e.g., *sh*, *ch*, and *th*). The discussion of these words will show students some of the flexibility and ambiguity related to English pronunciation. Also, of course, it will familiarize them with some of the more common sounds in the language. After covering some basic digraphs, the teacher can move on to short-vowel words beginning with consonant blends like *bl*, *sl*, and *st*. These blends require students to remember the individual sounds of the consonants, but also to combine them into a slightly new form. Work with consonant blends helps accelerate pronunciation for many students, as they begin to combine several letters into a single sound.

### Long vowel sounds and multisyllabic words

After addressing short vowel sounds, the teacher can move on to words featuring the long vowel sounds. As much as possible, the teacher should focus on one-syllable words, like *row* and *mate*. Instruction can then move on to a look at diphthongs and other irregular verb formations. Some vowels sound different when they precede an *r* or an *l*: they are called *r*- and *l*- controlled verbs. Some examples of these words are *car*, *walk*, and *bird*. Such words should be discussed, though it is not necessary to give students an entire explanation of the linguistic phenomenon. Finally, once all of the above topics have been covered, the teacher can conclude by exploring some common multisyllabic words. For the most part, multisyllabic words are read just like combinations of one-syllable words. However, students should receive some guided practice before being asked to sound out these words on their own.

### Synthetic and analytic phonics instruction

The specific techniques of phonics instruction can be divided into two categories: those that build words out of sounds (synthesis) and those that break words down into their component sounds (analysis). These are reciprocal skills; the presence of one reinforces the development of the other. Activities that require students to make words out of disparate sounds are called synthetic phonics activities. In perhaps the most common synthetic phonics activity, the teacher writes an initial letter on the board and asks the students to pronounce it. Once students have mastered the sound of the letter or letters, the teacher should ask students to think of words that begin with that sound. This is an excellent way to demonstrate how the same sound can begin any number of words.

**Initial consonant, digraph, and blend cards**

Another synthetic phonics activity is for the teacher to distribute cards printed with initial consonants, digraphs, and blends. The teacher then writes a number of common rimes on the board and asks students to tape their cards where they combine with a rime to form a complete word. So, for instance, the teacher could write the rime *at* on the board, and students holding *b*, *c*, *s*, and *f* could tape up their cards to form a complete word. Students should be encouraged to attach their onsets to a number of different rimes, as this will reinforce the idea that many common words share an initial sound.

**Digraph, letter, and blend cards**

In sophisticated synthetic phonics activity, students are given cards printed with letters, digraphs, and blends, and are asked to cooperate with one another to create short words. Every student should be given several cards, and there should be plenty of vowels. Once students have formed some short words, the teacher should ask them to attempt multisyllabic words. Of course, this activity is best suited to students who are well into the analytic phase of phonics knowledge. An advantage of it, though, is that it requires students to consider not only the onset or initial sound in the word, but also the medial and end sounds. In another activity, a teacher combines letter recognition with synthetic phonics instruction by writing a letter on the board and asking students to name objects in the class that begin with that letter. So long as this activity is conducted orally, it will be a good exercise for phonics skills. Any activity that requires students to consider the initial sound of a vocabulary word is a reinforcement of phonic skills.

**Underlining**

Whereas synthetic phonics instruction encourages students to build words out of sounds, analytic phonics instruction requires them to break words apart into discrete sounds. One easy introductory activity is to present students with a short text and ask them to underline all of the appearances of a given letter or digraph. For example, students might be asked to underline all the instances of the letter *p*. The teacher will then reread the text aloud, pointing at the words as they are pronounced, so that students can see how the *p* is used in each different case. This activity helps to build understanding of how letters function in words.

**Repeated consonant sound**

One advanced phonics exercise begins when the teacher writes several sentences on the board, each of which contains the same consonant sound. The words that contain the consonant sound should be underlined. Students will be asked to read the underlined words, and then to identify the sound these words have in common. (The activity is more effective if the words only have one sound in common.) Once the sound has been identified, the teacher writes the consonant, digraph, or blend next to the list of sentences. This activity moves the students' attention from the entire sentence to the individual words and finally to the recurrent sound. In essence, it helps students "zoom in" on phonics as it occurs in real language.

**Word sort**

One method of analytic phonics instruction is a word sort, in which students are given cards on which short words have been printed. Students are then asked to organize the cards according to some criterion: for instance, they may be asked to put all of the cards beginning with a *sh* sound together. Later, the teacher might ask the students to group words that have a *sh* sound in any position. If the teacher prefers students to work by themselves on a word sort, the activity can be recreated on paper: the teacher simply passes out a list of words and asks the students to underline those that meet the criterion.

**Decoding and encoding**

Phonics assessments are typically categorized depending on whether the student is putting sounds together to make a written word or converting written words into sounds. The former is called encoding and the latter is called decoding. In an encoding exercise, the student writes down words as the teacher says them. The traditional spelling test, in which the word is read aloud by the teacher several times and the student must attempt to spell it on paper, is a classic encoding assessment. This type of assessment is excellent for spelling, of course, but it is also good at pinpointing basic phonics problems.

**Encoding assessments**

With more advanced students, it is useful to require encoding assessments that place words in context. In a typical exercise, students are asked to transcribe a few sentences spoken by the teacher. A longer writing sample helps the teacher spot recurrent errors that may be based on faulty correspondences between sound and symbol. For instance, a student may consistently use a *d* when he means to use a *t*. This sort of error can be spotted rapidly when encoding is performed in context. Encoding in context tends to work better with older students, who are capable of generating a text long enough to be analyzed.

**Decoding assessments**

Whereas encoding assessments require students to write down words as they are spoken, a decoding assessment requires them to pronounce the words they read. For obvious reasons, it is more difficult to administer a formal decoding assessment to a large class, so teachers tend to perform most of their decoding assessments informally, by having students read words aloud or name the letters written on the board. In a more defined decoding assessment, however, the teacher should be given a list of simple, similar words and asked to read them aloud. The list of words should systematically isolate different letters, for instance by including several words with the same ending but different initial letters. This will allow the teacher to pinpoint problems related to particular letters.

One common feature of formal decoding assessments is a series of nonsense words, like *gop*, *bam*, and *rud*. These words are included because, since they could not be a part of the student's sight vocabulary, they provide a clearer look at phonics skills. The value of including such words is debated among educators: some feel that the words serve a useful purpose, while others feel that phonics assessments should focus on words that actually appear in the English language. When they are used, the teacher should note any disparity between performance on real and made-up words, as a large drop-off related to fake words may indicate serious problems with phonics.

**Reading aloud**

While beginning students will only be able to decode words in isolation, more advanced readers should be asked to read sentences, short passages, and even complete stories. Once a student has mastered the fundamentals of phonics, any residual problems will only become evident during prolonged sessions of reading aloud. For this reason, teachers tend to perform this assessment piecemeal by calling on various students to read aloud during the course of a content-area lesson. Of course, this technique is counterproductive when students have not obtained sufficient fluency, because listening to a peer stumble through a long paragraph about science is a bad way for the rest of the class to learn. In a more formal version of this exercise, often included as part of an Informal Reading Inventory, the student and teacher are separated from the rest of the class, and the student is asked to read a long section of text out loud. The teacher should keep careful notes of any mispronunciations made by the student. Specifically, the teacher should take note of how words are mispronounced, as repetition of the same mispronunciation will indicate the problem to be resolved.

**Reliability and validity**

For assessments to be effective, they need to be reliable and valid. In testing, reliability is the consistency between scores from different administrations of the assessment. If you use the same assessment on the same student twice and get wildly different results, the assessment is unreliable. Validity, on the other hand, is the degree to which a test measures what it was intended to measure. A test with questions about reading comprehension, for example, is an invalid assessment of phonemic awareness. It is essential that an assessment target the specific knowledge and skills the teacher is trying to identify.

**Formal assessment**

There are a few important terms related to the scoring of formal assessments. When an assessment is norm-referenced, the student's score is compared with those of his peers. Scores from norm-referenced tests are often presented as a percentile. A percentile indicates the percentage of students who scored worse than the student in question. So, if a student scores in the 78th percentile, she has performed better than 78 percent of the other students in her grade. Percentile scores are a good way of seeing how students compare to their classmates; they help identify trends in performance. Another way of presenting formal assessment results is as a grade-equivalent score. In this case, the score is translated into a grade level. A high-achieving third grader might be assigned a grade-equivalent score of 5.2, meaning that his level of knowledge and skill is the same as that of an average fifth grader in the second month of school. Grade-equivalent scores are a handy way of expressing scores in academic terms. Finally, some formal assessments use stanine scores. Stanine, short for standard nine, is a nine-point scale, with one lowest and nine highest. The stanine system provides a general look at performance.

**Informal assessment**

Whereas formal assessments generate objective results, informal assessments contribute more generally to the teacher's understanding of the student's strengths and weaknesses. Informal assessment is an extremely broad concept: it includes any observation made by the teacher that does not generate a concrete score. For instance, when a teacher asks her class questions about a story they have read together, she is performing an informal assessment of the class. She may not be grading the class' answers, but she is surely taking note of the students who understood the story and those who did not. When a teacher asks students to read aloud, she is collecting information about their ability. Informal assessment can also include assignments completed during class, homework, class presentations, and student conferences. Any interaction between student and teacher that helps the teacher gauge the student's progress can be considered informal assessment.

**Theoretical orientation**

In the promotion of biliteracy in the ESL classroom, teachers have to juggle a number of competing interests. They want to maintain and develop reading skills in the primary language, but they also want to improve academic language proficiency in English. They may also be constricted by the elements of the ESL program design. In order to organize their efforts, many teachers subscribe to a specific theoretical orientation to reading instruction. The theoretical orientation is simply a set of assumptions and beliefs that prescribe goals and expectations for students. Many teachers use a specific theoretical orientation as a guide to choosing instructional procedures and materials. Teachers will select a theoretical orientation that creates the type of environment they believe is most conducive to expansion of reading skills. There are three main types of theoretical orientation in reading instruction: the phonics approach; the skills or balanced approach; and the whole language approach.

**Phonics approach**

The phonics approach to ESL reading instruction emphasizes the importance of the relationship between sound and comprehension. A teacher who uses this approach starts out with the basic units of spoken language, phonemes, and gradually increases complexity to include word units, phrases, and sentences. A teacher using this approach goes to a great deal of trouble to outline and make explicit the correspondences between sounds and letters. Instruction on recognizing specific words by sight is only used for words that cannot be decoded by phonics. English is notorious for having a large number of exceptions to the rules of phonics. The phonics approach emphasizes language units smaller than word level, so students typically do not begin reading out loud until they have developed a strong foundation.

**Skills/balanced approach**

The skills/balanced approach to reading instruction in a secondary language focuses on giving students a set of tools with which to make sense of simple texts. Students in a class that uses this approach will find themselves reading authentic texts in English much faster than will students in a classroom using the phonics approach. The skills approach emphasizes building a large vocabulary of words that can be recognized on sight, with less priority placed on the systematic teaching of phonics. The teacher will try to give students the ability to recognize words by root, prefix, suffix, or configuration. Over time, students will be given the tools to recognize a word by context. At first, however, the teacher will concentrate on introducing vocabulary words with a concentration on the first and last consonant sounds. Teachers need to perform constant assessment when using this approach to ensure that students are not overwhelmed by the plunge into texts in English.

**Whole language approach**

Teachers who use the whole language approach to ESL reading instruction concentrate on the specific functions of language. From almost the very beginning of instruction, students are provided with quality children's literature. There is a strong emphasis on communication skills in the whole language approach, with students encouraged to participate in dialogues and role-plays in the English. Students are often encouraged to generate their own stories, and one of the priorities of instruction is to develop an overarching sense of narrative structure before teaching smaller units of language. To the extent that they are used at all, phonics and word attack skills are incorporated in the general reading experience. They are typically mentioned only when they have a direct correlation to a part of the assignment. This approach is especially popular for teaching older students and adults.

**Graphophonemic cueing systems**

Teachers will often have to use what are known as cueing systems in their interactions with students. There are three basic kinds of cueing system. In the graphophonemic system, the teacher concentrates on explicating grapho-phoneme-morpheme relationships to speed word recognition. In other words, students are encouraged to declare the similarities and differences between written and spoken forms of a sound. Over time, the teacher seeks to extend phonemic awareness based on sounds in the student's primary language that are different from sounds in English. In general, it is a good idea to conduct this kind of cueing after students have developed a small sight vocabulary. Cueing should follow a logical sequence, and should be sure to inculcate rules thoroughly before presenting any exceptions. Students should be encouraged to apply what they learn about phonics to their independent work.

### Semantic/syntactic cueing

The second kind of cueing system that many teachers will need to use is known as the semantic/syntactic cueing system. This involves asking the student to predict the meaning of a word based on syntax and grammar clues. Obviously, this kind of cueing can only work with students who have achieved a moderate level of linguistic knowledge. It is especially valuable with students who need a little practice in discovering context clues and solidifying their understanding of the structure of English syntax. The final kind of cueing system is referred to as discourse or deep structure cueing. In this process, students are encouraged to associate relevant background knowledge with the words that are being discussed. Through creating these associations, it has been found that students improve their chances of memorizing new vocabulary. The discourse method of cueing also enables students to discover underlying patterns of exposition and discourse; that is, it familiarizes them with the ways in which arguments are made in different languages.

### Yopp-Singer Test of Phonemic Segmentation

Because sound segmentation is considered the most difficult test of phonemic awareness, many teachers use the Yopp-Singer Test of Phonemic Segmentation as a general measure. In this oral test, the teacher reads 22 words aloud and the student states the component sounds in order. The test should be composed of simple, one-syllable words that the student is likely to know already. The Yopp-Singer Test is a good yardstick for general progress in phonemic awareness, but in order to get a comprehensive look, a teacher needs to assess each of the six phonemic awareness skills. This can be done in similar fashion to the Yopp-Singer, by providing the student with a list of about twenty words and asking him to perform the phonemic task. Of course, the words are to be read aloud to the student.

### Sound blending, deletion, isolation, matching, and substitution

To test sound blending the teacher might read words slowly, one phoneme at a time, and ask the student to say the word at regular speed. In the assessment of sound deletion, sound isolation, sound matching, and sound substitution, separate examinations need to be given for beginning, medial, and end phonemes. A sound matching test, for instance, must include twenty cases in which the phonemes are at the beginning of the words, twenty in which the phonemes are in the middle, and twenty in which the phonemes are at the end. Also, it is important to use different phonemes in the exercises. For example, there should not be a long /a/ sound at the beginning of all the words used in a sound matching exercise. Students need to demonstrate that they can perform these phonemic awareness tests with all of the phonemes in the English language.

### Emergent literacy model

Three of the most common approaches to providing balanced instruction are the emergent literacy, language acquisition, and reading readiness models. The emergent literacy model suggests that children have a natural tendency towards language learning. In other words, children are constantly exposed to the concepts of print, reading, and oral language, and therefore do not need a great deal of explicit instruction on these subjects. According to the proponents of emergent literacy, students do not need a great deal of external motivation to acquire literacy. Instead, adults and other teachers should create a good environment for learning and then stay out of the way.

**Language acquisition model**

The language acquisition model is slightly different from the emergent literacy model. Proponents of this model agree that students have a predisposition to become literate, but disagree about the influence of direct instruction. The language acquisition model emphasizes the role of educators in solidifying students' natural understanding of language and literacy. A teacher who subscribes to the language acquisition model would use a greater mix of explicit teaching strategies, so that students can examine their assumptions about language. The language acquisition model, then, includes a great deal of metacognition, or thinking about thinking. Students are encouraged to self-correct their learning processes.

**Reading readiness model**

The reading readiness model for balanced teaching is opposite to the emergent literacy model. It places a great deal of emphasis on the direct instruction of reading skills, going so far as to suggest that some students will remain illiterate unless they are given explicit instruction in the basics of reading. The proponents of reading readiness deny that literacy can spontaneously emerge from long exposure to texts and language; on the contrary, they claim that certain reading skills are prerequisite to literacy. That is, students must be ready to learn how to read. This model is somewhat undermined by instances of self-teaching, but for most students, it is true that explicit attention must be paid to concepts of literacy.

**Basic concepts of print**

According to the influential researcher Marie M. Clay, there are four basic print concepts: the meaning of print; the direction of text; letter, word, and sentence representation; and book orientation. The fundamental concept of print is that it has meaning. Some students will arrive in the classroom with this understanding, but others, especially those who do not come from a print-rich home, will not. It is possible to understand that print has meaning without being able to read. Indeed, many students who have not yet obtained literacy demonstrate print awareness by improvising words and narratives for illustrated books. The child cannot read the text, but is aware that it is telling a story related to the illustrations. Such a child has mastered the fundamental concept of print. There are innumerable teaching activities that reinforce this concept: writing on the board, reading a book aloud, and pointing out the words on common traffic signs, for instance. It is important for students to understand that print appears in many places besides books and magazines. Billboards, signs, and product labels all contain meaningful print.

**English print orientation**

Once a child has mastered the concept that print carries meaning, he can begin to appreciate the style in which English print is written. Specifically, the child can begin to see that English is read from left to right, and that lines of print are read in descending order. The movement from the right end of one line to the left end of the line beneath is known as a return sweep. When a student can perform the return sweep, he has mastered the directionality and tracking of printed English. This concept can be assessed rather easily by following the student's eyes as print is read.

### Recognition of letters and sentences

Having obtained some basic orientating principles, students can discover the units of printed English: letters, words, and sentences. Before they can learn to read, students must understand that letters make up words, and that words make up sentences. Students must be able to identify how many letters are in a word, as well as how spaces indicate the boundaries of a word. Provided they have sufficient counting ability, students should be able to enumerate the letters in the word and the words in a sentence. Students should be able to identify the marks of punctuation that indicate the end of a sentence (namely the period, question mark, and exclamation point). Moreover, students should be able to recognize how these rules of print exist in different formats, such as on books, signs, and labels. Of course, students do not need to be literate to demonstrate all of these skills. On the contrary, most students acquire a basic knowledge of print units long before they can read, much less identify specific letters and words.

### Features of a book

The last of the basic print concepts outlined by Clay is the features of a book. Students need to be able to identify the various book parts, like the cover, the pages, and the back cover. Students should know how a book is held and how it is stored. Eventually, students should be able to distinguish between the name of the book and the name of the author on the front cover. The student should know that a book is read from the front to the back and from the left page to the right page. Picture books are especially good at demonstrating these concepts, because the sequence of the pictures corresponding to the action is the same as the sequence of print locations. In other words, the illustrations can be followed throughout the book in the same way as the print. Almost all students will have a basic idea of how a book is handled while it is being read. A teacher, though, needs to ensure that students understand the steps in reading a book, as well as the parts of a book.

### Letter recognition

Along with these four concepts, many educators include letter recognition as a fundamental part of early print awareness. Letter recognition is simply the identification of the letter in both uppercase and lowercase forms. Accurate and rapid uppercase and lowercase letter recognition is an essential component of reading development. Letter recognition does not entail writing the letter or even knowing the sound produced by the letter. All it entails is seeing the letter and being able to give its name. Some teachers do combine letter recognition with basic letter production, though it is not necessary to do so. Letter recognition develops along with the alphabetic principle: that is, the idea that English words are made up of individual letters, each of which has an identity of its own.

### Alphabetic principle

The alphabet in a language is the set of letters that make up all the words. One of the first things that most students learn in their linguistic studies is the alphabet. For one thing, students need to be familiar with all the letterforms before they can begin producing written expressions. As students are learning their letters, the teacher needs to ensure that they make the connection between the way a letter is written and the way it sounds. Even when this connection is primitive, it paves the way for a more sophisticated understanding of language in the future. At this point, teachers are attempting to promote the so-called alphabetical principle: specific sounds are consistently associated with specific letters.

One of the problems with implementing the alphabetic principle in English is that English does not always do a very good job of following the alphabetic principle. There are innumerable examples of letters that have multiple sounds or words in which particular letters make no sound at all. To avoid burdening students with these exceptions to the basic alphabetic rules, a teacher needs to be good at selecting solid examples for early class instruction. As students progress, it may become appropriate to begin discussing the complexity of the English language as it relates to the alphabet. The only way to determine when it is appropriate is to have a solid mastery of informal and formal assessment.

For some students, establishing the alphabetic principle is quite difficult. For this reason, teachers need to have on hand a broad spectrum of instructional materials, including books, drawings, and manipulatives. Furthermore, teachers need to be able to use all of these materials appropriately. Some students learn more effectively through the use of touch, and should be given manipulatives in the shapes of the letters. The ability to effectively implement a wide variety of instructional strategies obviously depends on accurate assessment. Other good sources of information about instructional methodology are coworkers and research journals.

**Reading aloud**

The easiest way to solidify print concepts is to read aloud to the class. Reading aloud demonstrates how books are held, how pages are turned, and, most important, how those mysterious symbols on the page become spoken words with meaning. Of course, the students will not be thinking such dry thoughts as the story is being read. Nevertheless, simply reading an interesting storybook to a group of students is a great way to indicate the basic concepts of print. This process is strengthened when the teacher points at the words as they are read and moves slowly through each line of text. Even when students have little letter recognition, they will quickly figure out that the hand movements of the teacher correspond to the words coming out of her mouth. Also, before beginning the book, the teacher can show students the cover and point to the title and the name of the author.

Sometimes, reading aloud is undermined by the size of the class. If there are too many students, the ones farthest away from the teacher may not be able to see her point to each word as it is read. Thus, some of the value of the exercise is lost. Some ingenious publishers have surmounted this problem by creating enormous books with extra-large type, so that even students in the very back row can see the layout clearly. When these books are not available, however, teachers should be ready to use some alternate strategies. For instance, many teachers just divide the class into groups and read the story to the groups in turn. One advantage of this strategy is that the teacher has more opportunity to observe each of the students. Also, students in a small group are more likely to pay attention to the book. (Of course, this presumes that the remaining students will stay on task!) Reading aloud to small groups is a great job to give teaching assistants and parent volunteers. The reader should move slowly through the book, pointing at every word as it is read.

**Developing sound matching skills**

Sound matching is the identification of identical phonemes. In other words, sound matching requires the student to discern when two words contain the same sound. This is not the same as rhyming, because the identical sounds can appear in different parts of the words and need not appear at the end. For instance, a teacher might ask students to name the sound the words *apple*, *pear*, and *peach* have in common. If the students can see that the /p/ sound is present in all three of these words, then they are adept at sound matching. Another way to teach sound matching is to have students identify classroom objects that begin with a certain sound. For instance, a teacher might make the /p/ sounds and see if students can point out the posters, plants, picture frames, and other items that begin with a *p*. To work on sound matching with phonemes in the medial or end positions, the teacher could pronounce a phoneme and then three words, only one of which contains the given phoneme. This word should have the phoneme in the medial or end position. The teacher can then ask the students to identify the word containing the given phoneme.

**Sound isolation skills**

Sound isolation is the identification of the component sounds in a word. Even one-syllable words can have multiple phonemes. Students with no training in syllabification or word analysis may nevertheless be able to identify the series of discrete sounds that make up a word. To begin with, sound isolation can be taught by asking students to identify the sound at the beginning of a number of words with the same initial letter. For example, the teacher might determine whether students can identify that *girl*, *gift*, and *gear* all start with the /g/ sound. A teacher might ask her class to isolate the sounds in the word *flag*. This word contains four separate sounds, one for each of its letters. To be competent at sound isolation, students must be able to identify the beginning, medial, and end phonemes. Of course, some phonemes (like diphthongs) are more difficult to identify. So long as students are capable of identifying simple phonemes in all the possible positions within a word, they are judged to have phonemic awareness. It is a good idea to show students how the same phoneme can appear in different words, so that students do not too closely associate a phoneme with a particular word.

**Sound blending skills**

Sound blending is the combination of disparate phonemes to create a word. When teachers slowly pronounce a word, one sound at a time, they are essentially modeling sound blending for their students. Students demonstrate sound blending by speeding up this slow pronunciation and using the word as it is normally spoken. For instance, a teacher could model the word *ball* by saying *b*, then *aw*, then *ll*. Students should be able to combine these sounds to form the entire word. One common technique when modeling this pronunciation is to include a drawing or photograph of the object being pronounced. Also, sound blending often occurs as part of a phonics lesson, in which students pronounce the parts of the word as the teacher points at the various letters. However, for the purposes of phonemic awareness, it is not necessary to have the written version of the word. All that matters is that the students can identify how the constituent phonemes join to create a word.

**Sound substitution skills**

Sound substitution is the transfer of different phonemes into a given position in a word. For example, a student with phonemic awareness could hear the word *boy* and would know that if a /k/ sound were used instead, the resulting word would sound like *coy*. Once again, a student does not need to have any understanding of print or written language in order to master sound substitution. Also, it is perfectly acceptable for the class to create nonsense words when practicing sound substitution. One common method of reinforcing this skill is with the song, "I Like to Eat Apples and Bananas." This song has very simple lyrics, but in each verse all of the vowel sounds are replaced with a single sound. So, after the initial verse of "I like to eat apples and bananas," the song proceeds to "A lake tay ate apples and bananas," with all of the *a* sounds being long. The song then moves on to *e*, *i*, *o*, and *u*. Of course, the lyrics of the song become gibberish when all of the vowel sounds are the same, but students will soon find it easy to substitute phonemes.

**Sound deletion skills**

Sound deletion is the identification of what results when a phoneme is removed from a given word. This task is a little bit more difficult, because it requires students not only to understand that words are composed of individual sounds, but that sounds can be taken away from words. As an example, a teacher might ask the class to pronounce the word *boy*, and then to pronounce what is left when the /b/ sound is removed. It is a good idea to begin by removing initial phonemes, but students should eventually be able to delete medial and end phonemes as well. Many teachers have found that sound deletion is best introduced with consonant blends (such as in the words *spray* and *glade*), perhaps because the removal of the initial consonant does not drastically change the structure of the word.

### Sound segmentation skills

Sound segmentation is the identification of all the component phonemes in a word. This is considered by most education experts to be the most difficult task in phonemic awareness. Most students can easily identify the beginning phonemes but have a harder time with the medial and end phonemes. It is best to start with simple words. For instance, a teacher might pronounce the word *tub* and see if students can identify the /t/, /u/, and /b/ sounds. In order for sound segmentation to be complete, the student must identify all three of the sounds. It is not a good idea to begin sound segmentation with multisyllable words or words with diphthongs. Also, sound segmentation should not be confused with syllabification, in which words are divided into their component syllables.

### Promoting phonemic awareness

Several activities promote phonemic awareness. Even children in the early stages of literacy will have an intuitive understanding of rhyme, so a teacher could ask students to come up with rhymes for a simple word like *cat*. Similarly, a teacher can use simple songs to illustrate rhyming and promote phonemic awareness. Many books for children are written in verse or feature alliteration (the repetition of initial sounds), both of which can be used to introduce phonemic concepts. Assonance, which is the repetition of a vowel sound, can also be used to demonstrate phonemic awareness.

### Identification of the main idea

Literal comprehension is an understanding of the explicit elements of the text. In other words, it is the comprehension of the author's direct message. There are four component skills in literal comprehension. To begin with, a student must be able to identify an explicit main idea. Of course, in many texts (for instance, in stories), there will be no main idea as such or the main idea will not be stated directly. When reading an expository or informational text, however, students must be able to ascertain the author's central message. Even when a main idea is not explicit, a reader should be able to describe the tone of the message.

### Identification of details, sequence of events, and causal relationships

The second literal comprehension skill is the ability to identify important details in the text. As with the main idea, some texts will not permit ready identification of important details. Nevertheless, a student should be able to identify some important supporting elements in the text and be able to articulate why they are important. The third skill is identifying the sequence of events in a story or the sequence of argument in an expository text. If the student has mastered the identification of main idea and supporting details, recognizing the sequence should not pose any problems. Finally, literal comprehension requires the identification of cause-and-effect relationships. This is similar to identifying the sequence of events, though it forces the student to look for specific and explicit reasons for the events.

### Inferential comprehension

Inferential comprehension, meanwhile, is the understanding of the implicit elements of the text. Everything that is not written by the author but can be guessed by the reader is in the realm of inferential comprehension. Inferential comprehension skills are essentially the same as literal comprehension skills, except they rely on the perception of implied ideas and events. The two components of inferential comprehension are inferring an implicit main idea and inferring details, sequence of events, and cause-and-effect relationships. For most students, inferential comprehension lags behind literal comprehension. This is to be expected: students who are still solidifying the mechanics of reading have no thought to spare for implied messages. Nevertheless, even at a young age, students can be encouraged to begin thinking of the implications of what they read, so that once their basic skills have evolved, they will be primed to think about texts in a more sophisticated manner.

**Evaluative comprehension**

The third set of reading comprehension skills, those of evaluative comprehension, is probably the most advanced. Evaluative comprehension is the ability to consider the text as a whole and to make judgments about it. Students must achieve fluency in all areas of reading before they can evaluate a text effectively. Three specific skills combine in evaluative comprehension. To begin with, a student must be able to recognize an author's bias. This is similar perhaps to inferential comprehension, insofar as it requires the reader to look beyond the explicit message in the text. When making an ostensibly objective argument, an author will often reveal his personal inclination through details, passing comments, and subtle characterizations. It takes a great deal of perception on the part of the reader to detect bias.

**Detecting propaganda**

A significant component of evaluative comprehension is the detection of propaganda. Propaganda is argument or information communicated for the sole purpose of helping or harming a particular group. Although the word has acquired a negative connotation in English, not all propaganda is destructive. A leaflet outlining the reasons to help the poor, for instance, might be propaganda on behalf of a charity organization, but not many people would criticize it. Often, however, propaganda is not explicitly declared as such. When this is the case, students need to be able to identify it.

**Fact and opinion**

The final component of evaluative comprehension is distinguishing between fact and opinion. In the first few years of reading instruction, a student is unlikely to encounter texts in which the boundary between fact and opinion is ambiguous. As students grow up and begin reading texts of greater complexity, however, it will sometimes be difficult to tell when an author is stating an established truth and when he is simply giving an opinion. It is essential for students to recognize the difference, so that they can make informed decisions about what is being said. As with propaganda, it should be noted that subtle or implied opinion is not necessarily a bad thing. In many cases, students will agree wholeheartedly with the opinion of the author. The important thing is to recognize when an opinion is being given. Students need to cultivate this skill so that they can think critically about advertising, editorial messages, and other opinionated communications.

**Syntax and comprehension**

Syntax (the order of the words in a sentence) can facilitate or impede reading comprehension. English is an uninflected language, which means that the grammatical use of words is not denoted by their ending. Unlike inflected languages like Latin, then, the words in an English sentence must be in a particular order to make sense. As students begin to encounter texts of greater sophistication, however, they will see increasingly complex sentence structures. Some of these may be inscrutable to developing readers. It is very important for students to understand complex grammatical structures. This understanding can be aided by sentence diagramming, though oral presentation of complex sentences can also have a positive effect. If a teacher reads a complex sentence with appropriate prosodic emphasis, the student receives a model for comprehension.

### Independent reading

Independent reading can be a great help in the reinforcement of comprehension skills and strategies. Students who read by themselves become self-reliant with respect to comprehension. To this end, teachers should provide frequent opportunities for sustained silent reading in class. As students grow older, these sessions may increase in duration. Students should be encouraged to select books related to their interests or books that they will enjoy. Independent reading texts should always be at grade level. Education experts agree that the promotion of purposeful independent reading is the foundation of healthy reading habits for life.

### Self-monitoring and reading comprehension

A teacher needs to have some explicit instruction strategies for improving comprehension and helping students monitor their own comprehension. Reading is not as simple as moving the eyes across the page and following the word-for-word meaning of the message. It also includes relating sentences, paragraphs, and chapters to one another, weighing the argument or style of the author, and evaluating the message in its totality. This is a tall order, and students need to become accustomed to self-monitoring their performance in order to ensure optimal comprehension. Students should get into the habit of continually asking themselves, "Do I understand this?" If the answer is no, the student needs to reread and possibly ask for assistance. Students should be taught that there is no shame in not understanding a text, but that failing to recognize this and respond is unacceptable.

### Self-monitoring

There are a number of activities that students can use to self-monitor. If a student truly understands a text, he should be able to paraphrase its message. This means that the student should be able to articulate the main ideas without direct reference to the text. Also, the student should be able to put these ideas in his own words. This can be done orally or in writing. When the student's self-monitoring indicates that comprehension is suboptimal, the student should know to slow down. Sometimes, students feel pressure to finish a reading assignment quickly, and so they short-change comprehension. When this is the case, the teacher should relax any time constraints and allow the student to take as much time as necessary with the text. There is no benefit to reading unless there is comprehension, so simply skimming a text that needs to be learned is a waste of time. Students would be better off reading a short passage closely than merely glancing over the entire text.

### Taking notes

One way to ensure comprehension during the reading process is to take notes. In many cases, it will not be appropriate for students to write directly in the book, but they may write key ideas and questions on their own paper. Simply writing out the ideas from a text can be a major spur to comprehension. Students should be encouraged to write down any questions they develop while reading. It is a good habit to read with a pen and paper handy, since even the best readers cannot achieve total recall. At the very least, students should mark sections that ought to be reread, either because of their significance or their obscurity.

### Class discussion

After reading is complete, the teacher should use different instructional strategies to reinforce and cultivate comprehension. As much as possible, the teacher should lead class discussions of texts immediately after they are read and while they are still fresh in the minds of the class. Articulating the ideas of the text and listening to the reactions of classmates is a great way for students to solidify their understanding. In particular, the teacher should encourage students to make text-to-self, text-to-text, and text-to-world connections; that is, students should be encouraged to relate the ideas and events of the text to themselves, to other texts, and to the world in general. Comprehension requires critical as well as creative thinking.

### Pictures, semantic maps, and Venn diagrams

One of the most popular methods for increasing creative thinking about texts is to lead students in the creation of pictures, semantic maps, and Venn diagrams. Works of fiction often lend themselves to interpretation through drawing or painting. Students might be asked to draw a main character based on the description in the text, or perhaps to depict a major scene from the story. A semantic map is more appropriate for an expository or informational text, in which ideas and new vocabulary are presented in a network of relationships. A Venn diagram, finally, is composed of overlapping circles. For instance, an article about Congress might inspire a Venn diagram with two circles: one representing the Senate, and one representing the House of Representatives. These circles should partially overlap. The functions that are exclusive to each body would be written in the non-overlapping part, and the functions that are shared or performed by both bodies would be placed in the overlapping part.

### SQ3R

SQ3R stands for survey, question, read, recite, and review. This formula for in-depth reading has been around since 1946. It breaks the process down into five simple steps, in part as a way to demystify the experience of deep reading. The student begins by surveying the entire passage to be read, noting the title and section headings, any key words in bold, and any pulled quotes. Next, the student writes down a few questions that he expects will be answered by the text. This helps the student to structure his thinking about the text. The student then reads the text, all the while considering the questions he has posed. After reading, the student recites the material in the text, and in particular seeks to answer the questions posed earlier. Finally, the student reviews the material a few times in the future.

### KWL charts

KWL charts are used to improve reading comprehension and textual analysis. The chart is divided into three parts: what students already **know** about the subject, what they **want** the text to teach them about the subject, and, after they finish reading, what they have **learned** about the subject. The titles of the three sections (**K**now, **W**ant to know, and **L**earned) give the chart its name. A KWL chart helps students approach a text in such a way that they will obtain maximum benefit from reading. These charts are a simple way to organize one's thoughts about a text.

### QAR system

The QAR (question-answer relationships) system is an easy way for teachers to guarantee that they are asking a healthy range of reading comprehension questions. The QAR system distinguishes four types of question: right there; think and search; author and you; and on my own. A "right there" question probes literal comprehension by asking student to identify explicit details from the text. A "think and search" question requires the student to draw information from different parts of the text. Such a question might require the student to support his answer with examples from all over the text. An "author and you" question assesses inferential comprehension by asking the students to draw on their own knowledge and experience to answer a question about the text. This is distinct from an "on my own" question, which encourages the students to think about their own lives in the context of issues raised by the text. An "on my own" question takes the text as a starting point and asks the student to consider examples from his own life.

### CLOZE tests

CLOZE (short for "closure") tests are used to determine whether students will be able to understand a given text. Teachers often use them before beginning work with a particular textbook in a content area like science or social studies. The teacher takes a passage from the beginning of any chapter besides the first. He then enters the passage into a word processor and deletes every fifth word. The teacher hands out copies of the modified passage to the students and asks them to read the passage in its entirety, and then go back and attempt to fill in the blanks. If the student gets at least 40 percent of the answers correct (the only correct answer is the word in the original text), then the teacher should be able to use the text successfully. The passage must be at least 275 words so that there will be sufficient blanks.

### Read-alouds

Listening comprehension is the foundation of reading comprehension development. To this end, teachers need to incorporate oral language activities in the development of comprehension skills. For example, teachers can lead strategic, purposeful read-alouds. A read-aloud is the guided oral presentation of a story, with pauses at key points for questioning and discussion. As the class proceeds through the text, the teacher might pause to ask them to evaluate what has happened or predict what is about to happen. The teacher might also pause just to ask students to identify some main ideas or details from the text.

### Methods of text-based discussion

Text-based discussions, such as instructional conversations, questions for the author, and think-pair-share exercises, can enhance reading comprehension. In an instructional conversation, the teacher helps the student develop an approach to comprehension by asking questions about the main idea and details. This is a sort of Socratic dialogue, in which the teacher probes the student's knowledge and tries to make the student evaluate his assumptions and judgments. Another method is to have students come up with questions for the author. This exercise is good for demonstrating that texts do not just provide answers, they also generate questions. In a think-pair-share exercise, the teacher asks the entire class a question about the text they have just read. Students then arrange themselves into pairs, where they discuss their answers to the question. The student pairs then share their answers with the class at large. This progressive activity gives students a chance to refine their insights.

### Letter recognition

Letter recognition can be reinforced through reading aloud, but it will probably require some more direct instruction at first. The tried and true method of developing letter recognition is to lead children slowly through the alphabet song while pointing to each letter as it is sung. Research has indicated that students learn unfamiliar material much more quickly when they are given a mnemonic, or memory aid. In this case, the alphabet song is such a mnemonic. Of course, the song only primes the students' brains for more specific training in letter recognition. A teacher should also lead the class in activities that require more sophisticated letter recognition. For instance, a teacher might ask the students to identify individual letters in a storybook.

**Alphabet books**

There are a number of books that proceed through the alphabet in order, exemplifying each letter with a couple of objects ("A is for apple," etc.). Another way to build letter recognition is to hand out index cards printed with a letter and then write a message in large print on the chalkboard. Students will then be asked to tape their index card over the letter where it appears in the chalkboard message. The cards can be shuffled and distributed several times, so that students get to perform the exercise with different letters. It is important for students to recognize letters both in and out of the alphabetic sequence. In other words, if a student can only identify a *J* by saying to himself "H, I, J, K," then this student needs to improve his letter recognition.

**Concepts About Print**

One simple formal assessment for print concepts is the Concepts About Print test, developed by Marie M. Clay. This test requires special books, which are available from educational publishers or can be made easily by teachers. A CAP test book contains at least ten pages, some of which are upside down and on some of which the print is jumbled and oriented incorrectly. For instance, the print on one page might run from right to left or vertically up the page. However, the majority of the pages in the book should be laid out in the traditional manner. The book should be a simple story and should only include basic vocabulary. The cover and title pages should be positioned correctly.

To perform a CAP test, the teacher gives the book to the student and asks her to identify the cover, the title, and the author's name. The teacher then asks the child to open the book to the first page. Once there, the student should be asked to identify the starting word of the book. The teacher should read through the book slowly. At various times, the student should be asked where the teacher is to read next. Also, the student should be asked to count the letters in a word and the words in a sentence. If the student is advanced enough to have developed some sight vocabulary, he should be asked to identify some elementary words. If possible, the student should hold the book and turn the pages throughout the test. As the test continues, the student should be asked to identify common punctuation marks and in particular those that end a sentence. When the student comes to later sections in which text has been jumbled or laid out improperly, the student should be asked how to resolve the situation.

**Print concept instruction**

Students whose first language is not English may require extra help with print concepts. In particular, students whose native language is fundamentally different from English should receive special attention. Differentiated instruction for English language learners should recognize that not all languages are alphabetic. Alphabetic languages are those in which words are composed of letters. The letters in an alphabetic language remain the same, but are arranged into thousands of words. Alphabetic languages are distinguished by how regular the correspondence is between symbol and sound. Spanish, for example, is described as a transparent language because the sound of each letter is very predictable. English, on the other hand, is called an opaque language because many letters can make a variety of different sounds. If a child has experience only with transparent alphabetic languages, he may need some help in understanding that English letters are capable of producing a range of sounds.

**Problems with print concepts**

Native English speakers are often surprised to learn that only some languages adhere to the alphabetic principle. Many languages, such as Chinese, are not alphabetic at all. Chinese is a logographic language, which means that it is composed of pictures that represent entire words. A Chinese character is not a sequence of letters; it is an entire entity representing one word alone. Children who have grown up in a logographic linguistic culture will need more instruction with regard to print concepts in English. In many of these languages, the direction of print is different as well, so this too may necessitate instruction.

**Fluency and reading**

Fluency plays an important role in all stages of reading development. Indeed, fluency, word analysis skills, vocabulary, academic language, background knowledge, and comprehension are all related. For instance, fluency helps connect word analysis skills and comprehension. Once a child is fluent enough to decode words automatically, he will also be able to comprehend text much more quickly. According to the automaticity theory, fluency is directly responsible for reading comprehension improvement. In particular, students seem to demonstrate rapid advances in comprehension once they are fluent enough to read at a rate similar to that at which words are spoken. Once it is possible for a student to read at this normal rate, it becomes much easier to concentrate on the message of the text. Indeed, many authorities state that prosody and comprehension have a reciprocal relationship; that is, the improvement of prosody will contribute to the development of reading comprehension skills. The addition of the dramatic phrasing and intonation of prosody makes basic comprehension much easier. Indeed, phrasing and intonation communicate information as surely as words do: by spacing out blocks of words and placing emphasis on certain parts of a sentence, these prosodic elements tell the listener or reader what is important and what is not.

**Accuracy, rate, and prosody**

There are three interrelated indicators of reading fluency: accuracy, rate, and prosody. Accuracy is the correct decoding and recognition of words. Rate is the speed at which words are recognized correctly. Automaticity, then, is a combination of exceptional accuracy and a rapid rate of reading. Prosody, meanwhile, is the dramatic and artful reading style that improves the attention and understanding of the listener. Prosody may include applying the appropriate stresses or emphases, varying pitch and intonation, and pausing at appropriate times. All of the devices that an experienced speaker can use to present a text artfully fall under the heading of prosody. To do this, a speaker must have mastered the basics of written language. In order to phrase well, for instance, one must have a good knowledge of syntax and mechanics.

**Fluency disruption**

Unfortunately, a number of factors can disrupt fluency. They include a lack of familiarity with vocabulary, weak word analysis skills, a lack of background knowledge, a lack of familiarity with complicated syntactic structures, and an encounter with a text that has a number of seldom-used, multisyllabic content words. Fluency cannot be developed by repeated exposure to sophisticated texts. Instead, it must be cultivated gradually by repeated exposure to texts of ever-increasing sophistication. It is very important to give students decodable texts in order to promote fluent reading, especially while students are developing basic phonics skills. Over time, students should be shifted to texts of greater sophistication.

### Repeated reading and choral reading

As with other elements of reading instruction, systematic and explicit instruction is very important in promoting fluency development. A number of activities promote fluency. One is repeated reading, in which the teacher or students read the same text aloud two or more times in a row. Repeated reading allows students to anticipate words and phrases, which means they are more likely to improve their accuracy and rate and incorporate elements of prosody. Another way to improve fluency is through choral reading, in which the class reads a text aloud in unison. Choral reading will be dominated by the most advanced students in the class; however, as long as they are not discouraged, other students will improve their fluency in their effort to keep up. Choral reading should be performed slowly and should be led by the teacher.

### Dramatic reading and reading with a recording

In dramatic reading exercises, students are encouraged to act out the narrative described in the text. Students will need to be familiar with the text before they can provide a decent dramatic reading, but once they do so, they may gain appreciation for the ways that reading can resemble performance. Encouraging students to think of a text as a message with emotional and dramatic content is a great way to develop fluency. Dramatic reading works well for developing fluency, but it requires a great deal of class participation. In some cases, it may be better to have students work individually. A great individual activity to improve fluency is to have students follow along with a recorded reading of a book. Students can read silently while listening to the recorded version on headphones. It is essential that the recorded book be easily decodable for the student.

### Reading silently vs. reading aloud

In the past, many education authorities recommended independent reading for improving fluency. However, independent, silent reading can only create so much in the way of automaticity. Students tend to skip over words they do not understand without spending any time trying to decode structure or context. Before students acquire automaticity, they need to work on reading aloud, even if only to themselves. The act of reading aloud forces students to confront every word in the text and to try pronouncing it at least. Repeated attempts in this manner will eventually result in automaticity.

### Improving fluency

Developing the fluency of English language learners creates some unique challenges. For English learners and speakers of nonstandard English, it may be necessary to give extra instruction with English patterns of intonation, phrasing, syntax, and punctuation. In particular, students who come from logographic linguistic communities may need assistance with these uniquely English elements of written and spoken language. One easy way to provide such an opportunity is to show these students movies in English. In many cases, students live with non-English speakers and have had much less incidental exposure to the rhythms and conventions of spoken English.

### Informal reading inventory

One of the most common versions of informal assessment is called the informal reading inventory, or IRI. The precise contents of an informal reading inventory vary by student ability, but the following tests are frequently included: word recognition list; graded reading passage; reading interest survey; print concepts test; phonemic awareness test; phonics test; structural analysis test; CLOZE test for content-area reading; vocabulary test; and spelling test. These assessments make up a comprehensive assessment of reading.

Informal reading inventories are typically administered individually, so that the teacher can observe the student's performance. In some cases, the informal reading inventories administered to two students in the same class will be different. There is more flexibility in informal assessment; the teacher has more freedom to select the precise array of assessments that will be most helpful.

The purpose of the informal reading inventory is to establish the student's independent, instructional, and frustration reading levels. At the independent reading level, the student understands and can pronounce 95 percent of the words in the text and answers 90 percent of grade-level reading comprehension questions correctly. Students reading at this level do not need any help from the teacher or from their classmates. This is a good level for pleasure and research reading. At the instructional reading level, the student understands and can pronounce 90 percent of the words in the text and answers at least 60 percent of grade-level reading comprehension questions. A student reading at the instructional level will need some help, though he ultimately will be capable of reading the text. A textbook or basal reader should be at the student's instructional reading level, so that he will be challenged but not overwhelmed.

The protocol for performing an informal reading inventory with an ESL student is only slightly different. Because these students may have comprehension skills that far surpass their vocabulary, they should be given an opportunity to demonstrate understanding in ways other than language. For instance, ESL students might be asked to draw a picture or short comic strip depicting the events of a story. Indeed, illustrated stories can be a particular help with ESL students, because the connections between illustration and text reinforce fluency. ESL students may also benefit from hearing a story read aloud, since otherwise they may develop bad pronunciation habits based on their native language.

**Frustration reading level**

At the frustration reading level, the student cannot understand or pronounce at least 90 percent of the words in the text and cannot answer at least 60 percent of grade-level reading comprehension questions. Children should not be made to read at their frustration level without assistance. It should be noted that children are perfectly able to listen to and obtain meaning from texts they themselves would read at the frustration level. However, children will not obtain any benefit from reading such advanced texts on their own or aloud. On the contrary, prolonged exposure to frustration-level texts can be damaging to self-esteem and the development of literacy.

**Assessing the components of fluency**

The assessment of fluency is generally holistic, since fluency itself is an integration of disparate language skills. There are unique assessments for the components of fluency, however. A teacher needs to be able to use all types of assessments with respect to all three components of fluency. Accuracy and rate can be easily assessed by having the student read a grade-level text aloud. The accuracy of reading can be determined by calculating the number of words read correctly as a portion of the total words read. The rate of reading can be calculated on a per-minute basis by timing the student as he reads. Students should not be encouraged to read quickly, but rather to read with as much expression as they can. Prosody is a little more difficult to measure directly. Students may be asked to read a narrative aloud with as much expression as possible. Various generic rubrics are available that allow teachers to grade all areas of prosody: intonation, phrasing, etc. Many teachers audiotape these readings so that they can assess in more depth.

**Holistic methods**

The holistic assessment of fluency can be accomplished many different ways. Teachers often use dramatic or choral readings as informal assessments of fluency. Fluency should be assessed with regard to both unfamiliar and familiar texts. When students are being assessed on their reading of a text with which they are unfamiliar, the text must be at grade level. If a text is too difficult for the student to read fluently, the results of assessment will be useless. This is because a student's performance on a text that is just a little too hard is liable to be indistinguishable from his performance on a text that is way too hard. It is also worthwhile to assess students as they read texts that they have read a few times. Students who have a concept of prosody but do not yet have enough accuracy or speed to make use of this knowledge will demonstrate much more fluency when they are working with a familiar text.

**Phonemic instruction for ELL**

There are not many changes in phonemic instruction for English language learners. It is likely that most of the English phonemes will be present in the student's native language. The teacher should consult a reference to determine which phonemes the student is unlikely to know already. These phonemes should receive extra attention during instruction. Other than that, the instructional methods for English language learners are the same as for native English speakers. If necessary, the teacher may begin activities by working in the student's first language, though the transition to English should be made as soon as possible.

**Problems learning phonics**

Students for whom English is a second language may have some initial trouble with phonics. Long exposure to their native language will have created certain "habits of listening," which may make it difficult for the students to identify subtle variations in the way English letters (in particular vowels) are pronounced. These students may be well served by extra exposure to English rhymes and word families, though simply receiving greater exposure to English as it is spoken will inevitably bring them up to speed. Indeed, most experts assert that English language learners ought to acquire basic oral fluency before turning to written language. In large part, this is because the habits of speech contribute to an intuitive understanding of orthography and spelling. In addition, however, the comfort and confidence derived from oral fluency will be important during what is often a difficult transition. Some languages, including Spanish, use a similar alphabet and have significant overlap with English phonics. Teachers should reinforce these similarities while spending more time going over the differences. It should be assumed that advanced English language learners already have competence in phonics in their first language, so instruction in English can focus on specific problem areas.

**Sight vocabulary**

The assessment of sight vocabulary is fairly simple and can be conducted either formally or informally. The student should be presented with the word and asked to read it aloud. If the word is in sight vocabulary, the student should be able to read the word without hesitation and without sounding it out. If the word has more than one phoneme or syllable, there should be no gaps or pauses during pronunciation. Sight vocabulary should be assessed both in and out of context. In other words, the teacher should observe the student reading sight vocabulary words as part of a sentence as well as on their own. Sometimes, students automatically pronounce isolated words that they might stumble over in the midst of a complex sentence. For a word truly to be in sight vocabulary, it must be read almost reflexively, no matter how it is presented.

### Teaching multisyllabic words

Instruction must begin by covering multisyllabic words that are formed by the addition of a common prefix or suffix to a base word. One of the most common strategies for improving word identification is to teach students the common morphemes and affixes (prefixes and suffixes). This strategy is especially useful with words derived from Latin, because they have a more regular structure. Structural analysis can be taught through a phonics-centered method or through the balanced literary approach. Either way, the teacher should be familiar with the basic word parts: root words, prefixes, suffixes, inflectional endings, and contractions.

### Root words, affixes, and contractions

Root words are the bases from which complex words are developed. In the word *working*, for instance, the root word is *work*. The other part of this word, *–ing*, is both a suffix and an inflectional ending. A suffix is any ending attached to a root word, while an inflectional ending is a suffix that alters the meaning of the word. In this case, the addition of the suffix *–ing* changes the tense of *work*. A prefix, meanwhile, is attached to the beginning of a word. Adding the prefix *re-* to the start of *working*, for instance, would make the word mean "working again." Prefixes have regular meanings and can be taught easily. Contractions are abbreviated combinations of two words, like *don't* for *do not* or *would've* for *would have*. In a contraction, the deleted letters are replaced by an apostrophe.

### Teaching affixes

There is a recommended sequence for the instruction of affixes. The teacher should begin by focusing on the correspondence between letters and sounds. Once this has been established, the teacher should introduce the affixes in isolation. Some of the most common prefixes are *pre-*, *re-*, *un-*; some of the most common suffixes are *–ing*, *-tion*, and *–ment*. Students should become familiar with these affixes by themselves at first. Then, the teacher can give examples of how they are used in specific words. Once students have learned some examples of these common affixes, the words can be taught as they appear in context. One way to expand on discussion of common word structures is to guide students in the creation of word webs. A word web has at its center a common root, like *port*. Students can then draw lines out from this hub to other words that share that root, like *deport*, *important*, *import*, and *portable*. Many students benefit from this kind of depiction of the relationships between words.

### Syllabic analysis

Structural analysis will be useful with many types of words, but students also need to have syllabic analysis skills. Instruction should cover multisyllabic words with the common syllable patterns. In particular, students should receive special instruction related to compound words. Compound words comprise two or more base words. Some common compound words are *mailbox*, *bookmark*, and *butterfly*. Some students will benefit here from special instruction on syllabification. Although students may have developed solid phonemic awareness, they may not yet understand the division of a large word into syllables. There are many ways to teach this lesson, but perhaps the easiest is through song. In a song, notes are correspondent not to words but to syllables. By singing along with a simple song, children can learn to appreciate how words are divided. In addition, the teacher might ask students to pronounce multisyllabic words one syllable at a time, clapping on each syllable. Creating a rhythm of syllables helps many students understand the structural characteristics of words.

## Natural order hypothesis

In developing the secondary language writing skills of students, teachers should keep in mind the natural order hypothesis introduced by Krashen. This hypothesis suggests that there is a typical order of linguistic acquisition. In general, the ability to write will lag one or two levels behind oral proficiency level. Students will take a bit longer to develop a sense of form in their writing, and it may take them even longer to describe events and things accurately in their writing. Students will begin by learning to write words and simple phrases; with time, they will be able to compose sentences and eventually simple narratives. Bilingual students will often exhibit a strong reliance on their primary language proficiency in their English compositions. Some of the syntax errors that the individual makes in oral speech are likely to appear in writing as well. It is also common for bilingual students to spell words according to the letter-sound correspondence common to their primary language.

## Development of written communication

The ability to create thoughtful and meaningful written communication is one of the last elements of literacy to develop. Teachers need to be patient with students as they develop these skills. Although the development of written communication skills may lag behind the development of reading and speaking skills, teachers should not ignore the many connections between these aspects of literacy. For instance, through reading, students can develop an appreciation for the various letterforms. Speaking and listening to language can help students develop a feel for the rhythms and intonations of English sentences, so that when they begin to compose their own written work, they will intuitively mimic these qualities.

## Writing activities that improve reading comprehension

Writing activities can help to support and reinforce comprehension. For example, summarizing, outlining, and responding are all very useful. Summarizing is the brief recapitulation of the main points or events in a text. It can be performed orally or in writing. Outlining is the organization of main points or events in a text, typically according to a system of Roman numerals, numbers, and letters. In an outline, the main points are distinguished from supporting details. Responding is an immediate description of how the story or text made the reader feel. A student response might include questions generated by the text or experiences from the student's own life that can be related to the text.

## Importance of writing

Throughout instruction, the teacher should include activities that require students to write. Research has confirmed that there is a strong relationship between orthographic knowledge and word analysis. In other words, students who have ample practice writing out long words are more likely to learn the basics of structural and syllabic analysis. This stands to reason, as the process of writing forces students to consider the way in which words are constructed. After a time, students should be able to apply orthographic generalizations to unfamiliar words. One example of an orthographic rule is a change from *–y* in the singular to *–ies* in the plural. Many of these changes in written English occur according to regular patterns, so that students may be able to guess correctly when they encounter an unfamiliar pattern.

## Dialogue, double-entry, reader response, and personal

In a dialogue journal, the student makes an entry and receives a written response from another student or the teacher. A dialogue journal will take on the character of a conversation, in which the student and his interlocutor ask questions, compare experiences, and trade information. In a double-entry journal, students divide the page in half and write down different types of information on either side. For instance, on one side of the page the student might make a list of characters, and on the other side, he might detail the statements and actions of each character. In a reader response journal, students describe their emotional and intellectual reactions to a text. In a personal journal, students record their personal feelings and thoughts. The entries in a personal journal should only be read by the teacher, so that students feel comfortable recording ideas they may be embarrassed to share with their classmates.

**Stages of composition**

Many teachers break the composition process down into four stages. Pre-writing is the first stage. It includes the selection and narrowing of a topic, the determination of the audience, and, in some cases, the creation of an outline. During the pre-writing stage, students will narrow their topic and determine their target audience. In the second stage, drafting, the student composes a first version of the text. In the third stage, revising/editing, the student looks over the first draft and makes changes. Sometimes, it is useful to bring in another person, like a teacher or classmate, to make suggestions. This stage can also be called the proofreading stage. In the fourth stage, final draft, the student makes all necessary revisions and polishes the final version of the text.

**Pre-phonetic stage spelling development**

Pre-phonetic students may understand the alphabetic principle and yet not have developed letter recognition: such students will use any letter that comes to mind in their attempts at spelling. Students at this level are sometimes called semi-phonetic. Semi-phonetic spellers are also prone to omitting syllables, so their writing may be virtually unreadable. The instruction of students in the pre-phonetic stage largely focuses on the alphabetic principle. At this point, spelling cannot be addressed directly; to the contrary, spelling instruction should be a byproduct of instruction in the alphabet, phonics, and phonemic awareness. This makes sense: students cannot begin to arrange letters correctly (i.e., spell) until they have learned the alphabet and the correspondence between sounds and symbols. So, there is no need to develop or implement spelling lessons while students are in the pre-phonetic stage.

**Phonetic stage spelling development**

A student in the phonetic stage will have basic letter recognition skills and some basic knowledge about the common sounds made by the letters. During the phonetic stage, spelling instruction may become more direct. Students in the phonetic stage will be learning about the correspondences between letters and sounds, and so they will naturally be receptive to spelling-centered lessons. Spelling instruction should be limited to words with common consonant patterns and short vowel sounds. In addition, students can begin to learn common prefixes, suffixes, and rimes. Much of this information will also be a part of phonics and phonemic awareness instruction.

**Transitional stage spelling development**

During the transitional stage, spelling instruction becomes more variable. Some students may respond well to lessons about etymology or morphology, while others will improve their spelling simply by reading and writing as much as possible. Teachers have a great deal of freedom when working with students in the transitional stage, and so informal assessment should guide the development and implementation of lesson plans. This is a great time for lessons that cater to tactile or kinesthetic learners. For instance, students could be asked to mold letters out of clay or to chant the letters in a word while bouncing a ball. Some students respond very well to odd lessons like this. At the same time, transitional spellers are more receptive to detailed information about spelling. Indeed, many teachers wait until the transitional stage of spelling development to begin discussing homophones (words that sound the same despite having different spellings, like *bare* and *bear*).

**Word walls**

One common instructional method for students in the phonetic stage of spelling development is the creation of a word wall. A word wall is a large sheet of paper, taped to the wall, at the top of which is written a common word. The word at the top of the word wall should feature a common pattern of vowels or consonants. Students should then be encouraged to write on the paper other words with the same spelling pattern. As an example, a teacher might write the word *chair* at the top of the word wall. This word features the unique but commonplace rime *–air*. Underneath *chair*, students could write words like *air*, *pair*, *stair*, and so on. Teachers will often leave a word wall posted for days or weeks at a time, so that students can continue to find new words for inclusion. Word walls are a great way to encourage students to think about common spelling patterns and thereby promote strategic spelling.

**Word banks**

One task that teachers often assign conventional spellers is the creation of a word bank. Students are asked to keep an ongoing list of words they spell incorrectly or find confusing. For even the best conventional spellers, a few words cause consistent trouble. Students can use their word bank as a quick reference when they come upon one of their problem words, or they can spend some time consciously committing these words to memory. In one easy system for memorizing a difficult word, the student begins by saying the word aloud. Then, the student silently mouths each letter in the word. The student then shuts his eyes and attempts to spell the word aloud. Next, the student writes the word down and checks his spelling. If the spelling is incorrect, the student starts over. If the spelling is correct, the student writes the word one more time and then moves on to the next one. This memorization method perhaps seems laborious, but it involves a number of the senses and forces the student to become an active learner.

**Spelling test**

The traditional mode of assessment for spelling is the written test, in which the teacher reads a list of words aloud and students attempt to spell them. This is an acceptable method of assessing spelling, but it should be supplemented by assessment that is more rooted in everyday language use. Too often, spelling lessons consist of a word list handed out on Monday, studied on Thursday, tested on Friday, and forgotten by Saturday. Increasingly, education experts are asserting the importance of context for spelling instruction. Spelling books now organize word lists by letter pattern or theme: for instance, a list may be devoted to words associated with geology. Spelling lists should also include words that the student is likely to encounter in his reading, since this subsequent meeting will help to reinforce what has been learned. In general, early spelling tests conducted in the traditional style should only include words with common orthographic patterns; that is, words with regular roots, affixes, rimes, blends, diphthongs, and digraphs.

**Spelling assessments**

Despite the utility of the traditional spelling test, it is necessary for spelling assessment to encompass other methods as well. In particular, spelling assessment should focus on language as it is used in context. Students' writing should be evaluated not only for its diction, syntax, and content, but also for its spelling. It is while looking at a student's spelling in context that a teacher can develop a full appreciation for the student's competence. For instance, it should become clear when a student has not entirely mastered the correspondence between a particular sound and symbol. Also, some students (especially those with dyslexia) will invert the order of letters in common words. It is not enough to note that a word has been spelled incorrectly: the teacher needs to determine *how* it was spelled incorrectly. Spelling amounts to a series of choices, and a poor choice made in one instance is likely to be duplicated in similar situations unless there is an intervention. In other words, simply correcting a student's mistake is not effective. A teacher must demonstrate the applicable rule of spelling, or, if the student has erred with regard to a word that is an exception to the rule, must indicate this to be the case. Just as the context in which the error was made informs the assessment, so must the intervention provide context to the student.

**Structural and syllabic analysis vs. word analysis and spelling**

Regardless of whether these skills are explicitly taught, structural analysis and syllabic analysis are essential to accurate word analysis and the successful spelling of multisyllabic words. Students who develop excellent spelling will have obtained these skills, though they may not be able to articulate their principles. Structural analysis is the decoding of multisyllabic words that have a prefix or suffix attached to a root. Syllabic analysis, on the other hand, is the decoding of a multisyllabic word that follows one of the common syllable patterns, such as open and closed syllables. An open syllable ends with a vowel, typically a long vowel. A closed syllable has a vowel but ends with a consonant. In a closed syllable, the vowel is much more likely to be short. By learning this trick of syllabic structure, students can improve their spelling skills and word recognition.

**Contextual redefinition, semantic mapping, and semantic feature analysis**

In contextual redefinition, the teacher writes out the sentence in which the new word first appears and then asks the students to use the context to guess the meaning of the new word. In some cases, it may be necessary to include a couple of surrounding sentences. In semantic mapping, the teacher guides the students in the creation of a diagram demonstrating the relationships between the new word and other known words. Semantic feature analysis is a common method for teaching a group of related words. The teacher makes a grid, with the new words along the left side and a series of questions along the top. The students then answer the questions for each new word.

**Cognitive academic language learning**

One of the common approaches to helping students understand content-area instruction in their second language is known as the cognitive academic language learning approach. This approach relies on explicit teaching of learning strategies and endeavors to involve students in all aspects of their education. Advocates of this method believe that learning academic strategies in one area will translate into success in other areas. This method assumes that learning is an active and dynamic process in which information is selected and retained when it is made important to the learner. This method also emphasizes the need to make clear associations in content material. This approach is sometimes referred to as a metacognitive learning strategy, because it requires students to "think about thinking." Students are told explicitly the learning objectives, and help to develop the structure of the lesson to meet these objectives. Students are encouraged to relate learning processes to linguistic demands in the domains of listening, speaking, reading, and writing.

## Cognitive approaches

Many teachers endorse cognitive approaches to teaching a second language because they feel that making students as active as possible in their own education is advantageous. In order to do this, teachers need to be constantly making associations with students between current and prior instruction. Students may be asked to group words or concepts according to their attributes, or may be asked to elaborate how new ideas and concepts connect to their own lives. Teachers who use the cognitive approach often refer students to textbooks, dictionaries, and encyclopedias. Students will frequently be asked to make mental, oral, or written summaries of information. Teachers should frequently ask students to make inferences from the instructional material they have learned. Cognitive approaches do a good job of engaging advanced and motivated students, but they run the risk of alienating less-active types.

## Scaffolding

One of the instructional techniques frequently utilized by successful instructors is scaffolding, in which students receive occasional but timely support from the teacher, with the eventual goal being student independence. Scaffolding can be either verbal or procedural. In verbal scaffolding, teachers outline a subject, model it, and then allow students to practice until they achieve mastery. As the students get better, the teacher should provide less instruction. Procedural scaffolding, on the other hand, is the process whereby students are placed into different grouping configurations as they gain greater proficiency. Students will begin work as part of the whole class and then will be broken into small groups. Once a reasonable level of proficiency is achieved, students will work with a partner, with the eventual goal being proficient work as an individual.

## Tying curriculum to universals

When providing content-area instruction in English, the ESL teacher must be sure to maintain the connections between subjects. It is especially important for students working in their second language to get an explicit account of the associations between various subjects, as this tends to increase engagement and motivation. Whenever possible, teachers should illustrate the connections between disparate content areas and use overlapping vocabulary. Teachers should endeavor to connect specific content with overarching questions that pertain to all areas of study, and should encourage students to discuss these issues in class. By making connections between seemingly disconnected content areas, teachers can naturally foster fluency in English.

## Reciprocal teaching

Reciprocal teaching is an instructional strategy wherein teacher and students alternate leading a discussion about a piece of text. In other words, the teacher will lead the discussion for a while, and then students will take over. There are four basic steps in reciprocal teaching: summarizing, questioning, clarifying, and predicting. During the summarizing period, students will identify and discuss the most important parts of the text. At first, students will probably only be able to discuss and integrate themes on the sentence and paragraph levels. As they become more adept at summarizing, however, they should be able to evaluate and integrate information at the paragraph and passage levels. The teacher will guide students through this summarizing process at first, and then will allow students to take over.

There are quite a few advantages to reciprocal teaching. For one thing, it gives students the tools they will need to read independently with comprehension and insight. Also, the interactive nature of the instruction forces all the students in the class to participate. Many teachers find that reciprocal teaching encourages the formation of new relationships between low- and high-functioning students. Reciprocal teaching is especially effective for students who are good at decoding but have poor comprehension skills. Reciprocal teaching is also good for nonreaders. Reciprocal teaching seems to help good and poor students alike. Good students benefit from constructing elaborate questions, while poor students learn effective strategies for improving their own comprehension. Again, the interactive nature of reciprocal teaching seems to keep more students involved.

When incorporating the instructional strategy of reciprocal teaching in a lesson, the teacher will have to incorporate slightly modified strategies for assessment. In the main, teachers will have to rely on their listening skills to determine which students are learning the strategies. Teachers should be especially looking for students who make the transition from decoding to sophisticated comprehension. In some cases, the teacher may require students to write out questions and summaries. Some students may require additional scaffolding before they can successfully execute the strategies of reciprocal teaching. Over time, the teacher should try to eliminate his direct influence as much as possible. The nature of reciprocal teaching is similar to modeling in that teachers will demonstrate a method of self-instruction that students will learn to execute on their own.

**Questioning**

The questioning component of reciprocal teaching involves developing questions based on the content of the passage. Students will have to determine the essential information in the passage and then construct questions to test their own knowledge. Essentially, students are learning a self-assessment strategy for reading comprehension. In the clarifying stage, students will be asked to add detail to their summaries of the text. This component of reciprocal teaching is especially important with low-comprehension students, who may read automatically without much understanding. Usually, the clarifying process helps students to refocus their attention on the meaning rather than the sound of the text. In the final stage, predicting, students will speculate about what will happen next in the text. The ability to make a reasonable prediction depends on accurate comprehension.

**Challenges of ESL content-area instruction**

Many of the difficulties that English language learners have in reading literature in English have to do with differences of culture. If students do not have background knowledge of indigenous literary genres, they may have a hard time orienting themselves within the text. Students may also have a hard time with the abundance of idiomatic expressions in literature, as well as with the use of regional dialects. Some students will express confusion if a piece of writing docs not follow a clear and organized structure. Students may have a difficult time with figurative language and unorthodox sentence structures. Students may be unfamiliar with the language of literary analysis, and may have a tendency to literal-mindedness in their consideration of imagery and symbolism. Finally, English language learners may have a difficult time expressing their opinions or reactions to a story, especially when the setting or context is unfamiliar.

Mathematics

Often, students from other cultures emphasize getting the right answer to a mathematics problem at the expense of performing the right process. Students from other cultures may print their numbers differently and may have learned a different way to use the comma and decimal point. Many students will not have worked with manipulatives and may not understand the point of such activities. Many students will have never encountered a word problem and will be temporarily flummoxed by the process. Perhaps most important, many students will not be familiar with the jargon of mathematics. In many cultures, students are encouraged to perform mental math and so may not be used to demonstrating their calculations on paper. Similarly, many students will have learned math through memorization and will be inclined to repetition in their learning. Finally, many cultures do not teach math in a "spiral" fashion, so many students will not have any experience with geometry or algebra.

<u>Science</u>
In the United States, science classes tend to be much more interactive than in other countries. English language learners may not be comfortable thinking independently and drawing their own conclusions. They will also have to learn a tremendous amount of new vocabulary in order to understand scientific texts. Learning all of this new jargon, and being asked to learn new concepts as well, may be overwhelming for many students. Students may also be unfamiliar with basic scientific visual presentations and laboratory equipment. They may not have a firm background in the scientific method, and so may need explicit direction more often than other students do. Students may not be familiar with cooperating with another student in academic work. Finally, students may have a hard time with scientific texts, in which sentence structure is often complex and the passive voice is used frequently.

<u>Social studies</u>
Many ESL teachers claim that their students have the hardest time with social studies. This is usually because students who have arrived from other cultures have very little background knowledge to draw on in this content area. Students may be able to memorize information in preparation for a test, but without a real foundation of knowledge, this information is quickly lost. Students may also struggle to incorporate higher-level thinking skills on unfamiliar subjects. Students may be ignorant of social studies vocabulary. Students may not be used to expressing their personal opinions, and indeed may not have strong opinions on subjects covered in social studies. Some concepts that appear in American social studies classes are wholly foreign to incoming students. For instance, some students will struggle to understand democratic rights, privacy, and social mobility. Finally, the sheer amount of text covered in a social studies class may be overwhelming for many incoming students.

**Reading guides**

Creating a reading guide will help students organize and consider the material in an English textbook. It can be especially helpful when students want to compare their notes to the content of the course text. The first step in creating a basic reading guide is to have students look at the table of contents. Students should identify the basic structure of the book, including subtopics and sections within each major unit. Once they begin looking at the text, students should try to identify the thesis of each chapter and all the supporting arguments. Students should make a note of any unfamiliar vocabulary. It can be especially helpful to have students focus on an individual paragraph, to examine how it works. This exercise will often help students develop their ability to read quickly and understand academic language in English. Students can then write their own summary of the chapter, at whatever proficiency level they are capable. It is important that the construction of a reading guide be challenging but not impossibly frustrating for students.

**Evaluation of concepts**

When students are learning to read academic works in English, it is essential for the teacher to work through abstract concepts with them. When starting out, the teacher might want to isolate one important concept or idea from a content-area lesson. It is a good idea to choose an idea that allows for significant analysis. The teacher should then ask students to describe the characteristics of a concept. Some concepts are concrete, meaning that they can be directly experienced in the external world, while others are abstract. Teachers can ask students whether the concept has a broad application or whether it can only be applied to the narrow terms of the content-area lesson. The teacher can help students draw up a short list of ways in which this concept manifests itself in the world. Students often have a difficult time dealing with concepts in English because of the preponderance of figurative language; teachers should be prepared to help students understand the linguistic expressions used to describe the concept.

**Vocabulary acquisition vs. development of cognitive-academic language**

When teaching students to read academic texts in English, the teacher will have to address the matter of unfamiliar vocabulary on a regular basis. One way to do this is to teach word analysis skills, whereby the students will learn common prefixes, suffixes, and root words. A large portion of academic language in English is taken from Latin and has a set of regular prefixes and suffixes that can be learned easily and profitably. Another way to help students work through large amounts of unfamiliar vocabulary is by establishing cognate relationships. Teaching cognates gives students a way to relate new words in English to words they know in their native language. In many cases, uncommon English words will appear in slightly modified form in other languages (especially Spanish) much more often. It is important, however, to avoid setting up a habit of one-for-one translation that ignores the English idiom.

**Independent reading**

Once they have achieved a modicum of linguistic skill, children should read independently for increasing amounts of time. Teachers should maintain a special collection of books at various reading levels, so that students can find literature that is appropriate to their proficiency. It is hoped that children will develop an interest and ability to read in a variety of texts and genres. There are a number of benefits to independent reading. If it is successful, it builds confidence and increases fluency. It helps readers make personal connections with literature. It may start a lifelong habit of reading. In any case, independent reading forces students to apply reading strategies for a sustained amount of time.

**Reading aloud**

Reading aloud to children serves a number of purposes. When a teacher reads aloud, he is modeling fluent reading by emphasizing punctuation and features of the text. An expressive oral rendition of a text can go a long way to helping students learn basic linguistic patterns. The teacher can also ask students questions about what is then read, to stimulate critical thinking and reading comprehension skills. By providing some background knowledge before reading aloud, a teacher can help students to learn anticipatory and predictive skills. Research has shown that reading aloud develops knowledge of written language syntax and text structure. It also helps develop oral language and vocabulary. Reading aloud helps create a community of readers and introduces students to a variety of texts and genres which they may decide to explore on their own.

**Shared reading**

One of the activities that teachers often use to increase linguistic ability is called shared reading. In shared reading, members of the class take turns reading the same text aloud. Students who are not reading follow along in their own copy of the text. It is important that the text being read be comprehensible to students at all levels of proficiency. Shared reading explicitly demonstrates basic reading strategies like matching words with an oral rendition. It also helps students develop predictive skills and enhances their sense of narrative structure. Perhaps most important, shared reading provides social support during early reading attempts. As long as the teacher maintains a positive and supportive environment in the classroom, shared reading can be a great opportunity for students to help one another achieve greater understanding.

**Guided reading**

Guided reading can be one of the most useful activities for students with limited proficiency in academic language. In this activity, the teacher works with small groups of students with similar reading processes and needs. The teacher will select and introduce new books to each group, and then the group members will take turns reading the text out loud. As this is going on, the teacher will circulate throughout the room offering advice and support to the various groups. Guided reading gives students a chance to experience a wide variety of texts, and gives students a nice mixture of reading aloud and following along. The process of guided reading encourages students to develop their comprehension and analysis skills. Also, research suggests that when positive social communities are formed, students are more likely to strive for increased linguistic proficiency.

**Informal reading**

Reading instruction in the various content areas may require some modification of the textbook and materials. The teacher will likely have to select key vocabulary and concepts and cover these explicitly with students prior to the lesson. To be successful, students will need to learn the common organizational patterns and outlines used in academic prose. The teacher should help students to spot common textbook cues that indicate meaning and structure. Many teachers perform informal reading inventories to determine each student's skill at decoding and comprehending. This system places students into one of three categories: independent, instructional, or frustration. Students at the independent level recognize words with 97 percent accuracy, understand at least 80 percent of what they read, and can read aloud smoothly. Students at the instructional level can recognize words with 92-96 percent accuracy, understand 60-70 percent of what they read, and read aloud in a halting fashion. Students at the frustration level recognize less than 91 percent of the words in the text, understand less than half of what they read, and read aloud poorly.

**Patterns of exposition**

The sets of reading skills required to master academic texts will vary according to content area. All academic texts will require logic and critical thinking skills, but certain disciplines are notable for the presence of characteristic types of thought. For instance, social studies texts often emphasize cause-and-effect relationships and chronological sequence of events. These texts frequently ask the reader to compare and contrast events or people. In science texts, on the other hand, there is a great deal of classification and problem-solving rhetoric. Science texts also frequently deal with cause-and-effect relationships. In mathematics, the text often makes an assertion and then supplies evidence and supporting arguments at great length. Mathematical texts are riddled with symbolic relationships and operations. There is a great deal of jargon in mathematical texts. In literary texts, the language is often figurative or lyrical, which may be difficult for more literal-minded beginning students. Also, in order to adequately express their opinions about literary texts, readers will need to master the terminology of literature, such as plot, setting, character, etc.

**Matthew effect**

The development of vocabulary is more complicated than simply learning the definitions of obscure words. Teachers must understand all of the factors related to the development of vocabulary, academic language, and background knowledge, because the development of vocabulary at an early age, specifically from prekindergarten through second grade, is essential to students' future achievement in vocabulary and reading. When it comes to vocabulary learning, there is a tendency for more advanced students to make more progress than struggling students, thus widening the performance gap even further. This phenomenon is known as the Matthew effect, after a Bible verse that begins, "For to all those who have, more will be given." Teachers should be aware of the Matthew effect and understand how it affects the development of vocabulary, academic language, and background knowledge. Effective instruction and intervention can minimize the damage related to the Matthew effect.

## Vocabulary and content knowledge

Vocabulary knowledge and concept learning are intertwined, and it is impossible for one of these factors to improve without corresponding improvement in the other. For instance, the acquisition of vocabulary requires the learning of concepts, and the learning of concepts provides a framework for the development of vocabulary. In a sense, sophisticated words are a form of shorthand for difficult concepts. Also, effective vocabulary instruction is a major boon to the growth of background knowledge. As students develop the language of a new content area, they are likely to begin fitting these words together conceptually. It is futile to teach students vocabulary they are conceptually unequipped to handle.

## Reading and building vocabulary

In general, written language contains a larger and more sophisticated vocabulary and more complicated language structures than speech. For this reason, text is more important in the development of vocabulary, academic language, and background knowledge. A reader has time to go back and look at an unfamiliar word, while it may not be appropriate for a listener to ask the speaker to repeat or clarify. Independent reading, then, is essential in the development of vocabulary, academic language, and background knowledge. For instance, research has consistently shown that daily reading volume is directly correlated to academic achievement. Independent reading material does not need to be advanced or complicated; in fact, the most important criterion is that it interests the student. It is important to encourage independent reading at appropriate levels, because this will improve students' vocabulary, academic language, and background knowledge. Teachers should provide daily opportunities for sustained silent reading.

## Vocabulary instruction

There are a number of factors to consider when developing vocabulary, academic language, and background knowledge. To begin with, not all words should be given equal emphasis. Some words occur much more frequently and should therefore be of greater importance in instruction. This is yet another reason why the context of vocabulary and academic language is so important. It is a bad idea to find a list of difficult words and proceed through it alphabetically, because the students will have very little context for the words they are learning. Instead, teachers should approach vocabulary thematically. For instance, a teacher might spend one week teaching vocabulary words related to government, and the next teaching words related to legislation. It is a good idea to link new vocabulary to the lesson being covered in other content areas. The most important thing is to ensure that students have a context for new words, so that they will be able to incorporate them in their speaking and writing as soon as possible.

## Homophones

Students must be able to accurately recognize and incorporate common homophones.

Homophones are words that sound the same but have different spellings. Two of the most common homophones in English are *sail/sale* and *bare/bear*. Students are likely to confuse these words unless they receive relevant and explicit instruction. Teachers should begin by presenting these words in isolation and ensuring that students are familiar with both spellings. Then, teachers should help students differentiate these homophones by linking the written version of the word with a picture or example of its meaning. Finally, the words should be presented in context.

**Semantic and syntactic approaches**

Word analysis instruction should be balanced and comprehensive. It is a good idea to let students approach unfamiliar words from both the semantic and syntactic perspectives. A semantic approach emphasizes the meaning of words. A child is using the semantic approach when he thinks about context and about what type of word would make sense in a given sentence. A teacher can guide the student towards an appreciation of semantics by asking questions about the meaning of the sentence and the likely meaning of an unfamiliar word. The syntactic approach, on the other hand, emphasizes the order of the words in a sentence. English has fairly regular syntax, so the reader can often predict what type of word (e.g., noun, verb) will appear next in a sentence. A teacher can stimulate students to think about syntax by asking the student to read a sentence and determine whether it makes sense. A teacher can ask the student whether the words in a sentence appear to be in the right order.

**Activities that reinforce**

Students should read a number of texts containing words with the affixes, syllable patterns, and orthographic patterns and rules that have been discussed in class. It is important for students to encounter these words in different contexts, including expository, literary, and reference works. In addition, students should be given plenty of writing opportunities to apply their knowledge of multisyllabic spelling and complex orthographic patterns. Descriptive writing exercises are a great way to elicit the use of just-learned words, as students will search for the right words to express their thoughts. Also, reading and personal journals can be a good venue for students to use the more complicated words they have recently learned.

**Differentiation of word analysis instruction**

Word analysis can be a challenge for many students, and so there is likely to be a great range of performance in the same class. Teachers must be able to address the strong and weak students in the class. In particular, teachers need to provide differentiated instruction for students who are struggling or have reading difficulties or disabilities. For instance, a teacher needs to be able to go back and focus on key skills and knowledge, like syllable patterns and morphemes that occur frequently. Some students need to have the same material approached from different perspectives before they fully master it. The teacher should be able to outline a number of real-world examples for an abstract concept. The use of songs and poems to illustrate syllabification is one helpful way to bring struggling students up to speed. Finally, a teacher should be able to provide differentiated practice situations for the skills that have been taught.

Instruction related to word analysis should be differentiated for English language learners. Most of the time, these students require extra training in the common English roots, prefixes, and suffixes. Many foreign languages do not include these morphemes, and so students may not have heard them in conversation throughout their lives. Moreover, many languages do not include affix systems, and so students may need some basic training in how these word parts can alter meaning. For this reason, it may be necessary to provide these students with more exposure to morphemes that are second nature to native English speakers. Some students benefit from the use of flashcards that cover common English morphemes.

### Improving reading rate

There are some excellent strategies for building reading rate. For instance, when decoding is not automatic, the student should be asked to whisper read while being monitored. Whisper reading is essentially just reading aloud to oneself. Because the student is reading aloud, he is forced to read each word. Whisper reading allows the entire class to get the benefits of reading aloud without distracting one another. Once decoding has become automatic, students should be asked to read silently by themselves and should be held accountable for their comprehension. In other words, the teacher should at the very least ask the student some questions that test whether the student has obtained the literal message of the text.

### Modeling, phrase-cued reading, and intentional, teacher-directed instruction

Some strategies for improving fluency with respect to prosody include modeling, phrase-cued reading, and intentional, teacher-directed instruction in a specific subject area in order to build content knowledge and academic language. Modeling is the demonstration of the task to be learned. Repeated reading and choral reading are examples of modeling. Phrase-cued reading, which is similar to modeling, is a system in which the teacher reads a text in phrase-sized chunks. The text being read by the teacher needs to be visible to the class; this can be accomplished either by holding up a book or by projecting the text on a screen. In any case, the students need to be able to follow along with the teacher, who will be pointing at each successive phrase with a finger or pen. The idea is for students to begin looking at sentences as collections of phrases rather than as discrete words or groups of letters. When students begin to organize their oral production by phrases rather than letters or words, they will have obtained some degree of fluency. Finally, in some cases, prosody may be improved by explicit instruction in the content area to be discussed. Some priming with respect to vocabulary and subject matter will help students anticipate the content of the text and will enable the emergence of prosody.

### Synonyms and antonyms

To begin with, instruction should include definitions that can easily be understood by students. Much of the vocabulary in content areas is difficult necessarily because it is representative of difficult concepts. In order to understand the words, students must understand the concepts. It is important, then, that instruction include meaningful examples in context. Words should not be presented simply in list format without any explanation as to how they are used. The teacher should describe the sorts of text in which a word is used, and should demonstrate its use in a sentence. Students especially need these examples when dealing with new concepts, lest they become disoriented. Whenever appropriate, guided discussions should include the identification of synonyms and antonyms. A synonym is a word that means the same thing, while an antonym is a word that means the opposite. So, for instance, *arid* is a synonym for *dry*, while *moist* is an antonym for *dry*. Students should be encouraged to come up with examples of synonyms and antonyms for new vocabulary words.

### Concept maps

Teachers should incorporate explicit oral and written strategies to promote the integration of word knowledge. It is important for students to take several different approaches to a new word, so that they develop a little dexterity in handling it. The teacher should help the students work out the relationships between words, and, if it is useful, should depict these relationships graphically. A concept map, in which lines representing relationships are drawn between the words, is one way to illustrate relationships of vocabulary. In an even more sophisticated concept map, students write verbs on the connecting lines to describe the relationship between the words: for example, in a concept map about Congress, the word *passes* might be written on the line connecting *Senate* to *legislation*.

**Cluing**

Another popular technique for teaching new vocabulary is cluing. In this method, the teacher writes four sentences on the board for each new word. The first sentence uses the target word in a sentence: "Larry's *celerity* made it possible for the job to be done by 5." At this point, the students will not have been taught the definition of the target word. The second sentence describes the target word in some way: "Rabbits, runners, and racecars are all known for their *celerity*." The third sentence defines the target word: "*Celerity* means swiftness or speed." Finally, the fourth sentence asks a question with the target word: "Can you name something that moves with *celerity*?" The cluing technique may seem over-simple, but it effectively slows down the introduction of new words so that students can develop a context almost immediately. Through cluing, the student is shown how the word is used, given some examples, told the definition, and encouraged to use the word to answer a question. Rather quickly, the student has made four approaches to mastery of the word.

**Word logs**

Another method of vocabulary instruction is the creation of word banks and word logs. These are lists of new vocabulary words, either those explicitly taught by the teacher or those the student comes across in his own academic work. This list is referred to frequently, so that the student has multiple exposures to each new word. At the same time, the student should be asked to perform some tasks with the new words, such as using them in a sentence or looking up the definition in the dictionary. The creation and maintenance of a word bank or log helps personalize vocabulary instruction and allows the student to focus exclusively on the words he needs to learn.

**Challenges of teaching vocabulary**

A teacher must be able to provide differentiated instruction for English language learners. This may require reactivating prior knowledge by creating explicit connections between prior and new knowledge. Often, students will have mastered the concepts associated with vocabulary and academic content, but will not yet have the words in English. As much as possible, the teacher should capitalize on the transfer of cognates. The teacher should build on the students' current language skills and reinforce their knowledge of basic, functional grammar to make reading comprehension easier. When necessary, this may include some instruction in the student's native language. The teacher should emphasize reading instruction that encourages the development of academic language. This will likely include the explicit instruction of more complex language structures and the key vocabulary in the relevant text. Also, a teacher needs to contextualize new vocabulary and concepts. This can be done with visual aids, like pictures, charts, word organizers, and graphic organizers. Many teachers find success with a sequence of preteach-reteach-practice-review. Teachers should work to build morphological knowledge, including the meanings of the common root words used in academic language.

**Assessing vocabulary**

As with other forms of assessment, vocabulary assessment should take place before, during, and after instruction. One of the most common methods of formal or informal assessment is to ask students to use new vocabulary words in a sentence. If a student knows the definition of a word but cannot incorporate it in real linguistic production, he has not yet fully acquired it. Other, slightly more sophisticated vocabulary assessments ask students to identify synonyms, antonyms, or analogies for new vocabulary words. When constructing these sorts of assessments, the teacher should be sure that there are acceptable answers (for instance, not all words have a ready antonym). With vocabulary instruction, it is essential to use this sort of assessment as a point of departure for further exploration and instruction. It requires detailed analysis to determine exactly where a student is falling short of his potential. Instruction should be responsive to the results of assessment and should incorporate as much informal assessment as possible.

**Differentiating assignments**

When an informal or formal assessment indicates a significant discrepancy between students, teachers can modify assignments so that they become suitable for a broad spectrum of abilities. For students functioning at a low level, the objectives of the assignments can be simplified, either by reducing the number of required parts or by making the required parts easier. Students may be asked to compose a drawing instead of a written response. The teacher may find that it is appropriate to divide students into small groups based on ability level, and then allow students to conduct discussions in lieu of individual written responses. The teacher may also find it is appropriate to adjust the length and difficulty of assignments; for reading comprehension exercises, for instance, the teacher may determine that it is appropriate to diminish the overall length of the reading assignment.

**Grouping**

In many cases, a teacher will determine that it is appropriate to separate students into small groups by ability level. This can be done a number of ways. One is by pairing high-functioning students with low-functioning students in a peer assistance program. It is often beneficial for both the superior and inferior student to examine material in a partnership of this kind. The teacher may also separate students into cooperative groups in which all the students are at roughly the same level. When doing this, teachers should ensure that content material is comprehensible to some degree to every member of every group. In some cases, teachers may divide students into small groups and then provide direct instruction to these groups individually. This is usually necessary in cases in which the discrepancy between the highest-functioning group and the lowest-functioning group is extreme.

**Small-group instruction**

There are a number of advantages to dividing students into small groups by ability level. For one thing, the teacher will be able to monitor student progress closely. In a larger group, it can be difficult to monitor the progress of individual students at the same time. When students are broken into small groups in which each member has specific responsibilities, it becomes much easier for teachers to assess the contributions of each member. Small-group instruction for this reason enables teachers to provide immediate feedback. By circulating throughout the room while students are working, teachers will be able to provide immediate responses to questions and concerns raised by the groups. The teacher will also be able to provide data-driven differentiated instruction. This is again because assessment becomes much easier when students are broken into small groups. When each individual in the class has a clear performance record, the teacher can collect data that is helpful in making future instructional decisions.

## Alternative assessments

It is essential that ESL teachers utilize alternative assessments to provide students with opportunities to demonstrate mastery of knowledge and skills. Alternative assessments are anything distinct from formal tests or examinations. These assessments often incorporate authentic classroom tasks in order to collect information about student achievement. Alternative assessments will allow the teacher to consider the performance of the student from a number of different perspectives, and will focus on the process performed as much as the results produced. Alternative assessments, because of their informal and improvisatory nature, can be developed to assess a broad range of knowledge and skills. Teachers who incorporate alternative assessments in their daily lesson are able to accumulate more data with which to make decisions about future instructional strategies.

## Speech organization

The process of speech organization entails selecting the elements that will make a speech, placing them into a coherent order, and arranging the supporting material for each message unit. One way to organize a spoken response mentally is to summarize each message unit in a simple sentence. This gives the speaker simple building blocks that can be easily rearranged. In general, a speech is to have a coherent introduction, body, and conclusion. The introduction should engage the interest of the audience and summarize the main points to be made. The body should contain the central points of the speaker's argument, as well as the supporting evidence. The conclusion should summarize the argument and give the audience food for thought.

## Proving a point

In a proof speech, the speaker introduces his argument and then attempts to prove it. Proof speeches abide by a consistent pattern. In brief, a proof speech has four components: introduction, argument, development, and conclusion. In a spoken response, one should follow these steps in order. A speech that follows this pattern allows the audience to become acquainted with the thrust of the speaker's arguments before substantiation is offered. The lengths of the various components of a proof speech will vary, depending on the speaker's interests and the amount of time available. Also, an audience that is already familiar with the subject matter may not require as much supporting material to be convinced.

## Idea vs. claim

A spoken response may try to disseminate information or persuade the audience. Another way of putting it is to say that a speaker will either deliver ideas or make claims. A speaker who is delivering ideas is expressing information and opinions for their own sake, and not necessarily to change the minds of the listener. Informative speeches are usually on subjects about which the listener is not expected to know very much. The purpose of the speech is to increase the knowledge of the listener, and not necessarily to convert him to any particular viewpoint. When a speaker makes claims, on the other hand, he is introducing opinions that may or may not be held by the listener. The intention of the speech will be to provide arguments and evidence to support the claims made by the speaker.

## Main idea

It is important when giving an oral response to lay out the main idea in a manner comprehensible to the listener. The main idea of an informative response should be presented near the beginning of the address, and therefore should not require understanding of any concepts that will be explained later in the response. The listener should be able to understand the gist of the main idea before the speaker goes on to elaborate. In the response, the speaker should define the main idea early on, so that he can proffer evidence and supporting arguments appropriate to that main idea. Too often, speakers introduce evidence and arguments that are not directly supportive of the main idea of the speech. The effect of this is that it confuses the listener and waters down the effect of the speech.

When a response is meant to present or advance a particular viewpoint, the speaker will need to pay special attention to the phrasing of the main claim. The main claim should be phrased in such a way that it will be comprehensible to a general audience, and will not offend casual listeners with a harsh or controversial tone. The degree of intensity appropriate to the claim will depend on the audience. A more strident tone can be used with an audience of like-minded listeners, while a diverse group of uncommitted listeners requires a more evenhanded tone. When constructing the main claim of a speech, the speaker should be sure to only present ideas that can be supported by general evidence and reasonable argument. If the main claim of a speech is far-fetched or unsupportable, even the more rational elements of the response may be dismissed by a skeptical audience.

**Well-organized oral response**

There are certain qualities that all well-organized responses have in common. For instance, a well-organized response is comprehensible, meaning that it can be understood by all members of the audience. A well-organized response also has a formal unity, which means that all of its parts contribute to its main idea. A unified response has no extraneous parts. A well-organized response is comprehensive, meaning that it covers all of the issues that a listener would expect to be treated by a response on the given subject. Finally, a well-organized response does not have any repetition. Every major point should be covered in its entirety, but no points need to be repeated once they have been clearly delivered.

**Narratives**

Speakers often incorporate narratives as a way of engaging interest and indirectly making a point. A narrative is simply a story. Narratives can be either fiction or nonfiction. As with examples, narratives tend to have more impact on an audience when they are true. However, an artfully told fictitious narrative can also captivate an audience. Recent scientific research suggests that listeners are mentally programmed to pay attention to information when it is presented as a story; that is, the human mind is naturally receptive to a narrative. Good speakers take advantage of this tendency by delivering information in the context of a narrative.

**Expository supporting material**

For the most part, speakers use expository supporting material. The word *expository* comes from the same root as *expose*, and describes information that seeks to shine a light on areas that may be unknown to the listener. Some of the common forms of expository information are examples, analogies, and narratives. Expository supporting material is distinguished from argumentative supporting material in that it strives to remain as objective as possible. When a speaker claims to be using objective and impartial information, he will be held to that standard by the listener. For this reason, it is especially important for speakers who use expository supporting material to verify their sources.

**Examples**

Successful responses may include both real and hypothetical examples. Real examples are appropriate in responses describing a particular historical or social topic that is grounded in reality. It would not do, for instance, to use a hypothetical example in an argument about the Revolutionary War. After all, we have plenty of real examples to illustrate points about that conflict. In more general responses, however, it may be necessary to use a hypothetical situation as an example. For instance, when describing the possible results of some decision, a speaker might invoke the case of some hypothetical person as a means of dramatizing his argument. In general, real examples are treated with more respect by an audience, and should be used whenever possible.

A good speaker knows that examples can be effective because they provide concrete case studies through which the listener can assess the arguments of the speech. Examples are also good at humanizing an abstract speech; for instance, a listener may not be very interested in a response related to economics unless the subject material is related to the lives of everyday people. A good speaker includes examples that are appropriate and interesting, but which do not distract from his main points. Also, examples should not dominate a response; they should simply add interest to the body of the speaker's message.

**Analogies**

An effective speaker will often elaborate and clarify his ideas with analogies. An analogy is simply an extended comparison between two things. For instance, a speech on economics might describe a current downturn in the economy as it relates to the Great Depression. In other words, the speaker is drawing an analogy between a current problem and a known historical event. The important thing about an analogy is to remember that the two things being compared will probably not be identical in all respects. The speaker should take care to indicate this, and should not make claims that suggest the analogy is perfect. On the other hand, an effective analogy can be a useful predictive tool, and can give the audience a way of engaging with the subject.

**Problem-solving pattern**

In a problem-solving speech, the speaker outlines a particular problem, attempts to diagnose the cause, and then suggests a potential solution. Problem-solving speeches are at their heart persuasive speeches, since they attempt to convince the listener of the merits of adopting a particular strategy to solve a given problem. In order to be effective, however, a problem-solving speech needs to follow a logical pattern. These speeches typically begin with an introduction and a definition of the problem in question. The speaker will then summarize the possible causes of the problem and discuss some of the possible solutions. The speaker will then make a case for one of the solutions and provide supporting evidence and argumentation. Finally, the speaker will attempt to rebut some of the possible counterarguments to the proposed solution.

# Cultural Awareness and Family and Community Involvement

## Culture

A culture is a comprehensive style of living that is developed in a society and maintained from generation to generation. Culture is manifested in a group's traditions, rituals, language, social norms, technology and economic structures. Broadly speaking, culture is everything which is learned by a member of a particular society, though it may include things that an individual learns but which become assumed and are never made explicit either in the individual's mind or in his social interactions. For this reason, many experts feel it is difficult to properly study one's own culture; they suggest that only the unclouded eyes of a foreign observer can perceive a society's most fundamental values.

## Material culture

A society's material culture is the set of all of the physical objects which the people of that society have either created or to which they assign cultural meaning. Material culture may therefore include objects like books, jewelry, buildings, and furniture, to name just a few; but can also include natural areas, if those areas have been considered by the members of the society in a special way. As an example of this latter kind of material culture, a sociologist might point to Native American society, in which the land itself held immense cultural value. Along with verbal culture, material culture makes up the sum total of that which sociologists have at their disposal for study.

## Nonmaterial culture

Nonmaterial culture is all of a society's customs, beliefs, political structures, languages, and ways of using material objects. In the United States, for instance, the emphasis placed on religious freedom and individual liberty might be considered an example of material culture. The boundary, however, between material and nonmaterial culture is never altogether clear; how, for instance, should one distinguish between the American flag and that for which it stands—the idea of freedom? The values and norms, as opposed to the physical things that are used to express values and norms, are that which make up a society's nonmaterial culture. Typically, nonmaterial culture is more difficult to change than material culture, though its change may be more difficult to observe. Teachers need to be aware of the material and nonmaterial elements of their ELL students' native cultures.

## Cultural cooperation and accommodation

The extent to which an English language learner thrives depends upon the relationship between ones culture and that of the school. Cooperation and accommodation refer to two ways in which the members of different cultures interact with one another. Cooperation is an agreement between two parties to work together towards a common goal; typically, cooperation refers to short-term goals which can be pursued without altering ones beliefs or values. Accommodation, alternatively, is an agreement between two conflicting cultures to acknowledge but ignore their differences and try to work together toward common goals, instead. Countries that have two or more cultural groups within them, such as Israel or Iraq, are always trying to work out some kind of accommodation, so that positive progress can be made for all the citizens of the nation despite their divergent systems of belief.

## Cultural assimilation

Assimilation is the process whereby individuals are absorbed into a particular society after having been members of a different one. Assimilation can either be voluntary, as in the case of people fleeing religious persecution to a friendly society, or forced, as in the case of some ethnic groups that have been required to observe national customs contrary to their own. The process generally includes learning a new language and a new set of social values and norms. For English language learners, assimilation is a necessary consequence of attending a new school. Typically, assimilation is easier for the young and for individuals who are educated and well-traveled. Many critics of the process argue that making cultures homogenous through forced assimilation stifles innovation and productive dialogue within a society.

## Cultural values

The values of a culture are its highest ideals. In the United States, for example, one might say that freedom and equality are two of our most important values. Values are usually very general concepts and may be complementary; for example, the values of hard work and material success seem to go together. Values are quite fluid and may come into conflict with one another, which can create social conflict and disorganization. An example of this is the conflict in mid-twentieth century America between the value of equal rights and that of segregation; ultimately, it was clear that only one of these values could remain. It is rare for American academic standards to challenge an ELL student's cultural values, but there is likely to be some conflict. Teachers should be sensitive to this conflict without seeking to avoid it.

## Cultural sanctions

Cultural sanctions are any rewards or consequences given to an individual or group to pursue or renounce a certain course of behavior. Sanctions may either be positive, as when a reward is promised for doing something properly, or negative, as when a punishment is promised for doing something wrong. Although the most common use of the word refers to international economic pressures (as in, for instance, the economic restrictions placed on Iraq during the 1990s), all societies place sanctions on their members in order to elicit approved behavior. People who uphold the values and norms of their society are rewarded by preferential treatment from their fellows, while those who transgress can be punished socially, economically, or legally. In a sense, ELL students are sanctioned to the extent that their native language and culture prohibits them from succeeding as students. A teacher's goal is to identify and eliminate these cultural sanctions.

## Cultural norms

Norms are specific rules regulating behavior in a culture. Norms may or may not be directly codified in the law of a society, but they are intended to encourage behavior which promotes the society's values. Taking again the example of the United States, one might say that treating men and women equally is a social norm, insofar as equality between the sexes is a value to which our culture aspires. This is not a norm in many other cultures, though, and some ELL students may display surprising behavior because of their familiarity with different norms. Norms depend on values for their justification, and values depend on norms for their enactment. Norms may vary greatly from society to society, such that the same behavior may be approved or condemned depending on where it is performed. Most of the time, norms are so customary for the members of a society that they are performed automatically.

## Formal and informal norms

Norms may be considered formal or informal depending on whether they are codified in the laws of the society in which they apply. Formal norms are written law; for example, the prohibition of murder, the forced payment of taxes, and the sanctity of the institution of marriage. Informal norms, on the other hand, are unwritten codes of conduct. Examples of informal norms might include the prohibition of spitting in public or the encouragement of deference to women. Typically, a society formalizes the norms which are most important, and for which violators should be punished. Formal norms tend to be much more consistent among various societies than informal norms.

## Social markers, laws, and folkways

A social marker is any part of behavior that indicates the identity, character, or way of understanding of a particular group of people. Social markers can be laws, folkways, traditions, or other patterns of behavior. A teacher should be on the lookout for the social markers displayed by ELL students. Laws are simply social norms that have been made explicit and are enforced by the government. There are plenty of norms, however, which are encoded in law but are also internalized-- the prohibition of murder, for instance. Folkways are social norms that have become habitual or traditional in a society. In the United States, for instance, we are accustomed to tipping a waiter or waitress for their service: that this is so ingrained in our daily life makes it an American folkway.

## Cultural pluralism, subcultures, and reference groups

Cultural pluralism exists when multiple distinct cultures exist within the same society after a process of accommodation. These self-contained cultures should not be confused with subcultures, which are smaller cultures within a large culture. Subcultures usually have a set of norms and values that are different from those held by the larger society to which they are a member. In the United States, we might consider punk rockers or hippies as subcultures, because they have different values than Americans on the whole, but do not really have a self-sustaining or separate society of their own, either. Reference groups are those groups to which individuals aspire and compare themselves, and against which one evaluates one's own qualities. For example, a man who considers himself to be wealthy might purchase a yacht or an expensive sports car because of a desire to resemble those whom he aspires to imitate, rather than necessarily desiring said objects.

## Dominant culture and ethnocentrism

In any society, the dominant culture is the group whose norms, values, and behavior patterns are forced on the rest of the society. Many nations, including the United States, have laws that are designed to restrain the dominant culture from extinguishing minority cultures. In the United States, for example, the English-speaking culture is the dominant culture. Ethnocentrism describes the tendency to view one's own cultural patterns as superior and to judge all others only as they relate to one's own. This philosophy has been at the root of some of humanity's worst atrocities, including the Holocaust, which was perpetrated by Germans who believed they must maintain the purity of their superior race, and colonial conquests, in which Western nations brutally imposed their customs on various indigenous peoples. Obviously, a teacher of ELL students must strive to promote assimilation without ethnocentrism.

## Cultural relativism

Cultural relativism is the idea that any particular part of a given culture can only be understood in relation to the rest of the culture, and as a product of its context. In large part, cultural relativism is a reaction to Western ethnocentrism, or the belief that Western culture is superior to all others. Some critics argue that cultural relativism inevitably leads to the absence of any standards at all, and makes judgment (and hence constructive criticism and progress) impossible. Its proponents counter that the general similarity in moral code between various cultures implies that there is a set of innately human values, and that cultural relativism offers the only approach wherein the sociologist can explore the nature of his own assumptions.

## Progress, cultural lag, and diffusion

The idea of progress is the idea that social and technological progress is inevitable. A cultural lag is created when a change in one part of society is not immediately answered by corresponding changes in the other parts. A typical example of this is when new technology brings rapid progress to the day-to-day lives of the citizens, and the religious institutions do not adjust their practices to incorporate it. This typically produces a period of relative inactivity in the society. Diffusion is the process by which technological, political, and social innovations spread from one society to another. The process of diffusion is usually accelerated in pluralist societies that are accustomed to a healthy internal debate.

## Acculturation

Acculturation is an extensive borrowing by one group of cultural traits from another group. Acculturation can also describe the exchange of cultural traits between two cultures that are in close contact for a long period of time. Acculturation may occur such that the recipient culture incorporates new traits without significantly altering its own culture; an example of this is the acquisition of Chinese linguistic characters into Korean and Japanese society. Of course, acculturation may also have a devastating effect on one of the cultures, as in the savagely unequal exchange between Europeans and Native Americans. Many groups are currently trying to resist the acculturation encouraged by globalization. In the ELL classroom, a certain amount of acculturation is inevitable, but the teacher should be sure to affirm the worth of both English-speaking culture and the native cultures of the students.

## Syncretism

Syncretism is the conscious adopting of the cultural elements of a dominant group by a subordinate group. One classic example of this kind of syncretism is the economic transformation of Japan after World War Two. The Japanese, with help from the Western powers, rapidly developed an industrial base and market economy modeled after that of the United States. Syncretism has often been used to describe the interplay of religions within a society; for example, it is invoked hopefully by those who would like to see reconciliation between the Protestant and Catholic churches. There is a danger in syncretism of losing elements of culture that are unique to the subordinate culture, and thus discouraging debate and innovation. In the classroom, some argue that syncretism should be avoided, as it can be perceived to devalue the native culture of the ELL student.

## Culture shock

Culture shock is the feeling of disorientation that a person may feel when they encounter cultural values, norms, or practices that are contrary to their own. Culture shock may occur when an individual goes to another country, moves to a different environment, or simply encounters something with which he is unfamiliar in his own culture. Culture shock typically has four phases: the honeymoon, in which the new thing is perceived as good; the shock, in which the individual becomes disoriented; the negotiation, in which the individual labors to make the new thing acceptable to him or herself; and acceptance, in which the positives and negatives of the new culture have been absorbed and reconciled. It may be assumed that ELL students will have already passed through the honeymoon and shock periods, and will need assistance with negotiation and acceptance.

## Convergent cultural evolution

When different cultures develop similar cultural traits because they live in similar environments, it is known as convergent cultural evolution. For example, societies that developed in tropical environments have been shown to have arrived at similar agricultural practices independently. Similarly, cultures that develop in densely-populated areas tend to be different from those that arise in rural areas. For one thing, rural cultures tend to place more emphasis on the strength of the family unit, because there are fewer people readily available to care for the young. In urban culture, there may be more emphasis placed on specialization and division of labor, as the size of the population allows for a diverse market economy. For teachers of English language learners, the manifestation of convergent cultural evolution may at first be surprising. Often, students from distant regions will have more in common with their new classmates than one would expect. The danger for a teacher is to assume that the presence of some convergent cultural evolution obviates the need for further assimilation.

## Cultural determinism

Cultural determinism is the assertion that the potential for variation in human societies is unlimited, and that cultural forces can shape human nature into almost any form. This idea has manifested itself in a number of different societies, typically as a source of the culture's sense of uniqueness. For example, the ancient Greeks attributed their self-proclaimed superiority to their language, and actually coined the term "barbarian" to describe foreigners (literally, those who, to the Greeks, made gibberish sounds like "bar-bar"). Even today, many Americans feel that the democratic system has somehow made them unique in history. A teacher of English language learners should be aware of the deterministic effect of language, but should avoid attributing superiority to any linguistic culture.

## Cultural gatekeepers

The cultural gatekeepers of a society are the people who permit or forbid the introduction of new elements of culture into their society. Specifically, cultural gatekeepers are people who have control over the means by which ideas are distributed in a society, and therefore decide which ideas are distributed. For example, radio executives can decide which new songs will get airtime, and in effect control which songs will become a part of the popular culture. Of course, cultural gatekeepers like movie and radio executives, fashion buyers, and editors are subject to the demands of the market, and therefore cannot always introduce the things which they personally find worthy; instead, cultural gatekeepers often simply mimic elements of the culture that are already present. The idea of the cultural gatekeeper is an interesting one for ELL instruction, because it suggests that some students will be especially instrumental for encouraging their fellows. In other words, some students will have the charisma and acknowledged authority to convince others of the necessity of adopting elements of English-speaking culture.

## Cultural universals

Cultural universals are the elements of culture that are found in virtually every society. The anthropologist George Murdock once compiled a list of these universals, and it included sports, cooking, courtship, dancing, family, games, language, music, religion, and restrictions on sexual activity. Although these elements appear in every culture, the particular forms in which they emerge are quite various. Most of them have a clear role in perpetuating the society; it is easy to see, for instance, why cooking, courtship, and language should be universal. Sociologists are still debating, however, why it is that more trivial things like sport and music should be found in every society, and what role these things play in the continuation of the social group.

## Cultural pluralism for English language learners

Cultural pluralism exists when several distinct cultures thrive alongside one another. There may be a dominant culture, but it does not seek to eliminate the others, and indeed often looks to absorb useful elements from them. The ELL classroom should aspire to cultural pluralism, because it creates the most value for students. When the various members of the class are eager to learn about and incorporate aspects of each other's culture, efficient and accelerated learning is possible. Cultural pluralism can be explicitly encouraged by teachers by creating an inclusive learning environment in which students feel comfortable sharing their backgrounds and cultural traditions. Cultural pluralism is undermined by instruction that directly or indirectly values one culture over another.

## Intra- and intergroup differences

In the ELL classroom, it is useful to distinguish intragroup differences from intergroup differences. Intragroup differences exist within a particular cultural or linguistic community. For instance, within the community of Spanish-speaking people are Argentineans and Mexicans, who may not have a great deal in common besides language. It is important for a teacher to recognize these differences and not simply to lump all the members of a linguistic community together. Intergroup differences exist between the members of distinct cultural and linguistic communities. The differences between students from Haiti and students from Russia, for instance, are intergroup, because these students share neither a culture nor a language.

## Instruction for immigrants

In many ELL classrooms, the majority of the students are immigrants, meaning that they have moved to the United States during their lifetime. Teachers can expect that these students will have a more difficult time adjusting to American culture, including but not limited to language issues. Immigrant students are likely to have parents who are also unfamiliar with the United States, and so it may be necessary for the teacher to spend more time in communication with them. Immigrant students are more likely to have spent time in a distinct educational milieu, so a teacher may have to work on basic American academic skills like punctuality, taking turns, etc.

## Instruction for the children of migrants

Migrants are people who leave their home country in search of work. In the United States, there are many migrants from Central and South America who have come to work in agriculture and construction. These workers are often here illegally, and they therefore may be reticent to interact with a teacher. It is important to allay any concerns that these parents might have about dealing with school officials, who are concerned with educating children rather than citizenship. The children of migrants are often far below grade level, because their frequent travel has constantly interrupted their education. They may be unfamiliar with the rituals of school. Also, the children of migrants are likely to have spent the majority of their lives in a relatively small community, and therefore may be more shy about mixing with their peers. Teachers should be sensitive to these issues as they help the children of migrants adjust to the classroom.

## Instruction for refugees

Refugees have come to the United States to escape from religious, political, or other persecution. Their passage to the United States is typically orchestrated by the federal government, and, while efforts are made to place refugees in communities near others who share their culture, some may be feeling quite isolated when they enter school. Many refugees are placed in regions with a vastly different climate and topography than that to which they are accustomed, and this may be disorienting at first. Also, many refugees were traumatized by the events that drove them from their homeland, and may be dealing with psychological issues. In all, refugees can be among the most fragile classes of student for an ELL teacher. These students are typically familiar with formal education, but may need time to adjust to other aspects of life in the United States.

## Instruction for ELL students born in the United States

Of all the students in an ELL classroom, those who were born in the United States should be the easiest for a teacher to handle. However, these students often have grown up in communities where no English is spoken, so it should not be assumed that they will be any more fluent than their fellows. Students who were born in the United States should be conversant with the American academic system, and can be relied upon as resources for other students. These students may become bored with some of the remedial elements of ELL instruction, and therefore alternate activities should be established for when the main part of the class is concentrated on learning basic aspects of life and education in the United States.

## Teacher's cultural background and instruction

A teacher's cultural background can have an influence upon instruction in a number of ways. To begin with, a teacher may have adopted the assumptions and prejudices common to his culture, and may propagate these in the classroom. Most ELL teachers are aware of this possibility, however, and do a good job of preventing adverse influence. A less noticeable source of cultural influence is the teacher training program. Teachers earn their certification in programs that often have a pronounced bias towards the norms of white culture. Indeed, many critics have charged that the standardized tests required for admission to education programs have an inherent cultural bias. Because there are so few alternatives, many teachers are unaware of the potential for creeping bias. It takes effort to explore other paradigms for instruction.

Too often, discussions of multicultural education focus on the diversity of students, and fail to account for the unique cultural background of the teacher. However, the teacher's treatment of his own background is as important as discussions related to students'. A teacher should be upfront about any potential biases stemming from his background. More importantly, during preparation for instruction, a teacher should consider at length how his background might affect instruction. Of particular use would be any instances from a teacher's personal history in which he realized the assumptions or prejudices associated with his culture, and then used that awareness to develop a more expansive multicultural view.

## Nonverbal communication and turn-taking habits

Sometimes, ELL teachers are overly attuned to the linguistic differences between students, and they fail to recognize important nonverbal elements of communication. These include proxemics (the distance between interlocutors), posture, gestures, and eye contact. These nonverbal forms of communication can convey approval or disapproval, express personal identity, or conform to cultural ritual. It is important for a teacher to be aware of the elements of nonverbal communication common to different cultures, so that he can more accurately gauge student behavior and pinpoint potential problems before they occur. A particular area of emphasis is on the cultural norms surrounding turn-taking. In some cultures it is common for people to elbow their way forward rather than wait their turn. Such behavior is not considered rude. A teacher should be aware of this and should gently guide students towards the American norm of turn-taking.

## Promoting cooperation between students from different backgrounds

One of the inherent problems of the common pluralistic approach to multiculturalism is that it overemphasizes the distinctions between cultures and thereby tacitly encourages students to self segregate. To combat this problem, teachers should set up activities that require students from different cultures to cooperate. Once students have achieved a certain level of linguistic mastery, they should be able to work in collaboration with students with a different primary language. Another way to promote cooperation is to lead activities that emphasize the similarities between cultures. For instance, students could be asked to describe the traditional holidays in their cultures, and then to identify the common elements. In most cultures, holidays will be celebrated with special foods, dancing, and songs. These general characteristics are true of many cultures.

## Multiculturalism

Multiculturalism is the set of values and norms that suggest that different races in a pluralistic society should learn to understand and appreciate the differences between them, rather than seeking to impose one style of life upon another. The multicultural view emphasizes the inherent dignity in all human groups, and seeks to find ways to harmonize relations without compromising any group's beliefs. In the United States, multiculturalism exists in protection for the rights of minority groups to preserve their religious and cultural practices. Some critics of multiculturalism argue that it prevents assimilation and integration, and can thereby lead to disharmony in the society, or an under-performing and economically segregated labor force.

## Social role

A role is a person's particular niche within a society. Every role has a set of expectations and norms that define how the person holding it should behave. For example, in the case of the role of the father, most societies expect that a person will provide economic and material support for the rest of his family. It is quite possible to hold multiple roles at the same time, and indeed to acquire and cast off roles as one moves through life. Culturally acknowledged roles help to provide a society with its basic structure. Much of the trouble resulting from an individual's passage from one culture to another comes from the difficulty in discovering and occupying an accepted role in the new society. This transition can be facilitated by a knowledgeable and sensitive ELL instructor.

## Role performance, impression management, and studied nonobservance

Role performance is the way people holding a particular role actually behave, as opposed to the way they are expected to behave as holders of that role. Impression management is one's conscious manipulation of one's role performance. Successful role management requires that an individual has an accurate understanding of his role, as well as the expectations society has for him. Studied nonobservance is the sociological term for when members of a society ignore lapses in one another's role performance, in the interest of preserving harmony within the society.

## Role set, role strain, role exit, and role-taking

The role set is the full group of roles associated with any particular status. A college professor, for instance, must by turns be a mentor, expert, friend, and colleague. Role strain is the difficulty an individual may have in meeting the social obligations of a role. Most sociologists would say that every individual experiences role strain to some degree, as no person is perfectly suited to any role. Role exit is the process of leaving a role that formerly had been integral to the individual's personality. Everyone exits roles throughout their life, for example leaving behind the role of son when one's parents die, or leaving the role of student when one graduates. Role-taking is the process whereby an individual imagines himself in the role of another, and tries then to understand the meaning of what the other is expressing. Developing this sense of empathy is an important first step towards enabling students to inhabit roles in both their native culture and English-speaking culture.

## Socialization

Socialization is the process through which individuals born into a society gradually become participating members of that society. This involves learning the culture, including the prevailing social values and norms, and learning to assume the behavior appropriate to a specific societal role. Experts usually distinguish between primary socialization (the period in which an infant acquires the rudiments of language), and secondary socialization (in which the individual is trained to join a particular social group). Socialization is impossible without the active participation of the society, especially the family, education, and religious groups. Most experts concur that socialization continues in some degree throughout an individual's entire life, though it is most crucial in childhood. For ELL students, of course, transition to English-speaking culture is another instance of intense socialization.

## Gender socialization

Gender socialization is the process through which an individual learns about the various gender roles in his society and comes to take one. Sociological research has shown that boys and girls are treated quite differently in most societies; parents encourage their children to act in gender-appropriate ways, and are embarrassed or angry when children display traits of another gender. Peer pressure also subtly lets children know what clothing and behavior is appropriate to their gender. Studies of American schools during the 1990s showed that teachers generally assigned different tasks to boys and girls. It has also been observed that most children's books and television programs present stereotyped gender roles.

## Class socialization

Sociologists have determined that there are fundamental differences in the ways children are socialized depending on their social class. In fact, research has shown that the specific values stressed by parents vary depending on their class. Middle-class parents tend to emphasize responsibility, self-control, and curiosity about why things happen, whereas working-class parents are more interested in teaching their children manners, neatness, honesty, and obedience. The inference drawn by sociology is that individuals in higher classes tend to place more emphasis on self-direction and obeying internal standards, as opposed to conformity and obeying external standards. There is speculation that this difference is the result of working-class parents being so thoroughly involved in slavish work that they come to identify with the ethics of conformity and obedience. One of the emphases of critical multiculturalism has been to extend the treatment of bias in the ELL classroom beyond race and ethnicity to socioeconomic status.

### Primary socialization

Typically, an individual's primary socialization occurs among his family. The family is the first mirror a child develops for himself, and it is the family's reactions to his behavior that forms the behavioral habits he will take into the society at large. Mothers and fathers typically have complementary ways of relating to children, which provides for a more balanced socialization process. The presence of siblings can give the child some experience at conflict, cooperation, and competition. Generally, however, primary socialization in the family means the child is born into a particular social status, and will absorb a particular set of values, attitudes, and beliefs.

### Secondary socialization

Secondary socialization is that socialization that the individual undergoes outside of the family unit: from friends, at school, and from the media. An ELL student undergoes a variation of secondary socialization in the classroom. A child's peer group provides him with experience dealing with others of relatively equal status. In this setting, children can take some power in their relationships, and learn about friendship and conflict resolution. Socialization at school is important as well because it places the child in a subordinate relation to someone other than his parent, and prepares him for life among bureaucratic, impersonal organizations. Television is probably the most important socializing agent among the mass media; most research shows that it tends to reinforce stereotypes about social roles and norms.

### Anticipatory socialization and desocialization

When an individual begins to alter his beliefs or norms because of an expected socialization process he is about to undergo, it is known as anticipatory socialization. One possible example of anticipatory socialization might be a college graduate who, before actually getting a job, adopts the dress and lifestyle of a member of the business community. Some ELL students will demonstrate this behavior. Desocialization is the process of casting off one version of self and one set of values. Desocialization is followed by resocialization into another set of values and norms. Sociology asserts that as individuals move through life, taking on and casting off various roles, they are constantly altering the set of values and norms that are most in line with their status. Therefore, they are constantly engaged in a process of desocialization and resocialization. To some extent, this process should be expected in the ELL classroom, but it should not be accelerated through the denigration of the student's native culture.

### Internalization of norms

The internalization of norms is basically the development of a conscience. It refers to the condition whereby the members of a society accept the norms of that society as correct, to the point that they no longer even need to think of them explicitly. Internalization is crucial because it means that the governing authority does not have to make sure individuals are policed at all times. In the United States, for instance, most citizens simply *feel* that stealing from one's neighbor is wrong; the immorality of theft is a norm that has been fully internalized in American society. Some sociologists have speculated that genetics may be intertwined with the internalization of norms, as many common norms promote survival and successful propagation of the species. An ELL teacher should expect that most students will share norms, regardless of their native culture. However, there may be some small but important differences.

### Differential socialization, horizontal socialization, and vertical socialization

Differential socialization is the way in which different members of the same society may develop markedly different traits, depending on what role their society intends for them to assume later in life. This differentiation can occur in one of two ways. When sociologists are referring to a fundamental difference in the socialization, for instance the different requirements that a society has for doctors and teachers, they call it horizontal differentiation. When sociologists are referring to differences in socialization caused by varying social status, for instance the socialization of the wealthy compared to that of the poor, they use the term vertical socialization. Every individual is subject to both kinds of differentiation in his socialization. It is important for an ELL teacher to understand this concept so as to avoid pigeonholing students.

### Attachments, investments, involvements, and beliefs

Attachments are the bonds formed between individual members of a society, as for instance the love between family members or friends. Investments are the material and emotional costs that a person expends in order to make his place in a society and, hopefully, secure the future rewards of participation in that society. For students, learning English makes an investment in the English-speaking culture. A person's involvement in his society is the amount of time they spend engaged in nondeviant activities, and a person's beliefs are their ideas about how the members of their society should behave. The development of involvements and beliefs will be a consequence of the formation of attachments and investments by students.

### Family

The family is the basic unit of society. The size and configuration of the family varies from culture to culture, but the general functions remain the same. The most obvious and important function of the family is to nurture and socialize the young, but the stability provided by family life is also a benefit to the society at large. In the United States, family structure was extremely rigid and stable during the colonial period, as adverse economic conditions made family members very dependent on one another. As the country became more prosperous, however, family life became more and more improvised and careless, resulting in a rise in crime. In the early-eighteenth century, however, the traditional family roles that survive somewhat today (that is, father as breadwinner, mother as caretaker) appeared, and the family structure became much more stable. The students in an ELL class are likely to emerge from vastly different family structures.

A nuclear family is a family group consisting of one adult couple (one male and one female) and their children. The strong bond among the members of a nuclear family is a consistent feature of almost every society, with one notable exception being the Israeli kibbutz, in which children are raised by the entire community without any particular parents. An extended family consists of more than one adult couple, often the parents, brothers and sisters of a particular heterosexual couple. In many human societies, people live among their extended families, rather than just in a nuclear family unit. This is especially typical in societies where people do not have to move particularly quickly (that is, in agrarian or industrial rather than hunting and gathering societies).

## Patrilineality and matrilineality

In a culture operating on the principle of patrilineality, a person inherits his title and property from his father's side of the family. Patrilineal descent is much more common that matrilineal descent, in which things are inherited from the mother's side. In fact, societies that operate on matrilineality often transfer property not to the women themselves, but to the male heirs of a woman. For this reason, even in such a woman-based system, women see little material benefit. In a society operating on a patrilocal rule of residence, married couples will live either with or close to the man's family. In a culture observing a matrilocal rule of residence, married couples will live with or near the woman's family.

## Endogamy, exogamy, polygamy, polyandry, and polygyny

There are several distinctions within the institution of marriage, to account for differences in arrangement and configuration. Endogamy is the practice of forcing someone to marry within his own group. The group in question could be the individual's religious, tribal, racial, national, or other group. Exogamy, on the other hand, is the practice of marrying outside the group. Polygamy describes any marital group that consists of one man or woman and his or her multiple spouses. Within polygamy, polyandry is the practice of forming marital groups consisting of one wife and two or more husbands. Polygyny, on the other hand, is the formation of marital groups of one man and two or more wives.

## Soliciting cultural information

English language learners come from various and diverse backgrounds, and a teacher cannot be expected to have familiarity with each student's native culture. However, a teacher should know how to go about acquiring some degree of familiarity, particularly with regard to those cultural aspects that will affect the student's progress. The first and best resource for a teacher is the student and the student's family. Even within a general culture or ethnicity, a family is likely to have specific characteristics and idiosyncrasies that relate to education. For instance, a teacher might assume that all students from the Middle East have a patriarchal view of gender relations, only to discover that there are countries in the region with a more westernized attitude about such things than one might expect.

A great deal of useful information can be obtained from the artifacts of a culture: that is, the music, film, and literature produced by its members. Many teachers have found that exploring the art of their students' native culture has a broadening effect on every aspect of their lives, not only their instruction. Insofar as it is possible to incorporate these artifacts into the work of the class, it can be greatly beneficial. Another resource is the Internet: there are scores of English-language websites and chat rooms for every culture, and a teacher can often solicit advice from people who represent or are expert in a particular culture. Finally, a teacher can visit the reference department of a local library. Reference librarians are trained to point out useful books and articles that can help a teacher become oriented to a culture.

## Applying cultural knowledge

Having obtained an understanding of the native cultures of his students, a teacher should apply this knowledge to instruction. Perhaps the most important aspect of culture to consider is the concept of education. In some cultures, particularly those in Africa and Asia, it is typical for students to passively receive information. These students will not be used to thinking creatively or offering their opinions in class. A teacher should avoid putting them on the spot in the first weeks of class. Many students will be used to a disorganized school structure, particularly those who come from impoverished or semi-literate backgrounds. Such students may need more instruction on basic elements of being a student, like taking notes, adhering to a schedule, and raising one's hand before talking. For a teacher, it is easier to exercise patience with students who struggle to adjust to American-style education when the reasons for the struggle are understood.

## School culture vs. student's native culture

When education experts refer to the degree of cultural congruence, they mean the extent to which the culture of the student overlaps with the culture of the school. It is assumed that high cultural congruence is a positive, but this is not always the case. When a student's native culture is very similar to the predominant culture at the school, the student may be disincentivized from learning about the school culture. The student may have the idea that their current cultural orientation is "good enough," and that there is no reason to attempt to master elements of the school culture. A teacher's role is to underscore the differences between cultures without passing judgment or stigmatizing either side. A teacher should encourage students to explore cultural differences without preference or bias. Of course, a teacher's job is made somewhat easier by a high degree of cultural congruence, because students will need less instruction in the basics of being a student in an American-style program.

## Cultural values in the classroom

Bilingual educators need to be especially sensitive to the educational needs of culturally diverse learners. This is because these needs can manifest themselves in ways that are not normal for the culture in which the teacher has been raised. All students need not only cognitive and linguistic education, but psycho-social and affective education. On top of that, students need to be receiving professional and vocational skills so that they can hold a job in the future.

Teachers need to be aware of the way in which cultural values are formed. Individuals develop cultural perceptual patterns which determine the stimuli that reach their awareness, and go a long way to determining their judgments of people, objects, and events in their lives. Individuals from different cultures will literally think differently. These differences are the results of environmental adaptations, contact with other cultural groups, historical factors, and socio-economic evolution. Students will also develop their personal values based on their relationships with their family, religious group, and peers.

## Promoting cultural diversity

Teachers are responsible for creating an effective learning environment for ELL students by remaining sensitive to the cultural values of all students. Teachers should be aware that many students will have a negative predisposition toward authority figures. At times, a teacher may find that his own values and beliefs are in conflict with the values and beliefs of the student. Regardless, a teacher needs to maintain high expectations for his students. Significant research has indicated that the nature of a teacher's expectations for students has a direct relation to performance. When students feel that the teacher has low expectations for their performance, it tends to diminish their self-confidence and makes failure more likely. In contrast, when teachers have high expectations for their students, students are more likely to take risks and experiment with new methods of study. Students are also more likely to set clear goals and work hard to achieve them.

## Structural considerations related to a multicultural classroom

Teachers need to be aware of how the structural aspects of the learning environment will affect the performance of bilingual students. Often, school systems that are entrenched in traditional methods will be especially resistant to making changes to benefit bilingual students. Some schools use aggressive tracking programs, meaning that students are placed into groups based upon ability. In other schools, students will be mixed seemingly at random. Some schools will rely heavily on standardized testing to categorize students, while others will depend more heavily on future evaluations. Finally, the curriculum mandated by the school will have an effect on the learning environment for ELL students. It is essential that the curriculum be as relevant as possible to the needs, interests, and environment of the students. Too many school systems have ethnocentric curricula that alienate foreign students. Also, it is a common practice for the ELL curriculum to simply be a diluted version of the normal course of study.

## Respect for diversity

At all times, teachers need to indicate their respect for the cultural heritage and the values of every student in the class. Teachers should always treat students as individuals, and should make a concerted effort to learn about their cultural and personal values. At the same time, teachers should strive to identify the idiosyncratic learning styles of students, and should incorporate instructional strategies and materials appropriate for each student. One of the best ways to indicate respect for students' heritage is to foster communication with the student's family; often the best source for information about a student's heritage and cultural values will be his parents. Finally, a teacher should become aware of his own teaching and learning style, so as to be better able to accommodate the diverse learning styles of students. The best teachers are those who recognize their own strengths and weaknesses, and adapt to best meet the needs of their students.

## Basics of multicultural education

Multicultural education is a specific program of curricula and instructional techniques designed to be inclusive of all racial, ethnic, religious, and linguistic backgrounds. This program was developed to promote democracy by empowering the members of all demographic groups to become informed and participate in the community. It was motivated by the recognition of the changing population in the United States, with an ever increasing and varying mix of minority groups. Elements of a multicultural educational philosophy have found their way into almost every school in the country. However, the ascendancy of this philosophy has not been without some controversy. Some critics charge that the multicultural education program emphasizes the distinctions between cultures, but pays very little attention to the abundant similarities.

## Five dimensions of multicultural education

The intention of multicultural education is to advance democracy by empowering minority groups and explicitly challenging students to become active citizens. To this end, the multicultural educational philosophy works in five dimensions. Firstly, multicultural education emphasizes content integration, meaning that different subject matter is related to underscore similarities and differences between cultures. This pedagogical style also emphasizes the knowledge construction process, which means that teachers focus on the ways that students form ideas and opinions, and try to remove any implicit bias. The third dimension is attention to prejudiced reactions, and the fourth is the so-called equity pedagogy, which is an explicit attempt to create a level playing field for all minority groups. Finally, multicultural education promotes a school culture and social structure that is empowering to all students.

## Hidden curriculum

A hidden curriculum is a set of informal and implicit rules that a school teaches children in order to help them succeed both academically and socially. Specifically, the hidden curriculum is that set of rules which a child needs to learn in order to survive outside the family, in a larger social organization. Sociologists frequently cite self-discipline as the foremost element of the hidden curriculum. Students must learn to work quietly, get along well with people they may not like, follow orders from someone else, and tolerate frustration. These skills are essential to becoming productive members of the economic community in later life. When polled, most Americans have supported this idea of the hidden curriculum by asserting that "discipline" should be the primary focus of school.

## Conservative multiculturalism

In their seminal work *Changing Multiculturalism*, educational experts Kincheloe and Steinberg made a critical study of the various forms of multicultural education. They explicitly favored critical multiculturalism. They claim that conservative multiculturalism makes assumptions that are detrimental to students; for instance, conservative multiculturalists assume that minorities are impoverished or culturally deprived. They tend to emphasize standardized testing that reinforces Eurocentric norms. IQ tests and the SATs are two such tests. According to Kincheloe and Steinberg, conservative multiculturalists believe that the status quo is basically equitable and should not be changed. In their formulation, white culture is not considered as a particular form of human experience, but is instead the standard by which all others are measured.

## Liberal multiculturalism

Kincheloe and Steinberg offered a penetrating critique of liberal multiculturalism, which they characterized as a well-intentioned but ultimately damaging attempt to help minorities. According to this critique, liberal multiculturalists assume that all people are the same, and that whatever racial inequality exists is due to a lack of opportunity. In their view, all people are responsible for themselves, and the playing field is essentially level. Liberal multiculturalists celebrate African-American and Hispanic culture, but critics like Kincheloe and Steinberg complained that this celebration is patronizing "tokenism." Also, they charge that the explicit coverage of discrimination and bias in the liberal multiculturalist curriculum is too divisive, and is ultimately destructive to cultural integration.

## Pluralist multiculturalism

In recent decades, pluralist multiculturalism has been one of the predominant forms of diversity education. Kincheloe and Steinberg criticize this approach for making certain assumptions that are damaging to students. According to their critique, pluralist multiculturalism assumes that diversity has an intrinsic value, and that a full curriculum will include coverage of other cultures as well as the prejudices and stereotypes that can be damaging to intercultural relations. According to Kincheloe and Steinberg, one of the main problems with pluralist multiculturalism is that it ignores differences of class, and creates a situation in which students are more likely to self segregate. The emphasis on pluralism necessarily means that the differences between cultures are discussed much more often and in greater depth than the more abundant similarities.

## Critical multiculturalism

In *Changing Multiculturalism*, Kincheloe and Steinberg promote the philosophy of critical multiculturalism. In this approach, discussion of cultural similarities and differences is merely one component of instruction related to social, institutional, and economic prejudices. Critical multiculturalists believe that justice is available for all people under the current rules, but it is not always distributed evenly. A critical multiculturalist also believes that different knowledge traditions must be explicitly discussed and approved within a school context. A critical multiculturalist does not entirely criticize white culture, but believes that the predominance of the white male view should be called into question in the classroom. Essentially, in the critical multiculturalist view, students should be encouraged to explore their own basis for knowledge and their constructed way of seeing the world.

**Student diversity**

Cultural identities are strongly embraced by adolescents but they also want to be recognized and treated as unique individuals. Teachers walk a fine line between respecting cultural differences and avoiding overly emphasizing them or disregarding them altogether. Responding to discriminatory comments immediately, using a wide variety of examples, quoting scholars from many cultures and identifying universal problems needing complex solutions can indirectly communicate appreciation of and respect for all cultures. Teachers must take care never to imply any kind of stereotype or make comments that might indicate a cultural bias. They must refrain from asking a student to respond as a member of a particular culture, class or country. Teachers should learn as much as they can about every racial, ethnic and cultural group represented in their classroom. It is also important that teachers respect students' commitments and obligations away from school, their family responsibilities and job pressures.

**Cultural influences**

Study after study has shown that a student's culture has a direct impact on learning. Since educational standards are based on white, middle class cultural identification, students who do not fall into that demographic face challenges every day. It's not that these students are incapable of learning; they simply judge that which is important and how they express that importance differently. Sometimes it is difficult for them to understand and relate to curriculum content, teaching methods and social skills required because their culture does things differently, emphasizes different choices and rewards different behavior. Adolescents identify with their culture; they become what they know. If teachers ignore cultural differences, it causes communication issues, inhibits learning and increases the potential for behavior problems. As long as a child has no physical or mental health issues, he is capable of learning. He simply needs that the information presented and examples used to be relevant to his life experiences; otherwise, it does not seem to make sense to him.

**Social environment**

The social environment is the set of people and institutions with which one associates and communicates. It has both a direct and indirect influence on behavior by the individuals within the group. It is sometimes defined by specific characteristics such as race, gender, age, culture or behavioral patterns. When defined by behavioral patterns it can lead to unproven assumptions about entire groups of people. In America's diverse society, it is essential that teachers recognize that various social groups exist within a classroom and thus determine the best strategies not only to facilitate the learning of "book" facts, but also to encourage understanding and acceptance between the groups. The learning theory called social cognitivism believes that people learn by observing others, whether they are aware of the process or not. Creating opportunities for students to interact with diverse social groups in a neutral, non-threatening situation can bring about positive interpersonal growth that could have long-term societal impact outside of the educational environment.

**Socialization**

Socialization is the process of learning the written and unwritten rules, acceptable behavioral patterns, and accumulated knowledge of the community in order to function within its culture. It is a gradual process that starts when a person is born and, in one form or another, continues throughout his life. There are many "communities" within a culture: e.g., family, school, neighborhood, military and country. There are six forms of socialization:

- Reverse Socialization: deviation from acceptable behavior patterns.
- Developmental Socialization: the process of learning social skills.
- Primary Socialization: learning the attitudes, values and actions of a culture.
- Secondary Socialization: learning behavior required in a smaller group within the culture.
- Anticipatory Socialization: practicing behavior in preparation for joining a group.
- Resocialization: discarding old behavior and learning new behavior as part of a life transition; e.g., starting school, moving to a new neighborhood or joining the military.

The agents of socialization are the people, groups and institutions that influence the self-esteem, emotions, attitudes, behavior and acceptance of a person within his environment. The first agents are the immediate family (mother, father, siblings) and extended family (grandparents, aunts, uncles, cousins). They influence religious affiliation, political inclinations, educational choices, career aspirations and other life goals. The school's role is explaining societal values, reinforcing acceptable behavior patterns and teaching necessary skills such as reading, writing, reasoning and critical thinking. Peer groups (people who are about the same age) share certain characteristics (attend the same school, live in the same neighborhood) and influence values, attitudes and behavior. The media (radio, television, newspapers, magazines, the Internet) have an impact on attitude, values and one's understanding of the activities of society and international events. Other institutions that influence people include religion, the work place, the neighborhood, and city, state and federal governments.

**Social ineptitude**

Social ineptitude is defined as a lack of social skills; in most societies, this term is considered disrespectful. There are medical conditions that may cause a deficiency in social skills such as autism and Asperger syndrome. Someone who believes himself socially inept may have an avoidant personality disorder. A shy person or an overly bold person may observe societal conventions but still exhibit social incompetence; the behavior is simply manifested in different ways. The criteria for social ineptitude are different in different cultures, which makes it difficult to cite specific examples. People trying to integrate into a new environment may unknowingly commit a social faux pas thereby earning the damaging label unfairly. In a culturally diverse classroom, it is critical to create an atmosphere of acceptance so if a student does something inappropriate, the behavior can be quietly and gently corrected without causing humiliation or embarrassment.

**Social skills**

Social skills are the tools used to interact and communicate with others. They are learned during the socialization process and are both verbal and non-verbal. These skills are integral to becoming an active and accepted member of any environment. There are general skills needed to complete daily transactions such as being able to ask sensible questions and provide logical answers and knowing how to read and write and understand simple directions. If these skills are missing or poorly executed, it can cause various problems and misunderstandings, some of which could have long-lasting and/or life-changing consequences. In smaller groups, other skills may be needed such as the ability to engage in interesting conversation, present ideas to peers, teach new concepts or actively participate in discussions. Using body language and gestures appropriate to the situation and the message, having the ability to resolve conflicts and being diplomatic when necessary are examples of advanced social skills.

**Meeting with parents**

Studies have shown that the more parents are involved in their children's education, the better the students learn and the fewer behavior problems one must handle. Teachers are an integral part of the process. It is up to them to keep parents informed about the academic and social progress of the students. Report cards only provide letter or number grades and are not designed to explore and explain how well the student is learning and progressing in the intangible skills like critical thinking, reasoning ability, study habits, attitude, communication with adults and peers and other social and interactive development. Sending home periodic progress reports is an effective way to keep parents abreast of changes. Meeting with parents regularly to discuss their child's particular progress and being available to answer questions are excellent ways to work together as a team to ensure the student benefits the most from his educational experience.

**Parent/student/teacher agreement**

If a teacher should wish to use a formal parent/student/teacher agreement as a way to involve parents, provide students with a written set of expectations and explain their commitment to a successful educational experience, there are several activities that can be included:

- Parent Priorities:
    - Show respect for and support of the student, teacher and the discipline policy.
    - Monitor homework assignments and projects.
    - Attend teacher conferences.
    - Ask about the student's day.
- Student Priorities:
    - Show respect for parents, teachers, peers and school property.
    - Put forth his best effort both in class and at home.
    - Come to class prepared.
    - Talk to his parents about school.
- Teacher Priorities:
    - Show respect for the student, his family and his culture.
    - Help each student strive to reach his potential.
    - Provide fair progress evaluations to students and parents.
    - Enforce rules fairly and consistently.

Many schools use some sort of parent/student/teacher agreement to ensure everyone understands the rules and agrees to abide by them. It can be as simple as requiring parents, students and teachers to sign a copy of the student handbook or it can be a formal contract drafted with specific activities each pledges to perform. Whichever format is used, it should detail each party's responsibilities. This accomplishes several goals:

- Parents are recognized as an important part of the educational experience. They are also made aware

of what is expected of them, their children, the teachers and the administration.
- Students are given written expectations, which prevent an "I didn't know" attitude. It encourages respect for himself, his parents, his teachers, his peers and the rules.
- Teachers make a written commitment to students and parents to provide an environment that encourages learning. They list specific, observable behavior which they pledge to perform.

**Levels of parental involvement**

Some parents are eager to participate in their child's education, some do so only when required, and others avoid involvement of any kind. All three approaches can be a challenge. Eager parents may bombard the teacher and administration with notes, phone calls, emails and requests for information and meetings. Setting reasonable, well-defined limits may be necessary. Parents who only show up when specifically requested (e.g., semi-annual parent/teacher conferences, meeting with the administration about a behavior problem), might only be going through the motions in order to keep their child enrolled in school. They may be incapable of or don't really care to address any underlying issues; they show up because they are required to do so. Parents who are never available and impossible to contact provide no help or insight and offer no support.

**Parent/teacher conferences**

Basics

Parent/teacher conferences can be stressful experiences for both parties. But with a positive attitude and much preparation, they can be pleasant, provide a forum for the exchange of information and improve the educational experience for the students. The first step is for the teacher to be rested. Fatigue can cause an inability to concentrate, unfortunate misunderstandings and inappropriate reactions. If a teacher thinks parents might be difficult to handle, it might be wise to ask an administrator to sit in. The teacher needs to have a plan prepared with discussion points and copies of the student's work available to review. He needs to keep in mind that the parents may have items to discuss as well, and therefore the plan needs to be flexible and allow time for questions. The discussion should focus on the positive and present negative information with a "we can fix it" approach.

In order to avoid wasting everyone's time during a parent/teacher conference, there are several things a teacher can do to set the scene for a productive meeting. Make initial contact early by sending a note or newsletter home briefly outlining plans and objectives for the year and providing contact information (e.g., phone number, email address, days and times available). This tells parents the teacher is willing to talk and/or meet when necessary. When a date for a conference is set, the teacher should be certain to invite both parents. It is the best way to gauge how involved they are, yet individual family circumstances need to be considered (one-parent families, parents' work commitments, et cetera). Schedule twenty to thirty minute conferences; if more time becomes necessary, schedule a follow-up meeting. Develop a flexible agenda and gather necessary paperwork. Verify parent and student names just before the meeting.

Encouraging parental involvement

Every teacher needs to develop ways in which to involve parents in the education of their children. Some communication methods may be more effective than others depending upon the age of the students, the educational level and time limitations of the parents, and the administrative support and resources available to the teacher. Some schools encourage a parent orientation program at the beginning of the year, in which the teacher informs parents what his expectations are concerning behavior and outlines classroom rules. He presents a broad picture of the material to be covered, projects that will be assigned and homework requirements. If a meeting isn't possible, the same information can be conveyed in a letter sent home just before school starts or during the first week. Besides regularly scheduled parent/teacher conferences, a periodic newsletter, perhaps when report cards are issued, can be sent to update parents.

Being prepared

Parent/teacher conferences are the best time for candid communication. For the encounter to be productive, both parties need to be prepared to discuss the student's strengths and weaknesses, share any concerns and decide upon the best way to help the student meet required goals and reach his potential. Some topics to consider in preparation for this important meeting:

- The skills and knowledge that should be learned and mastered.
- Required academic standards. Give parents a copy to which to refer during the year, and explain these standards.Projects planned and assignments required to complete academic requirements.The evaluation method, what data is considered and when progress reports are issued.How parents can help. Suggest concrete activities which they can do at home in order to encourage learning and support the teacher's efforts.Programs available for both fast and slow learners.What programs are available to prepare students for life after high school.

Things to remember

Try to use a table rather than a desk and chairs so that the parents and the teacher meet as equals; this creates a more relaxed environment. Start with a positive statement about the student and then briefly review the objectives of the meeting. The teacher should not do all of the talking; it should be a conversation, not a monologue. Avoid educational jargon. Many parents will not understand it or will interpret it incorrectly. Focus on strengths, give specific examples, provide suggestions for improvement and refer to actions rather than character. For example: "Sam turned in his essay the day after it was due," instead of "Sam is irresponsible." Ask for parents' opinions and listen to their responses. Use body language that shows interest and concern and make eye contact. Do not judge the parents' attitude or behavior, and consider cultural differences. Briefly summarize the discussion and end with a positive comment or observation about the student.

Conclusion

If either the teacher or the parents feel that there is more to discuss or that a follow-up meeting is necessary for an update on progress made, a time can be scheduled before the parents leave. As soon as possible after the conversation while the details are fresh, the teacher should make notes of the general discussion and record any specific actions that he or the parents agreed to take as well as the parents' attitude and willingness to offer support. Any private information and/or family issues which the parents shared should be kept in the strictest confidence. If a cooperative relationship is to be established, parents need to know that their family business will remain private. It is very important and even required in some states that teachers report any indication of or concerns about possible child abuse or endangerment to the authorities. All teachers and administrators need to be familiar with the pertinent statutes in their state.

## Pedagogy of the Oppressed

The most influential text in the development of multicultural education was *Pedagogy of the Oppressed* by Paolo Freire. This book is considered very radical, and has actually been banned in several countries. In it, Freire criticizes the traditional notion of students as empty vessels to be filled with the knowledge of the teacher. He claims that this idea, besides being incorrect insofar as it ignores the inherent knowledge of students, recreates the colonization process in which Eurocentric thinking is assumed to be superior. In Freire's model of education, students are the co-creators: that is, they collaborate with the teacher to explore ways of knowing and the assumptions inherent in each culture. Freire describes his method as "dialogic" (as in dialogue) instruction, meaning that the student and teacher engage in an instructional conversation and inform one another.

## Antibias curriculum

In recent years, some educational theorists have developed a pedagogical philosophy called the "antibias curriculum." This is in part a reaction to the multicultural curriculum, which is sometimes criticized for being too wide-ranging and scattershot. The antibias curriculum emphasizes the presence of discrimination in all areas: race, gender, linguistic background, ability and sexual orientation. In this curriculum, the emphasis is on explicit treatment of bias. A teacher who uses the curriculum will try to present each side of an issue in which bias is pervasive. For instance, in a discussion of American history, a teacher would be careful to explore how American and European historians have marginalized and deemphasized the contributions of minorities and Native Americans. The explicit goal of the antibias curriculum is social justice.

The theoretical foundation of the antibias approach is that there are two distinct curricula in education: the formal curriculum and the hidden curriculum. The formal curriculum is the set of explicit materials, books, syllabi, and instructional methods used in the classroom. The elements of a formal curriculum would be evident to any untrained observer. The hidden curriculum, on the other hand, is the set of ideas and prejudices that are indirectly or implicitly delivered to students. For instance, the traditional American school system distinguishes different subjects by organizing a class schedule in which students move from one subject to another. There is nothing bad about the system, but it is not necessarily followed in other parts of the world. In other places, there may be less distinction between subjects. Proponents of the antibias curriculum emphasize that teachers need to explore the elements of the hidden curriculum to ensure that they are not favoring one set of students over another. It is generally thought that there is more inherent bias in the hidden curriculum than in the formal curriculum.

### Goals of the antibias curriculum

Although the antibias curriculum has the broad goal of social justice, it also has some specific goals. For example, teachers who use the antibias curriculum want to improve the confidence and enhance the self perception of their students. In other words, the teachers want to help the students see themselves and their culture as they relate to others. Similarly, the antibias curriculum seeks to improve empathy by encouraging students to consider the mental and emotional situations of other people. By explicitly covering issues of bias, the antibias curriculum hopes to encourage students to think critically about the subject. Finally, teachers who employ the antibias curriculum aspire to have students who will stand up for themselves and for others against whom are being discriminated.

## Criticisms of the antibias curriculum

Although most educational experts acknowledge the validity of the critique offered by the antibias curriculum, there are some who complain that this curriculum swings the pendulum too far in the other direction. For instance, some critics charge that the antibias curriculum has an implicit bias against European ideas and cultural norms. Because these have long been dominant in the United States, it is natural that the antibias curriculum will spend more time problematizing them than it will spend on a critique of Native American ideology. The result, according to some critics, is an overabundance of identification with minority culture. The antibias curriculum has been called "too Afrocentric" by some. Another criticism of it is that it tends to omit the contributions of smaller minorities, like Eskimos and Native Americans.

## Cooperating with colleagues

To be successful, an ELL teacher must be constantly cooperating with and learning from colleagues. There are a number of ways to do this; one is to set up regular meetings with them. Many ELL teachers are part of a team of teachers who instruct the same group of students, and these meetings will therefore already be in place. If this is not the case, however, teachers should try to set up frequent meetings with colleagues who either teach the same students or the same subject. These meetings should not be the equivalent of teacher's lounge gripe sessions, but instead should be forums in which new teaching methods can be discussed, teaching content can be coordinated, and basic plans of behavior management can be established.

## Peer review programs for ELL teachers

Another way in which a community of ELL teachers can foster professional improvement is through peer review. In a peer review program, teachers observe one another and offer suggestions for improvement. This is especially helpful when it is done among teachers in the same grade level or subject. Another ELL teacher who is fluent in French, for instance, would be a great resource for a non-French-speaking teacher helping new immigrants from West Africa. Of course, in order for this sort of program to work, there needs to be a spirit of collaboration and constructive criticism among the teachers. Unfortunately, school politics and competitiveness often poison the relationships between colleagues, and make it difficult to offer or accept well-meaning suggestions. The best peer review programs establish a specific protocol for criticism and encouragement.

## Mentoring programs for ELL teachers

Mentoring is another professional improvement program that can be extremely valuable to an ELL teacher. In a mentoring program, experienced teachers develop relationships with beginning teachers. The schools that use these programs find that they are able to retain a larger proportion of their beginning teachers. When mentoring programs are not offered, new teachers should ask a veteran ELL teacher to act as a mentor, as a mentor can provide guidance on any aspect of teaching, from classroom management to lesson plans. New teachers get the most out of the relationship if they consciously remain open to constructive criticism. A mentor should observe his or her mentee directly in the teacher's classroom, but the mentee should also keep a list of concerns and questions to bring to private meetings. Teachers who accept advice and are willing to see things from a different perspective will grow immeasurably from the mentoring experience.

## Peer tutoring programs

Another way that ELL teachers can join with their colleagues in order to improve the quality of instruction is through peer tutoring. In a basic peer tutoring program, more advanced students work with the younger students on class work. For instance, the members of a second-grade ELL class might be paired with the members of a fifth-grade ELL class. The older children will still be using many of the concepts that they learned in second grade, thus it will be beneficial for them to explain and demonstrate these concepts. The younger children, meanwhile, will enjoy working with older children and may be more receptive to the material when it comes from a source other than the teacher.

Peer tutoring relationships are especially fruitful when they are between students from similar backgrounds. In a modern ELL class, there may be students from several different linguistic backgrounds. Some students may be the sole representative of their native culture in their grade level. If there are other students in the school with the same origin, however, they may be profitably united through peer tutoring. Also, peer tutoring programs are a great chance for students to develop their social skills; the older children will practice being generous and considerate of someone younger, while the younger children will practice being attentive and receptive to counsel. Of course, only those older students who have a good grasp of the content and are well-behaved should be involved in a peer tutoring program.

## Field trips with other classes

Another way that ELL teachers can band together is by arranging field trips with other teachers, as it is often easier to handle the logistics of a large field trip in cooperation with another teacher. Also, many field trips will have applications to multiple subject areas. For instance, a trip to a local battlefield could have relevance for American history, English, and Social Studies students. A visit to the local natural science museum could be pertinent to content in math, science, and history. It is always a good idea to encourage students to make associations between content areas. Furthermore, a field trip encourages ELL students to mix with other students, forming social connections that improve investment in the academic setting.

## Coordinating subject matter

One of the most positive ways for ELL teachers to work with their fellow teachers is by coordinating subject matter. This strategy is often used in teacher "teams" in elementary and middle school, but it can also be effective in high school. Let us consider a brief example of how teachers can coordinate subject matter with great results. Imagine that you are a sixth-grade ELL teacher. Before the school year begins, you could propose that the sixth grade uses "cities" as a theme. Each teacher can then construct lessons in their instructional domain that connect with this theme. As the ELL teacher, you could look at texts that focus on life in the city. The history teacher could teach students about the rise of the big urban centers during the Industrial Revolution. The math teacher could incorporate some study of the various statistics and charts that are used to describe and learn about cities. If your school is located in or near a large city, you might also take some field trips so students can observe first-hand the things that they have learned.

## Coordinating instructional content

The net effect of coordinating content seems to be that ELL students learn more. Educational research suggests that all knowledge is associative, and people therefore tend to remember those things that they can easily fit into their existing store of information. If an ELL teacher and his colleagues can link diverse disciplines together by looking at the same subject from a number of different perspectives, they can help students develop a well-rounded and coherent way of intellectually exploring the world. This is especially true for ELL students, who will be encountering a dizzying amount of new information at school. If this material is disconnected and seemingly random, students will be more likely to forget it. Thematic content in multiple subjects helps avoid this problem.

## Communicating with colleagues

An ELL instructor should meet with his colleagues at some point during the year so that he can get a general idea of the structure and content of his colleague's classes. During the year, the ELL teacher should stay abreast of that which students are learning in their other classes, and should note associations between disciplines whenever they arise. A teacher should also know when his fellow teachers are assigning major projects or exams, so that he can avoid giving important assignments on the same day. Many schools assign a certain day of the week for tests in each subject; e.g., math tests on Monday, history tests on Tuesday, and so on. If the school does not do this, the ELL teacher should make sure that major projects and examinations are scheduled such that students are not overwhelmed with a flurry of work.

## Relationship with school administration

It is important for the ELL teacher to have a strong relationship with the school administration. The principals and support staff of a school are supposed to be there to make life easier, but they can only do this with cooperation. In order to maintain a happy partnership with the school administration, teachers should remember one guideline of great importance: namely, teachers should always report any significant problems immediately; these problems can include disciplinary matters, personal problems, or conflict with school protocol. In large schools where there is little one-on-one contact between the administration and the faculty, it is common for teachers to let their grievances fester in silence. The result is that what could be a cooperative relationship becomes poisoned by resentment and frustration. Teachers who have complaints or concerns about the way the school is being run, or who need help, should immediately discuss the problem with the principal.

## Meeting with the principal

An ELL teacher should try to avoid only visiting the principal when there is something wrong. A principal, like any person, will develop certain assumptions about a teacher whom they only see in times of crisis. Also, many principals will resent those teachers who they feel are constantly passing their problems onto the administration. ELL teachers should be referring problems to the principal only as a last resort. It is appropriate to let the principal know about concerns without necessarily asking for help. A teacher should try to check in with the principal periodically when things are going well in class, so that he or she can get a more balanced appreciation of the class' progress. When a teacher maintains a good relationship with the principal throughout the year, he or she will be much more helpful on those occasions of crisis.

## Scheduling an observation by the principal

One great way to cultivate a positive relationship with the principal is to invite him or her to sit in on a class. A teacher should invite the principal on a day when a particularly innovative and exciting lesson is planned. It is a good idea to let the students know ahead of time that the principal will be joining the class, so they need to be on their best behavior. During the observation, the teacher should invite the principal to participate whenever appropriate. Many principals were teachers at one time, and will welcome the opportunity to join in with the activities of the class. After the class, the teacher should ask the principal for his opinion. As in relationships with other teachers, teachers should try to remain open to criticism and accepting of advice. These kinds of observations can be very useful for beginning teachers, who may be unaware of some fundamental mistakes they are making.

## Relationships with teacher aides and assistants

Some teachers are lucky enough to have full- or part-time aides and assistants. When this is the case, the teacher should make sure that the aide is being used appropriately. For the most part, an aide should not be busy doing paperwork during class time. It is certainly useful to have another person to help with grading, but this can be done during the planning period or lunch. While the children are in the classroom, the aide should be another set of eyes and ears. In other words, the aide should circulate around the room while students are working. He can answer any questions students may have about the lesson, and can make sure that students stay on-task. Aides are also useful when some members of the class have fallen behind the others. The aide can assemble those students and give them a brief refresher on the recent material as the teacher instructs the rest of the class.

## Introductory note to parents

To ensure that one is able to effectively communicate with parents throughout the year, one should try to establish contact at the beginning of the term. Most teachers send a note to parents at the beginning of the year. In this note, one should introduce oneself and give some background information, such as ones educational background and personal interests. One can then describe the plans for the class as well as ones expectations for student conduct. Of course, an ELL teacher faces a unique challenge in composing such a note, because it is likely that many parents will not be fluent in English. To mitigate this problem, one should either make a translation into the parent's native language or provide access to a translator.

An introductory note at the beginning of the school year is a good place to inform parents as to how much homework students are likely to have during the course of the year, as well as what steps parents can take to ensure that their students are successful. For instance, one might indicate to parents that one is planning to administer a quiz every Friday, so that they can be sure to review material with their child on Thursday night. This note is also a chance to ask for parental involvement in the class. Parents may be called upon to help with supplies or with transportation on field trips. In an introductory note, one might detail some of the needs that the class will have during the course of the year, and ask parents to contact the teacher if they can help.

## Frequent updates to parents

After sending this first letter home, it is also helpful to send home periodic notes letting parents know how the class is proceeding. If one has a small number of students, one may even be able to make personal phone calls to each parent. Another way to stay in contact with many parents is through email; if one finds that all (or even some) of the parents in ones class have internet access, one may send out a short weekly update. Whatever format one chooses, one should try to keep parents informed of upcoming evaluations, field trips, and special events. If possible, one should personalize each message with some specific information about the child; this will convey the impression that one is taking a direct interest in the educational progress of each member of the class. It is important to make an effort to communicate both good news as well as bad. For many parents, the only contact they ever have with the school is when their child has gotten into trouble. One should occasionally make a call or drop a note to praise a student for improved academic performance. Parents will respond very positively to teachers who take the time to praise their children.

## Keeping parents alert to student performance

It is also important to let parents know how their children are faring in class by sending home their grades regularly. Many teachers require students to take home their major tests and have them signed by a parent. Increasingly, teachers are posting student grades on a class website so that parents and students alike can keep track. Whichever method one chooses, one should make sure that one does not wait until the end of the term to let a parent know that their student is in danger of failing. As soon as any student falls behind, it is imperative to alert his parents so that a strategy for improvement can be developed. Do not assume that students will keep their parents informed as to how they are doing in class. Many students will claim to be doing well even if they know that this will be disproved by their final grade. As a teacher, it is ones responsibility to keep parents informed.

## Parent-teacher conferences

Another important part of developing a positive rapport with parents is the parent-teacher conference. Most elementary schools schedule these near the beginning of the year, often at the end of the first grading period. In middle and high school, parent-teacher conferences are not always mandatory, though they are recommended. If one is a beginning teacher, one may approach ones first conferences with some anxiety. It is important to remember, however, that both the teacher and the parent both have the student's success as a goal. It is important to accurately communicate a student's standing within the class. It is also important for both parties to agree on a strategy for maintaining or improving the student's performance subsequent to the conference. Conferences are meant to be punishment for neither the instructor, the parent, nor the student.

## Discussing poor performance

Sometimes, it will be necessary for the teacher to contact a parent because of a student's disruptive behavior or poor academic performance. In these cases, one should plan ones talking points in advance. This is especially important as an ELL teacher, because it is quite possible that the parents will have only limited fluency in English. Under no circumstances should one call a parent while angry; this will only cause the parent to rally to their child's defense and ignore whatever the teacher has to say. One should be able to tell the parent specifically what the student has been doing wrong, and what he needs to do in order to improve. One should also ask questions, to see if there is something happening at home that would cause the student to act in a certain way.

## Teacher-parent phone call

When an ELL student is struggling, contacting his parents should not be a last resort. Rather, it should be done soon so that the student's course can be corrected. Many students act out at school because of problems they are having at home; learning about these motivating factors can not only help one understand the behavior, but can lead to possible solutions. In any case, when one calls a parent to communicate bad news, it is important to always maintain a focus on the steps that should be taken for improvement. Do not call a parent simply to gripe. At the end of the call, make plans to talk again in the near future, so that everyone can assess how the strategy for improvement is proceeding. Always treat the parent as part of a team whose aim is the success of the student.

## Open house

Another traditional means of making contact with parents is the open house. Most schools hold an open house at the beginning of the year so that parents can meet the teachers and see the classrooms. Besides being an opportunity to give information about the class, the open house is a chance for the teacher to present himself in a favorable light. The neatness and organization of the room is very important, as is greeting the parents as they enter. One should try to avoid getting bogged down in discussion with any one parent; discussions of individual students should be handled in another setting. The open house is a chance for one to sell oneself and the class. One should demonstrate the structure of one's class as well as present an appeal for help from parents.

## Inviting parents to class

Besides the open house, parents should be invited to school whenever their presence will have a positive impact on learning. For instance, if students are going to be putting on a group or individual presentation, parents should be invited to attend. This is especially important in elementary grades, where the presence of a parent can be extremely comforting and motivating to students. Other instances where parents could be invited to attend school are field days, class parties, and field trips. Too often, ELL students create a rigid separation between their school and home lives. Language differences reinforce this separation. By inviting parents to class, an ELL teacher breaks down the division between the academic and the family life, and encourages the student to incorporate what he is learning into all phases of his life.

## Incorporating parents into instruction

An ELL teacher should try to take advantage of parents' special skills or talents, especially as they relate to different content areas. For instance, if one is teaching a science-related unit and one of the students' parents is a botanist, you should invite him to speak to the class. If one is teaching a unit on Social Studies and discovers that one of the parents works for the federal government, it might be useful to invite him to speak. Whenever possible, one should be striving to make course content relevant to the daily lives of the students. There is no better way to do this than by incorporating their family members into the lesson.

## *Lau v. Nichols*

The Supreme Court ruling in Lau v. Nichols had a great influence on the expansion of bilingual education in the United States. A group of Chinese-American students in San Francisco claimed that they were receiving an inferior education because of their limited proficiency in English. Title VI of the Civil Rights Act of 1964 asserts that no individual can be discriminated against on the basis of national origin. The Supreme Court agreed that these students were being denied equal educational opportunities. One of the results of this decision was that language was now considered an inextricable part of ethnicity, and therefore any discrimination on the basis of language difference was considered a violation of the Civil Rights Act.

## *Meyer v. Nebraska* (1923)

In the United States, linguistic rights include the right to education, media, and administrative and judicial communication in a language of the recipient's choosing. The Equal Protection and Due Process clauses of the United States Constitution's Fourteenth Amendment prohibit racial and ethnic discrimination, and this prohibition has consistently been shown to extend to language. Minority groups have used the Constitution to protect their linguistic rights, and the courts have supported them. The landmark case in this regard was *Meyer v. Nebraska* (1923), in which the Supreme Court ruled that states cannot restrict foreign-language instruction. This was after World War I, and anti-German sentiment had led Nebraskan politicians to draft legislation banning the teaching of language other than English in any context. The Supreme Court ruled that this legislation violated the Due Process clause.

## Bilingual Education Act of 1968

In 1968, Congress enacted the Bilingual Education Act to provide local school districts with federal money for the establishment of English language programs for students whose primary language is Spanish. This act promoted the idea that non-English speakers should be instructed in English but should be allowed to maintain other distinctive aspects of their heritage. The first sum of money disbursed to schools for this purpose was $7.5 million, and was used for new materials, teacher training, and associations between parents and teachers. The Bilingual Education Act of 1968 declared that successful bilingual education programs would be guaranteed federal funds for at least five years.

Although many people saw the Bilingual Education Act of 1968 as a step towards multiculturalism, critics still charged that its terms were too vague and did not require the participation of all schools. After the Supreme Court case *Lau v. Nichols*, in which it was determined that Chinese students in San Francisco were receiving an inferior education, the federal government amended the Bilingual Education Act to mandate school districts to take definite steps towards English language instruction. Whereas before schools were only required to ensure that books and other educational materials were available for all students, now they were forced to establish specific programs to meet the needs of students of all backgrounds.

## *Castaneda v. Pickard* (1981)

In the case *Castaneda v. Pickard*, the United States Court of Appeals for the Fifth Circuit established three criteria for bilingual education programs in the United States. These criteria must be met in order for the program to align with the Equal Education Opportunities Act of 1974. According to this ruling, bilingual education programs must be "based on sound educational theory," must be "implemented effectively with resources for personnel, instructional materials, and space," and must prove to be effective at overcoming linguistic barriers. This case arose from a Mexican-American man's complaint that his three children were receiving an inferior education in south Texas. The man alleged that his children were being discriminated against because their school did not have sophisticated bilingual education programs, and therefore made it difficult for native Spanish speakers to participate in all school events.

## No Child Left Behind

The No Child Left Behind Act was signed into law on January 8, 2002, effectively terminating the Bilingual Education Act. The Bilingual Education Act had mandated the creation of native language programs for all students in public schools, whereas the No Child Left Behind Act did away with these programs and declared that students must be tested in English annually. Students whose first language is not English are not allowed to be tested in their native language. The right and responsibility to establish appropriate programs for students learning English as a second language is left to individual school districts.

## Subtractive and additive bilingualism

There has long been a controversy in ELL education over the hierarchical relationship between students' native language and English. Many advocates of English-only instruction believe that students are best served when they abandon their original language and culture. The intent of this idea is not necessarily to condemn the native heritage of the student, but to give him the best set of tools to survive in the American society and economy. Any form of bilingual education that places English above the students' first language in this way is known as subtractive bilingualism. In contrast, additive bilingualism exists in programs that seek to improve skills in both the first language and English, and indeed to use the two languages as reinforcements for one another. Additive bilingualism consciously avoids marginalizing the native language and culture of each student.

# English Language Arts and Reading

### Prose and poetry

Prose is language as it is ordinarily spoken as opposed to verse or language with metric patterns. Prose is used for everyday communication, and is found in textbooks, memos, reports, articles, short stories, and novels. Distinguishing characteristics of prose include:

- It may have some sort of rhythm, but there is no formal arrangement.
- The common unit of organization is the sentence.
- It may include literary devices of repetition and balance.
- It must have more coherent relationships among sentences than a list would.

Poetry, or verse, is the manipulation of language with respect to meaning, meter, sound, and rhythm. A line of poetry can be any length and may or may not rhyme. Related groups of lines are called stanzas, and may also be any length. Some poems are as short as a few lines, and some are as long as a book. Poetry is a more ancient form of literature than prose.

### Fiction and nonfiction

Fiction is a literary work usually presented in prose form that is not true. It is the product of the writer's imagination. Examples of fiction are novels, short stories, television scripts, and screenplays.

Nonfiction is a literary work that is based on facts. In other words, the material is true. The purposeful inclusion of false information is considered dishonest, but the expression of opinions or suppositions is acceptable. Libraries divide their collections into works of fiction and nonfiction. Examples of nonfiction include historical materials, scientific reports, memoirs, biographies, most essays, journals, textbooks, documentaries, user manuals, and news reports.

### Style, tone, and point of view

Style is the manner in which a writer uses language in prose or poetry. Style is affected by:

- Diction or word choices
- Sentence structure and syntax
- Types and extent of use of figurative language
- Patterns of rhythm or sound
- Conventional or creative use of punctuation

Tone is the attitude of the writer or narrator towards the theme of, subject of, or characters in a work. Sometimes the attitude is stated, but it is most often implied through word choices. Examples of tone are serious, humorous, satiric, stoic, cynical, flippant, and surprised.

Point of view is the angle from which a story is told. It is the perspective of the narrator, which is established by the author. Common points of view are:

- Third person – Third person points of view include omniscient (knows everything) and limited (confined to what is known by a single character or a limited number of characters). When the third person is used, characters are referred to as he, she, or they.

First person – When this point of view is used, the narrator refers to himself or herself as "I."

### Alliteration, assonance, and onomatopoeia

Alliteration is the repetition of the first sounds or stressed syllables (usually consonants) in words in close proximity. An example is: "Chirp, chirp," said the chickadee.

Assonance is the repetition of identical or similar vowel sounds, particularly in stressed syllables, in words in close proximity. Assonance is considered to be a form of near rhyme. An example is: the quiet bride cried.

Onomatopoeia refers to words that imitate sounds. It is sometimes called echoism. Examples are hiss, buzz, burp, rattle, and pop. It may also refer to words that correspond symbolically to what they describe, with high tones suggesting light and low tones suggesting darkness. An example is the *gloom* of night versus the *gleam* of the stars.

**Meter**

A recurring pattern of stressed and unstressed syllables in language creates a rhythm when spoken. When the pattern is regular, it is called meter. When meter is used in a composition, it is called verse. The most common types of meter are:

- Iambic – An unstressed syllable followed by a stressed syllable
- Anapestic – Two unstressed syllables followed by a stressed syllable
- Trochaic – One stressed syllable followed by an unstressed syllable
- Dactylic – A stressed syllable followed by two unstressed syllables
- Spondaic – Two consecutive syllables that are stressed almost equally

Pyrrhic – Two consecutive syllables that are equally unstressed

**Blank and free verse**

Blank verse is unrhymed verse that consists of lines of iambic pentameter, which is five feet (sets) of unstressed and stressed syllables. The rhythm that results is the closest to natural human speech. It is the most commonly used type of verse because of its versatility. Well-known examples of blank verse are Shakespearean plays, Milton's epic poems, and T. S. Eliot's *The Waste Land.*

Free verse lacks regular patterns of poetic feet, but has more controlled rhythm than prose in terms of pace and pauses. Free verse has no rhyme and is usually written in short lines of irregular length. Well-known examples of free verse are the King James translation of the Psalms, Walt Whitman's *Leaves of Grass*, and the poetry of Ezra Pound and William Carlos Williams.

**Short story**

A short story is prose fiction that has the same elements as a novel, such as plot, characters, and point of view. Edgar Allan Poe defined the short story as a narrative that can be read in one sitting (one-half to two hours), and is limited to a single effect. In a short story, there is no time for extensive character development, large numbers of characters, in-depth analysis, complicated plot lines, or detailed backgrounds. Historically, the short story is related to the fable, the exemplum, and the folktale. Short stories have become mainly an American art form. Famous short story writers include William Faulkner, Katherine Anne Porter, Eudora Welty, Flannery O'Connor, O. Henry, and J. D. Salinger.

**Primary and secondary research information**

Primary research material is material that comes from the "horse's mouth." It is a document or object that was created by the person under study or during the time period under study. Examples of primary sources are original documents such as manuscripts, diaries, interviews, autobiographies, government records, letters, news videos, and artifacts (such as Native American pottery or wall writings in Egyptian tombs).

Secondary research material is anything that is not primary. Secondary sources are those things that are written or otherwise recorded about the main subject. Examples include a critical analysis of a literary work (a poem by William Blake is primary, but the analysis of the poem by T. S. Eliot is secondary), a magazine article about a person (a direct quote would be primary, but the report is secondary), histories, commentaries, and encyclopedias.

**Emotions**

Poetry is designed to appeal to the physical and emotional senses. Using appeals to the physical senses through words that evoke sight, sound, taste, smell, and touch also causes the imagination to respond emotionally. Poetry appeals to the soul and memories with language that can be intriguingly novel and profoundly emotional in connotation. Poetry can focus on any topic, but the feelings associated with the topic are magnified by the ordered presentation found in poetry. Verse, however, is merely a matter of structure. The thing that turns words into poetry is the feeling packed into those words. People write poetry to express their feelings and people read poetry to try to experience those same feelings. Poetry interprets the human condition with understanding and insight. Children respond well to poetry because it has an inviting, entertaining sound that they are eager to mimic.

**Line structure**

A line of poetry can be any length and can have any metrical pattern. A line is determined by the physical position of words on a page. A line is simply a group of words on a single line. Consider the following example:

"When I consider how my light is spent,
E're half my days, in this dark world and wide,"

These are two lines of poetry written by John Milton. Lines may or may not have punctuation at the end, depending, of course, on the need for punctuation. If these two lines were written out in a paragraph, they would be written with a slash line and a space in between the lines: "When I consider how my light is spent, / E're half my days, in this dark world and wide."

**Stanza**

A stanza is a group of lines. The grouping denotes a relationship among the lines. A stanza can be any length, but the separation of lines into different stanzas indicates an intentional pattern created by the poet. The breaks between stanzas indicate a change of subject or thought. As a group of lines, the stanza is a melodic unit that can be analyzed for metrical and rhyme patterns. Various common rhyme patterns have been named. The Spenserian stanza, which has a rhyme pattern of a b a b b c b c c, is an example. Stanzas of a certain length also have names. Examples include the couplet, which has two lines; the tercet, which has three lines; and the quatrain, which has four lines.

**Literacy**

Literacy is commonly understood to refer to the ability to read and write. UNESCO has further defined literacy as the "ability to identify, understand, interpret, create, communicate, compute, and use printed and written materials associated with varying contexts." Under the UNESCO definition, understanding cultural, political, and historical contexts of communities falls under the definition of literacy.

While reading literacy may be gauged simply by the ability to read a newspaper, writing literacy includes spelling, grammar, and sentence structure. To be literate in a foreign language, one would also need to have the ability to understand a language by listening and to speak the language. Some argue that visual representation and numeracy should be included in the requirements one must meet to be considered literate. Computer literacy refers to one's ability to utilize the basic functions of computers and other technologies.

Subsets of reading literacy include phonological awareness, decoding, comprehension, and vocabulary.

**Phonological awareness**

A subskill of literacy, phonological awareness is the ability to perceive sound structures in a spoken word, such as syllables and the individual phonemes within syllables. Phonemes are the sounds represented by the letters in the alphabet. The ability to separate, blend, and manipulate sounds is critical to developing reading and spelling skills.

Phonological awareness is concerned with not only syllables, but also onset sounds (the sounds at the beginning of words) and rime (the same thing as rhyme, but spelled differently to distinguish syllable rime from poetic rhyme). Phonological awareness is an auditory skill that does not necessarily involve print. It should be developed before the student has learned letter to sound correspondences. A student's phonological awareness is an indicator of future reading success.

**Teaching phonological awareness**

Classroom activities that teach phonological awareness include language play and exposure to a variety of sounds and contexts of sounds. Activities that teach phonological awareness include:

- Clapping to the sounds of individual words, names, or all words in a sentence
- Practicing saying blended phonemes
- Singing songs that involve phoneme replacement (e.g., The Name Game)
- Reading poems, songs, and nursery rhymes out loud
- Reading patterned and predictable texts out loud
- Listening to environmental sounds or following verbal directions
- Playing games with rhyming chants or fingerplays
- Reading alliterative texts out loud
- Grouping objects by beginning sounds

Reordering words in a well-known sentence or making silly phrases by deleting words from a well-known sentence (perhaps from a favorite storybook)

**Alphabetic principle**

The alphabetic principle refers to the use of letters and combinations of letters to represent speech sounds. The way letters are combined and pronounced is guided by a system of rules that establishes relationships between written and spoken words and their letter symbols. Alphabet writing systems are common around the world. Some are phonological in that each letter stands for an individual sound and words are spelled just as they sound. However, there are other writing systems as well, such as the Chinese logographic system and the Japanese syllabic system.

**Language skill development**

Children learn language through interacting with others, by experiencing language in daily and relevant context, and through understanding that speaking and listening are necessary for effective communication. Teachers can promote language development by intensifying the opportunities a child has to experience and understand language. Teachers can assist language development by:

- Modeling enriched vocabulary and teaching new words
- Using questions and examples to extend a child's descriptive language skills
- Providing ample response time to encourage children to practice speech
- Asking for clarification to provide students with the opportunity to develop communication skills
- Promoting conversations among children

Providing feedback to let children know they have been heard and understood, and providing further explanation when needed

## Oral and written language development

Oral and written language develops simultaneously. The acquisition of skills in one area supports the acquisition of skills in the other. However, oral language is not a prerequisite to written language. An immature form of oral language development is babbling, and an immature form of written language development is scribbling.
Oral language development does not occur naturally, but does occur in a social context. This means it is best to include children in conversations rather than simply talk at them. Written language development can occur without direct instruction. In fact, reading and writing do not necessarily need to be taught through formal lessons if the child is exposed to a print-rich environment. A teacher can assist a child's language development by building on what the child already knows, discussing relevant and meaningful events and experiences, teaching vocabulary and literacy skills, and providing opportunities to acquire more complex language.

## Print-rich classroom environment

A teacher can provide a print-rich environment in the classroom in a number of ways. These include:
A. Displaying the following in the classroom:

- Children's names in print or cursive
- Children's written work
- Newspapers and magazines
- Instructional charts
- Written schedules
- Signs and labels
- Printed songs, poems, and rhymes

B. Using graphic organizers such as KWL charts or story road maps to:

- Remind students about what was read and discussed
- Expand on the lesson topic or theme
- Show the relationships among books, ideas, and words

C. Using big books to:

- Point out features of print, such as specific letters and punctuation
- Track print from right to left
- Emphasize the concept of words and the fact that they are used to communicate

## Print and book awareness

Print and book awareness helps a child understand:

- That there is a connection between print and messages contained on signs, labels, and other print forms in the child's environment
- That reading and writing are ways to obtain information and communicate ideas
- That print runs from left to right and from top to bottom
- That a book has parts, such as a title, a cover, a title page, and a table of contents
- That a book has an author and contains a story
- That illustrations can carry meaning
- That letters and words are different
- That words and sentences are separated by spaces and punctuation
- That different text forms are used for different functions
- That print represents spoken language

How to hold a book.

## Letters

To be appropriately prepared to learn to read and write, a child should learn:

- That each letter is distinct in appearance
- What direction and shape must be used to make each letter
- That each letter has a name, which can be associated with the shape of a letter
- That there are 26 letters in the English alphabet, and letters are grouped in a certain order

- That letters represent sounds of speech
- That words are composed of letters and have meaning

That one must be able to correspond letters and sounds to read

**Decoding**

Decoding is the method or strategy used to make sense of printed words and figure out how to correctly pronounce them. In order to decode, a student needs to know the relationships between letters and sounds, including letter patterns; that words are constructed from phonemes and phoneme blends; and that a printed word represents a word that can be spoken. This knowledge will help the student recognize familiar words and make informed guesses about the pronunciation of unfamiliar words. Decoding is not the same as comprehension. It does not require an understanding of the meaning of a word, only a knowledge of how to recognize and pronounce it. Decoding can also refer to the skills a student uses to determine the meaning of a sentence. These skills include applying knowledge of vocabulary, sentence structure, and context.

**Reading through phonics**

Phonics is the process of learning to read by learning how spoken language is represented by letters. Students learn to read phonetically by sounding out the phonemes in words and then blending them together to produce the correct sounds in words. In other words, the student connects speech sounds with letters or groups of letters and blends the sounds together to determine the pronunciation of an unknown word.

Phonics is a commonly used method to teach decoding and reading, but has been challenged by other methods, such as the whole language approach. Despite the complexity of pronunciation and combined sounds in the English language, research shows that phonics is a highly effective way to teach reading. Being able to read or pronounce a word does not mean the student comprehends the meaning of the word, but context aids comprehension. When phonics is used as a foundation for decoding, children eventually learn to recognize words automatically and advance to decoding multisyllable words with practice.

**Fluency**

Fluency is the goal of literacy development. It is the ability to read accurately and quickly. Evidence of fluency includes the ability to recognize words automatically and group words for comprehension. At this point, the student no longer needs to decode words except for complex, unfamiliar ones. He or she is able to move to the next level and understand the meaning of a text. The student should be able to self-check for comprehension and should feel comfortable expressing idcas in writing.

Teachers can help students build fluency by continuing to provide: reading experiences and discussions about text, gradually increasing the level of difficulty; reading practice, both silently and out loud; word analysis practice; instruction on reading comprehension strategies; and opportunities to express responses to readings through writing.

**Vocabulary**

When students do not know the meaning of words in a text, their comprehension is limited. As a result, the text becomes boring or confusing. The larger a student's vocabulary is, the better their reading comprehension will be. A larger vocabulary is also associated with an enhanced ability to communicate in speech and writing. It is the teacher's role to help students develop a good working vocabulary. Students learn most of the words they use and understand from listening to the world around them (adults, other students, media, etc.) They also learn from their reading experiences, which include being read to and reading independently.

Carefully designed activities can also stimulate vocabulary growth, and should emphasize useful words that students see frequently, important words necessary for understanding text, and difficult words such as idioms or words with more than one meaning.

**Promoting vocabulary development**

A student's vocabulary can be developed by:

- Calling upon a student's prior knowledge and making comparisons to that knowledge
- Defining a word and providing multiple examples of the use of the word in context
- Showing a student how to use context clues to discover the meaning of a word
- Providing instruction on prefixes, roots, and suffixes to help students break a word into its parts and decipher its meaning
- Showing students how to use a dictionary and a thesaurus
- Asking students to practice new vocabulary by using the words in their own writing
- Providing a print-rich environment with a word wall

Studying a group of words related to a single subject, such as farm words, transportation words, etc. so that concept development is enhanced.

**Affixes, prefixes, and root words**

Affixes are syllables attached to the beginning or end of a word to make a derivative or inflectional form of a word. Both prefixes and suffixes are affixes.

A prefix is a syllable that appears at the beginning of a word that, in combination with the root or base word, creates a specific meaning. For example, the prefix "mis" means "wrong." When combined with the root word "spelling," the word "misspelling" is created, which means the "wrong spelling."

A root word is the base of a word to which affixes can be added. For example, the prefix "in" or "pre" can be added to the root word "vent" to create "invent" or "prevent," respectively. The suffix "er" can be added to the root word "work" to create "worker," which means "one who works." The suffix "able," meaning "capable of," can be added to "work" to create "workable," which means "capable of working."

**Suffix**

A suffix is a syllable that appears at the end of a word that, in combination with the root or base word, creates a specific meaning. There are three types of suffixes:

- Noun suffixes – There are two types of noun suffixes. One denotes the act of, state of, or quality of. For example, "ment" added to "argue" becomes "argument," which is defined as "the act of arguing." The other denotes the doer, or one who acts. For example "eer" added to "auction" becomes "auctioneer," meaning "one who auctions." Other examples include "hood," "ness," "tion," "ship," and "ism."
- Verb suffixes – These denote "to make" or "to perform the act of." For example, "en" added to "soft" makes "soften," which means "to make soft." Other verb suffixes are "ate" (perpetuate), "fy" (dignify), and "ize" (sterilize).

Adjectival suffixes – These include suffixes such as "ful," which means "full of." When added to "care," the word "careful" is formed, which means "full of care." Other examples are "ish," "less," and "able."

## Context clues

Context clues are words or phrases that help the reader figure out the meaning of an unknown word. They are built into a sentence or paragraph by the writer to help the reader develop a clear understanding of the writer's message. Context clues can be used to make intelligent guesses about the meaning of a word instead of relying on a dictionary. Context clues are the reason most vocabulary is learned through reading.

There are four types of commonly used context clues:

- Synonyms – A word with the same meaning as the unknown word is placed close by for comparison.
- Antonyms – A word with the opposite meaning as the unknown word is placed close by for contrast.
- Explanations – An obvious explanation is given close to the unknown word.

Examples – Examples of what the word means are given to help the reader define the term.

## Comprehension

The whole point of reading is to comprehend what someone else is trying to say through writing. Without comprehension, a student is just reading the words without understanding them or increasing knowledge of a topic. Comprehension results when the student has the vocabulary and reading skills necessary to make sense of the whole picture, not just individual words. Students can self-monitor because they know when they are comprehending the material and when they are not. Teachers can help students solve problems with comprehension by teaching them strategies such as pre-reading titles, sidebars, and follow-up questions; looking at illustrations; predicting what's going to happen in the story; asking questions to check understanding while reading; connecting to background knowledge; and relating to the experiences or feelings of the characters.

## Improving comprehension

Teachers can model in a read-aloud the strategies students can use on their own to better comprehend a text. First, the teacher should do a walk-through of the story illustrations and ask, "What's happening here?" Based on what they have seen, the teacher should then ask students to predict what the story will be about. As the book is read, the teacher should ask open-ended questions such as, "Why do you think the character did this?" and "How do you think the character feels?" The teacher should also ask students if they can relate to the story or have background knowledge of something similar. After the reading, the teacher should ask the students to retell the story in their own words to check for comprehension. This retelling can take the form of a puppet show or summarizing the story to a partner.

## Prior knowledge

Even preschool children have some literacy skills, and the extent and type of these skills have implications for instructional approaches. Comprehension results from relating two or more pieces of information. One piece comes from the text, and another piece might come from prior knowledge (something from a student's long-term memory). For a child, that prior knowledge comes from being read to at home; taking part in other literacy experiences, such as playing computer or word games; being exposed to a print-rich environment at home; and observing examples of parents' reading habits. Children who have had extensive literacy experience are better prepared to further develop their literacy skills in school than children who have not been read to, have few books or magazines in their homes, are seldom exposed to high-level oral or written language activities, and seldom witness adults engaged in reading and writing. Children with a scant literacy background are at a disadvantage. The teacher must not make any assumptions about their prior knowledge, and should use intense, targeted instruction. Otherwise, reading comprehension will be limited.

**Literal vs. critical comprehension**

Literal comprehension refers to the skills a reader uses to deal with the actual words in a text. It involves skills such as identifying the topic sentence, main idea, important facts, and supporting details; using context clues to determine the meaning of a word; and sequencing events.

Critical comprehension involves prior knowledge and an understanding that written material, especially in nonfiction, is the author's version of the subject and not necessarily anybody else's. Critical comprehension involves analysis of meaning, evaluation, validation, questioning, and the reasoning skills a reader uses to recognize:

- Inferences and conclusions
- Purpose, tone, point of view, and themes
- The organizational pattern of a work
- Explicit and implicit relationships among words, phrases, and sentences
- Biased language, persuasive tactics, valid arguments, and the difference between fact and opinion

**Metacognition**

Metacognition is thinking about thinking. For the student, this involves taking control of their own learning process, self-monitoring progress, evaluating the effectiveness of strategies, and making adjustments to strategies and learning behaviors as needed.

Students who develop good metacognitive skills become more independent and confident about learning. They develop a sense of ownership about their education and realize that information is readily available to them.

Metacognitive skills can be grouped into three categories:

- Awareness – This involves identifying prior knowledge; defining learning goals; inventorying resources such as textbooks, libraries, computers, and study time; identifying task requirements and evaluation standards; and recognizing motivation and anxiety levels.
- Planning – This involves doing time estimates for tasks, prioritizing, scheduling study time, making checklists of tasks, gathering needed materials, and choosing strategies for problem solving or task comprehension.
- Self-monitoring and reflection – This involves identifying which strategies or techniques work best, questioning throughout the process, considering feedback, and maintaining focus and motivation.

**Metacognitive skills**

In terms of literacy development, metacognitive skills include taking an active role in reading, recognizing reading behaviors and changing them to employ the behaviors that are most effective, relating information to prior knowledge, and being aware of text structures.

For example, if there is a problem with comprehension, the student can try to form a mental image of what is described, read the text again, adjust the rate of reading, or employ other reading strategies such as identifying unknown vocabulary and predicting meaning.

Being aware of text structures is critical to being able to follow the author's ideas and relationships among ideas. Being aware of difficulties with text structure allows the student to employ strategies such as hierarchical summaries, thematic organizers, or concept maps to remedy the problem.

**Puppetry**

Using puppets in the classroom puts students at ease and allows them to enjoy a learning experience as if it were play. The purpose of using puppetry is to generate ideas, encourage imagination, and foster language development. Using a puppet helps a child "become" the character and therefore experience a different outlook.

Language development is enhanced through the student interpreting a story that has been read in class and practicing new words from that story in the puppet show. Children will also have the opportunity to practice using descriptive adjectives for the characters and the scene, which will help them learn the function of adjectives.

Descriptive adjectives and verbs can also be learned by practicing facial expressions and movements with puppets. The teacher can model happy, sad, eating, sleeping, and similar words with a puppet, and then ask students to do the same with their puppets. This is an especially effective vocabulary activity for ESL children.

**Drama activities**

Drama activities are fun learning experiences that capture a child's attention, engage the imagination, and motivate vocabulary expansion.

For example, after reading a story, the teacher could ask children to act it out as the teacher repeats the story. This activity, which works best with very young learners, will help children work on listening skills and their ability to pretend. The best stories to use for this passive improvisation are ones that have lots of simple actions that children will be able to understand and perform easily. Older children can create their own improvisational skits and possibly write scripts.

Visualization also calls upon the imagination and encourages concentration and bodily awareness. Children can be given a prompt for the visualization and then asked to draw what they see in their mind's eye.

Charades is another way to act out words and improve vocabulary skills. This activity can be especially helpful to encourage ESL students to express thoughts and ideas in English. These students should be given easier words to act out to promote confidence.

**Types of figurative language**

A simile is a comparison between two unlike things using the words "like" or "as." Examples are Robert Burn's sentence "O my love's like a red, red, rose" or the common expression "as pretty as a picture."

A metaphor is a direct comparison between two unlike things without the use of "like" or "as." One thing is identified as the other instead of simply compared to it. An example is D. H. Lawrence's sentence "My soul is a dark forest."

Personification is the giving of human characteristics to a non-human thing or idea. An example is "The hurricane howled its frightful rage."

Synecdoche is the use of a part of something to signify the whole. For example, "boots on the ground" could be used to describe soldiers in a field.

Metonymy is the use of one term that is closely associated with another to mean the other. An example is referring to the "crown" to refer to the monarchy.

**Graphic organizers**

The purpose of graphic organizers is to help students classify ideas and communicate more efficiently and effectively. Graphic organizers are visual outlines or templates that help students grasp key concepts and master subject matter by simplifying them down to basic points. They also help guide students through processes related to any subject area or task. Examples of processes include brainstorming, problem solving, decision making, research and project planning, and studying.

Examples of graphic organizers include:

- Reading – These can include beginning, middle, and end graphs or event maps.
- Science – These can include charts that show what animals need or how to classify living things.
- Math – These can include horizontal bar graphs or time lines.
- Language arts – These can include alphabet organizers or charts showing the components of the five-paragraph essay.

General – These can include KWL charts or weekly planners.

**Second language acquisition**

Since some students may have limited understanding of English, a teacher should employ the following practices to promote second language acquisition:

- Make all instruction as understandable as possible and use simple and repeated terms.
- Relate instruction to the cultures of ESL children.
- Increase interactive activities and use gestures or non-verbal actions when modeling.
- Provide language and literacy development instruction in all curriculum areas.
- Establish consistent routines that help children connect words and events.
- Use a schedule so children know what will happen next and will not feel lost.
- Integrate ESL children into group activities with non-ESL children.
- Appoint bilingual students to act as student translators.
- Explain actions as activities happen so that a word to action relationship is established.
- Initiate opportunities for ESL children to experiment with and practice new language.

Employ multisensory learning.

**Summarization, question generation, and textual marking**

It is important to teach students to use critical thinking skills when reading. Three of the critical thinking tools that engage the reader are:

- Summarization – The student reviews the main point(s) of the reading selection and identifies important details. For nonfiction, a good summary will briefly describe the main arguments and the examples that support those arguments. For fiction, a good summary will identify the main characters and events of the story.
- Question generation – A good reader will constantly ask questions while reading about comprehension, vocabulary, connections to personal knowledge or experience, predictions, etc.

Textual marking – This skill engages the reader by having him or her interact with the text. The student should mark the text with questions or comments that are generated by the text using underlining, highlighting, or shorthand marks such as "?," "!," and "*" that indicate lack of understanding, importance, or key points, for example.

**Theories of language development**

Four theories of language development are:

- Learning approach – This theory assumes that language is first learned by imitating the speech of adults. It is then solidified in school through drills about the rules of language structures.

- Linguistic approach – Championed by Noam Chomsky in the 1950s, this theory proposes that the ability to use a language is innate. This is a biological approach rather than one based on cognition or social patterning.
- Cognitive approach – Developed in the 1970s and based on the work of Piaget, this theory states that children must develop appropriate cognitive skills before they can acquire language.
- Sociocognitive approach – In the 1970s, some researchers proposed that language development is a complex interaction of linguistic, social, and cognitive influences

This theory best explains the lack of language skills among children who are neglected, have uneducated parents, or lives in poverty.

**Fairy tales, fables, and tall tales**

A fairy tale is a fictional story involving humans, magical events, and usually animals. Characters such as fairies, elves, giants, and talking animals are taken from folklore. The plot often involves impossible events (as in "Jack and the Beanstalk") and/or an enchantment (as in "Sleeping Beauty"). Other examples of fairy tales include "Cinderella," "Little Red Riding Hood," and "Rumpelstiltskin."

A fable is a tale in which animals, plants, and forces of nature act like humans. A fable also teaches a moral lesson. Examples are "The Tortoise and the Hare," *The Lion King*, and *Animal Farm*.

A tall tale exaggerates human abilities or describes unbelievable events as if the story were true. Often, the narrator seems to have witnessed the event described. Examples are fish stories, Paul Bunyan and Pecos Bill stories, and hyperboles about real people such as Davy Crockett, Mike Fink, and Calamity Jane.

**Preadolescent and adolescent literature**

Preadolescent literature is mostly concerned with the "tween" issues of changing lives, relationships, and bodies. Adolescents seeking escape from their sometimes difficult lives enjoy fantasy and science fiction. For both groups, books about modern, real people are more interesting than those about historical figures or legends. Boys especially enjoy nonfiction. Reading interests as well as reading levels for this group vary. Reading levels will usually range from 6.0 to 8.9. Examples of popular literature for this age group and reading level include:

- Series – Sweet Valley High, Bluford High, Nancy Drew, Hardy Boys, and Little House on the Prairie
- Juvenile fiction authors – Judy Blume and S. E. Hinton
- Fantasy and horror authors – Ursula LeGuin and Stephen King
- Science fiction authors – Isaac Asimov, Ray Bradbury, and H. G. Wells

Classic books: *Lilies of the Field, Charlie and the Chocolate Factory, Pippi Longstocking, National Velvet, Call of the Wild, Anne of Green Gables, The Hobbit, The Member of the Wedding,* and *Tom Sawyer*

**Topic sentence**

The topic sentence of a paragraph states the paragraph's subject. It presents the main idea. The rest of the paragraph should be related to the topic sentence, which should be explained and supported with facts, details, proofs, and examples.

The topic sentence is more general than the body sentences, and should cover all the ideas in the body of the paragraph. It may contain words such as "many," "most," or "several." The topic sentence is usually the first sentence in a paragraph, but it can appear after an introductory or background sentence, can be the last sentence in a paragraph, or may simply be implied, meaning a topic sentence is not present.

Supporting sentences can often be identified by their use of transition terms such as "for example" or "that is." Supporting sentences may also be presented in numbered sequence.

The topic sentence provides unity to a paragraph because it ties together the supporting details into a coherent whole.

**Cause and effect**

Causes are reasons for actions or events. Effects are the results of a cause or causes. There may be multiple causes for one effect (evolutionary extinction, climate changes, and a massive comet caused the demise of the dinosaurs, for example) or multiple effects from one cause (the break-up of the Soviet Union has had multiple effects on the world stage, for instance). Sometimes, one thing leads to another and the effect of one action becomes the cause for another (breaking an arm leads to not driving, which leads to reading more while staying home, for example).

The ability to identify causes and effects is part of critical thinking, and enables the reader to follow the course of events, make connections among events, and identify the instigators and receivers of actions. This ability improves comprehension.

**Facts and opinions**

Facts are statements that can be verified through research. Facts answer the questions of who, what, when, and where, and evidence can be provided to prove factual statements. For example, it is a fact that water turns into ice when the temperature drops below 32 degrees Fahrenheit. This fact has been proven repeatedly. Water never becomes ice at a higher temperature.

Opinions are personal views, but facts may be used to support opinions. For example, it may be one person's opinion that Jack is a great athlete, but the fact that he has made many achievements related to sports supports that opinion.

It is important for a reader to be able to distinguish between fact and opinion to determine the validity of an argument. Readers need to understand that some unethical writers will try to pass off an opinion as a fact. Readers with good critical thinking skills will not be deceived by this tactic.

**Invalid arguments**

There are a number of invalid or false arguments that are used unethically to gain an advantage, such as:

- The "ad hominem" or "against the person" argument – This type attacks the character or behavior of a person taking a stand on an issue rather than the issue itself. The statement "That fat slob wants higher taxes" is an example of this type of argument.
- Hasty generalizations – These are condemnations of a group based on the behavior of one person or part. An example of this type of argument is someone saying that all McDonald's restaurants are lousy because he or she had a bad experience at one location.
- Faulty causation – This is assigning the wrong cause to an event. An example is blaming a flat tire on losing a lucky penny rather than on driving over a bunch of nails.
- Bandwagon effect – This is the argument that if everybody else is doing something, it must be a good thing to do. The absurdity of this type of argument is highlighted by the question: "If everybody else is jumping off a cliff, should you jump, too?"

It is important for a reader to be able to identify various types of invalid arguments to prevent being deceived and making faulty conclusions.

### Inductive reasoning and deductive reasoning

Inductive reasoning is using particulars to draw a general conclusion. The inductive reasoning process starts with data. For example, if every apple taken out of the top of a barrel is rotten, it can be inferred without investigating further that all the apples are probably rotten. Unless all data is examined, conclusions are based on probabilities. Inductive reasoning is also used to make inferences about the universe. The entire universe cannot be examined, but inferences can be made based on observations about what can be seen. These inferences may be proven false when more data is available, but they are valid at the time they are made if observable data is used.

Deductive reasoning is the opposite of inductive reasoning. It involves using general facts or premises to come to a specific conclusion. For example, if Susan is a sophomore in high school, and all sophomores take geometry, it can be inferred that Susan takes geometry. The word "all" does not allow for exceptions. If all sophomores take geometry, assuming Susan does too is a logical conclusion.

It is important for a reader to recognize inductive and deductive reasoning so he or she can follow the line of an argument and determine if the inference or conclusion is valid.

### Theme

Theme is the central idea of a work. It is the thread that ties all the elements of a story together and gives them purpose. The theme is not the subject of a work, but what a work says about a subject. A theme must be universal, which means it must apply to everyone, not just the characters in a story. Therefore, a theme is a comment about the nature of humanity, society, the relationship of humankind to the world, or moral responsibility. There may be more than one theme in a work, and the determination of the theme is affected by the viewpoint of the reader. Therefore, there is not always necessarily a definite, irrefutable theme. The theme can be implied or stated directly.

### Types of characters

Readers need to be able to differentiate between major and minor characters. The difference can usually be determined based on whether the characters are round, flat, dynamic, or static.

Round characters have complex personalities, just like real people. They are more commonly found in longer works such as novels or full-length plays.

Flat characters display only a few personality traits and are based on stereotypes. Examples include the bigoted redneck, the lazy bum, or the absent-minded professor.

Dynamic characters are those that change or grow during the course of the narrative. They may learn important lessons, fall in love, or take new paths.
Static characters remain the same throughout a story. Usually, round characters are dynamic and flat characters are static, but this is not always the case. Falstaff, the loyal and comical character in Shakespeare's plays about Henry IV, is a round character in terms of his complexity. However, he never changes, which makes him a reliable figure in the story.

### Adjective, adverb, and conjunction

The definitions for these grammatical terms are as follows:

Adjective – This is a word that modifies or describes a noun or pronoun. Examples are a *green* apple or *every* computer.

Adverb – This is a word that modifies a verb (*instantly* reviewed), an adjective (*relatively* odd), or another adverb (*rather* suspiciously).

Conjunctions: There are three types of conjunctions:

- Coordinating conjunctions are used to link words, phrases, and clauses. Examples are and, or, nor, for, but, yet, and so.
- Correlative conjunctions are paired terms used to link clauses. Examples are either/or, neither/nor, and if/then.
- Subordinating conjunctions relate subordinate or dependent clauses to independent ones. Examples are although, because, if, since, before, after, when, even though, in order that, and while.

## Gerund, infinitive, noun, direct and indirect objects

The definitions for these grammatical terms are as follows:
Gerund – This is a verb form used as a noun. Most end in "ing." An example is: *Walking* is good exercise.
Infinitive – This is a verbal form comprised of the word "to" followed by the root form of a verb. An infinitive may be used as a noun, adjective, adverb, or absolute. Examples include:

- *To hold* a baby is a joy. (noun)
- Jenna had many files *to reorganize.* (adjective)
- Andrew tried *to remember* the dates. (adverb)
- *To be honest*, your hair looks awful. (absolute)

Noun – This is a word that names a person, place, thing, idea, or quality. A noun can be used as a subject, object, complement, appositive, or modifier.

Object – This is a word or phrase that receives the action of a verb.

A direct object states **to** whom/what an action was committed. It answers the question "to what?" An example is: Joan served *the meal.*
An indirect object states **for** whom/what an action was committed. An example is: Joan served *us* the meal.

## Preposition, prepositional phrase, pronoun, sentence, and verb

The definitions for these grammatical terms are as follows:

Preposition – This is a word that links a noun or pronoun to other parts of a sentence. Examples include above, by, for, in, out, through, and to.

Prepositional phrase – This is a combination of a preposition and a noun or pronoun. Examples include across the bridge, against the grain, below the horizon, and toward the sunset.

Pronoun – This is a word that represents a specific noun in a generic way. A pronoun functions like a noun in a sentence. Examples include I, she, he, it, myself, they, these, what, all, and anybody.

Sentence – This is a group of words that expresses a thought or conveys information as an independent unit of speech. A complete sentence must contain a noun and a verb (I ran). However, all the other parts of speech can also be represented in a sentence.

Verb – This is a word or phrase in a sentence that expresses action (Mary played) or a state of being (Mary is).

## Capitalization and punctuation

Capitalization refers to the use of capital letters. Capital letters should be placed at the beginning of:

- Proper names (Ralph Waldo Emerson, Australia)
- Places (Mount Rushmore, Chicago)
- Historical periods and holidays (Renaissance, Christmas)
- Religious terms (Bible, Koran)
- Titles (Empress Victoria, General Smith)
- All main words in literary, art, or music titles (Grapes of Wrath, Sonata in C Major)

Punctuation consists of:
Periods – A period is placed at the end of a sentence.
Commas – A comma is used to separate:

- Two adjectives modifying the same word (long, hot summer)
- Three or more words or phrases in a list (Winken, Blinken, and Nod; life, liberty, and the pursuit of happiness)

Phrases that are not needed to complete a sentence (The teacher, not the students, will distribute the supplies.)

## Colons and semicolons

Colons – A colon is used to:

- Set up a list (We will need these items: a pencil, paper, and an eraser.)
- Direct readers to examples or explanations (We have one chore left: clean out the garage.)
- Introduce quotations or dialogue (The Labor Department reported on unemployment: "There was a 3.67% increase in unemployment in 2010."; Scarlett exclaimed: "What shall I do?")

Semicolons – A semicolon is used to:

- Join related independent clauses (There were five major hurricanes this year; two of them hit Florida.)
- Join independent clauses connected by conjunctive adverbs (Popular books are often made into movies; however, it is a rare screenplay that is as good as the book.)

Separate items in a series if commas would be confusing (The characters include: Robin Hood, who robs from the rich to give to the poor; Maid Marian, his true love; and Little John, Robin Hood's comrade-in-arms.)

## Subject-verb agreement

A verb must agree in number with its subject. Therefore, a verb changes form depending on whether the subject is singular or plural. Examples include "I do," "he does," "the ball is," and "the balls are."

If two subjects are joined by "and," the plural form of a verb is usually used. For example: *Jack and Jill want* to get some water (Jack wants, Jill wants, but together they want).

If the compound subjects are preceded by each or every, they take the singular form of a verb. For example: *Each man and each woman brings* a special talent to the world (each brings, not bring).

If one noun in a compound subject is plural and the other is singular, the verb takes the form of the subject nearest to it. For example: Neither the *students* nor their *teacher was* ready for the fire drill.

Collective nouns that name a group are considered singular if they refer to the group acting as a unit. For example: The *choir is going* on a concert tour.

**Syntax**

Syntax refers to the rules related to how to properly structure sentences and phrases. Syntax is not the same as grammar. For example, "I does" is syntactically correct because the subject and verb are in proper order, but it is grammatically incorrect because the subject and verb don't agree.

There are three types of sentence structures:

- Simple – This type is composed of a single independent clause with one subject and one predicate (verb or verb form).
- Compound – This type is composed of two independent clauses joined by a conjunction (Amy flew, but Brenda took the train), a correlative conjunction (Either Tom goes with me or I stay here), or a semicolon (My grandfather stays in shape; he plays tennis nearly every day).

Complex – This type is composed of one independent clause and one or more dependent clauses joined by a subordinating conjunction (Before we set the table, we should replace the tablecloth).

**Types of paragraphs**

Illustrative – An illustrative paragraph or essay explains a general statement through the use of specific examples. The writer starts with a topic sentence that is followed by one or more examples that clearly relate to and support the topic.

Narrative – A narrative tells a story. Like a news report, it tells the who, what, when, where, why, and how of an event. A narrative is usually presented in chronological order.

Descriptive – This type of writing appeals to the five senses to describe a person, place, or thing so that the readers can see the subject in their imaginations. Space order is most often used in descriptive writing to indicate place or position.

Process – There are two kinds of process papers: the "how-to" that gives step-by-step directions on how to do something and the explanation paper that tells how an event occurred or how something works.

**Definition paragraph**

A definition paragraph or essay describes what a word or term means. There are three ways the explanation can be presented:

Definition by synonym – The term is defined by comparing it to a more familiar term that the reader can more easily understand (A phantom is a ghost or spirit that appears and disappears mysteriously and creates dread). Definition by class – Most commonly used in exams, papers, and reports, the class definition first puts the term in a larger category or class (The Hereford is a breed of cattle), and then describes the distinguishing characteristics or details of the term that differentiate it from other members of the class (The Hereford is a breed of cattle distinguished by a white face, reddish-brown hide, and short horns).

Definition by negation – The term is defined by stating what it is not and then saying what it is (Courage is not the absence of fear, but the willingness to act in spite of fear).

**Types of essays**

A comparison and contrast essay examines the similarities and differences between two things. In a paragraph, the writer presents all the points about subject A and then all the points about subject B. In an essay, the writer might present one point at a time, comparing subject A and subject B side by side.

A classification paper sorts information. It opens with a topic sentence that identifies the group to be classified, and then breaks that group into categories. For example, a group might be baseball players, while a category might be positions they play.

A cause and effect paper discusses the causes or reasons for an event or the effects of a cause or causes. Topics discussed in this type of essay might include the causes of a war or the effects of global warming.

A persuasive essay is one in which the writer tries to convince the audience to agree with a certain opinion or point of view. The argument must be supported with facts, examples, anecdotes, expert testimony, or statistics, and must anticipate and answer the questions of those who hold an opposing view. It may also predict consequences.

**Purpose and audience**

Early in the writing process, the writer needs to definitively determine the purpose of the paper and then keep that purpose in mind throughout the writing process. The writer needs to ask: "Is the purpose to explain something, to tell a story, to entertain, to inform, to argue a point, or some combination of these purposes?"

Also at the beginning of the writing process, the writer needs to determine the audience of the paper by asking questions such as: "Who will read this paper?," "For whom is this paper intended?," "What does the audience already know about this topic?," "How much does the audience need to know?," and "Is the audience likely to agree or disagree with my point of view?" The answers to these questions will determine the content of the paper, the tone, and the style.

**Drafting, revising, editing, and proofreading**

Drafting is creating an early version of a paper. A draft is a prototype or sketch of the finished product. A draft is a rough version of the final paper, and it is expected that there will be multiple drafts.

Revising is the process of making major changes to a draft in regards to clarity of purpose, focus (thesis), audience, organization, and content.

Editing is the process of making changes in style, word choice, tone, examples, and arrangement. These are more minor than the changes made during revision. Editing can be thought of as fine tuning. The writer makes the language more precise, checks for varying paragraph lengths, and makes sure that the title, introduction, and conclusion fit well with the body of the paper.

Proofreading is performing a final check and correcting errors in punctuation, spelling, grammar, and usage. It also involves looking for parts of the paper that may be omitted.

**Title and conclusion**

The title is centered on the page and the main words are capitalized. The title is not surrounded by quotation marks, nor is it underlined or italicized. The title is rarely more than four or five words, and is very rarely a whole sentence. A good title suggests the subject of the paper and catches the reader's interest.

The conclusion should flow logically from the body of the essay, should tie back to the introduction, and may provide a summary or a final thought on the subject. New material should never be introduced in the conclusion. The conclusion is a wrap-up that may contain a call to action, something the writer wants the audience to do in response to the paper. The conclusion might end with a question to give the reader something to think about.

**Introduction**

The introduction contains the thesis statement, which is usually the first or last sentence of the opening paragraph. It needs to be interesting enough to make the reader want to continue reading.
Possible openings for an introduction include:

- The thesis statement
- A general idea that gives background or sets the scene
- An illustration that will make the thesis more concrete and easy to picture
- A surprising fact or idea to arouse curiosity
- A contradiction to popular belief that attracts interest

A quotation that leads into the thesis

**Types of sentences**

A declarative sentence makes a statement and is punctuated by a period at the end. An example is: The new school will be built at the south end of Main Street.

An interrogative sentence asks a question and is punctuated by a question mark at the end. An example is: Why will the new school be built so far out?

An exclamatory sentence shows strong emotion and is punctuated by an exclamation mark at the end. An example is: The new school has the most amazing state-of-the-art technology!

An imperative sentence gives a direction or command and may be punctuated by an exclamation mark or a period. Sometimes, the subject of an imperative sentence is you, which is understood instead of directly stated. An example is: Come to the open house at the new school next Sunday.

**Parallelism, euphemism, hyperbole, and climax**

Parallelism – Subjects, objects, verbs, modifiers, phrases, and clauses can be structured in sentences to balance one with another through a similar grammatical pattern. Parallelism helps to highlight ideas while showing their relationship and giving style to writing.
Examples are:

- Parallel words – The killer behaved coldly, cruelly, and inexplicably.
- Parallel phrases – Praised by comrades, honored by commanders, the soldier came home
- a hero.
- Parallel clauses – "We shall fight on the beaches, we shall fight on the landing grounds, we shall fight in the hills." (Winston Churchill)

Euphemism – This is a "cover-up" word that avoids the explicit meaning of an offensive or unpleasant term by substituting a vaguer image. An example is using "expired" instead of "dead."
Hyperbole – This is an example or phrase that exaggerates for effect. An example is the extravagant overstatement "I thought I would die!" Hyperbole is also used in tall tales, such as those describing Paul Bunyan's feats.

Climax – This refers to the process of building up to a dramatic highpoint through a series of phrases or sentences. It can also refer to the highpoint or most intense event in a story.

**Bathos, oxymoron, irony, and malapropism**

Bathos – This is an attempt to evoke pity, sorrow, or nobility that goes overboard and becomes ridiculous. It is an insincere pathos and a letdown. It is also sometimes called an anticlimax, although an anticlimax might be intentionally included for comic or satiric effect.

Oxymoron – This refers to two terms that are used together for contradictory effect, usually in the form of an adjective that doesn't fit the noun. An example is: a "new classic."

Irony – This refers to a difference between what is and what ought to be, or between what is said and what is meant. Irony can be an unexpected result in literature, such as a twist of fate. For example, it is ironic that the tortoise beat the hare.

Malapropism – This is confusing one word with another, similar-sounding word. For example, saying a movie was a cliff dweller instead of a cliffhanger is a malapropism.

**Transitional words and phrases**

Transitional words are used to signal a relationship. They are used to link thoughts and sentences. Some types of transitional words and phrases are:

- Addition – Also, in addition, furthermore, moreover, and then, another
- Admitting a point – Granted, although, while it is true that
- Cause and effect – Since, so, consequently, as a result, therefore, thus
- Comparison – Similarly, just as, in like manner, likewise, in the same way
- Contrast – On the other hand, yet, nevertheless, despite, but, still
- Emphasis – Indeed, in fact, without a doubt, certainly, to be sure
- Illustration – For example, for instance, in particular, specifically
- Purpose – In order to, for this purpose, for this to occur
- Spatial arrangement – Beside, above, below, around, across, inside, near, far, to the left
- Summary or clarification – In summary, in conclusion, that is, in other words

Time sequence – Before, after, later, soon, next, meanwhile, suddenly, finally

**Pre-writing techniques**

Pre-writing techniques that help a writer find, explore, and organize a topic include:

- Brainstorming – This involves letting thoughts make every connection to the topic possible, and then spinning off ideas and making notes of them as they are generated. This is a process of using imagination, uninhibited creativity, and instincts to discover a variety of possibilities.
- Freewriting – This involves choosing items from the brainstorming list and writing about them nonstop for a short period. This unedited, uncensored process allows one thing to lead to another and permits the writer to think of additional concepts and themes.

Clustering/mapping – This involves writing a general word or phrase related to the topic in the middle of a paper and circling it, and then quickly jotting down related words or phrases. These are circled and lines are drawn to link words and phrases to others on the page. Clustering is a visual representation of brainstorming that reveals patterns and connections.

**Listing and charting**

Prewriting techniques that help a writer find, explore, and organize a topic include:

Listing – Similar to brainstorming, listing is writing down as many descriptive words and phrases (not whole sentences) as possible that relate to the subject. Correct spelling and grouping of these descriptive terms can come later if needed. This list is merely intended to stimulate creativity and provide a vibrant vocabulary for the description of the subject once the actual writing process begins.

Charting – This prewriting technique works well for comparison/contrast purposes or for the examination of advantages and disadvantages (pros and cons). Any kind of chart will work, even a simple two-column list. The purpose is to draw out points and examples that can be used in the paper.

**Purpose of writing**

Writing always has a purpose. Two of the five reasons to write are:

To tell a story - The story does not necessarily need to be fictional. The purposes are to explain what happened, to narrate events, and to explain how things were accomplished. The story will need to make a point, and plenty of details will need to be provided to help the reader imagine the event or process.

To express oneself - This type of writing is commonly found in journals, diaries, or blogs. This kind of writing is an exercise in reflection that allows writers to learn something about themselves and what they have observed, and to work out their thoughts and feelings on paper.

Three of the five reasons to write are:

To convey information - Reports are written for this purpose. Information needs to be as clearly organized and accurate as possible. Charts, graphs, tables, and other illustrations can help make the information more understandable.

To make an argument - This type of writing also makes a point, but adds opinion to the facts presented. Argumentative, or persuasive, writing is one of the most common and important types of writing. It should follow rules of logic and ethics.

To explore ideas - This is speculative writing that is quite similar to reflective writing. This type of writing explores possibilities and asks questions without necessarily expecting an answer. The purpose is to stimulate readers to further consider and reflect on the topic.

**Strategic arrangement**

The order of the elements in a writing project can be organized in the following ways:

Logical order - There is a coherent pattern in the presentation of information, such as inductive or deductive reasoning or a division of a topic into its parts.

Hierarchical order - There is a ranking of material from most to least important or least to most important, depending on whether the writer needs a strong start or a sweeping finish. It can also involve breaking down a topic from a general form into specifics.

Chronological order - This is an order that follows a sequence. In a narrative, the sequence will follow the time order of beginning to middle to end. In a "how to," the sequence will be step 1, step 2, step 3, and so on.

Order defined by genre - This is a pre-determined order structured according to precedent or professional guidelines, such as the order required for a specific type of research or lab report, a resume, or an application form.

Order of importance - This method of organization relies on a ranking determined by priorities. For example, in a persuasive paper, the writer usually puts the strongest argument in the last body paragraph so that readers will remember it. In a news report, the most important information comes first.

Order of interest - This order is dependent on the level of interest the audience has in the subject. If the writer anticipates that reader knowledge and interest in the subject will be low, normal order choices need to be changed. The piece should begin with something very appealing. This will hook the reader and make for a strong opening.

**Beginning stages of writing**

The following are the beginning stages of learning to write:

- Drawing pictures is the first written attempt to express thoughts and feelings. Even when the picture is unrecognizable to the adult, it means something to the child.
- The scribble stage begins when the child attempts to draw shapes. He or

she may also try to imitate writing. The child may have a story or explanation to go with the shapes.

- Children have the most interest in learning to write their own names, so writing lessons usually start with that. Children will soon recognize that there are other letters too.
- Children are learning the alphabet and how to associate a sound with each letter. Reversing letters is still common, but instruction begins with teaching children to write from left to right.
- Written words may not be complete, but will likely have the correct beginning and end sounds/letters. Children will make some attempt to use vowels in writing.

Children will write with more ease, although spelling will still be phonetic and only some punctuation will be used.

## Journals

Writing in a journal gives students practice in writing, which makes them more comfortable with the writing process. Journal writing also gives students the opportunity to sort out their thoughts, solve problems, examine relationships and values, and see their personal and academic growth when they revisit old entries. The advantages for the teacher are that the students become more experienced with and accustomed to writing. Through reading student journals, the teacher can also gain insight into the students' problems and attitudes, which can help the teacher tailor his or her lesson plans.

A journal can be kept in a notebook or in a computer file. It shouldn't be just a record of daily events, but an expression of thoughts and feelings about everything and anything. Grammar and punctuation don't matter since journaling is a form of private communication. Teachers who review journals need to keep in mind that they should not grade journals and that comments should be encouraging and polite.

## Revising

Revising a paper involves rethinking the choices that were made while constructing the paper and then rewriting it, making any necessary changes or additions to word choices or arrangement of points. Questions to keep in mind include:

- Is the thesis clear?
- Do the body paragraphs logically flow and provide details to support the thesis?
- Is anything unnecessarily repeated?
- Is there anything not related to the topic?
- Is the language understandable?
- Does anything need to be defined?
- Is the material interesting?

Another consideration when revising is peer feedback. It is helpful during the revision process to have someone who is knowledgeable enough to be helpful and will be willing to give an honest critique read the paper.

## Paragraph coherence

Paragraph coherence can be achieved by linking sentences by using the following strategies:

Repetition of key words – It helps the reader follow the progression of thought from one sentence to another if key words (which should be defined) are repeated to assure the reader that the writer is still on topic and the discussion still relates to the key word.

Substitution of pronouns – This doesn't just refer to using single word pronouns such as I, they, us, etc., but also alternate descriptions of the subject. For example, if someone was writing about Benjamin Franklin, it gets boring to keep saying Franklin or he. Other terms that describe him, such as that notable

American statesman, this printer, the inventor, and so forth can also be used.

Substitution of synonyms – This is similar to substitution of pronouns, but refers to using similar terms for any repeated noun or adjective, not just the subject. For example, instead of constantly using the word great, adjectives such as terrific, really cool, awesome, and so on can also be used.

**Verbs**

In order to understand the role of a verb and be able to identify the verb that is necessary to make a sentence, it helps to know the different types of verbs. These are:

Action verbs – These are verbs that express an action being performed by the subject. An example is: The outfielder caught the ball (outfielder = subject and caught = action).

Linking verbs – These are verbs that link the subject to words that describe or identify the subject. An example is: Mary is an excellent teacher (Mary = subject and "is" links Mary to her description as an excellent teacher). Common linking verbs are all forms of the verb "to be," appear, feel, look, become, and seem.

Helping verbs – When a single verb cannot do the job by itself because of tense issues, a second, helping verb is added. Examples include: should have gone ("gone" is the main verb, while "should" and "have" are helping verbs), and was playing ("playing" is the main verb, while "was" is the helping verb).

**Conjunctions**

There are different ways to connect two clauses and show their relationship.

A coordinating conjunction is one that can join two independent clauses by placing a comma and a coordinating conjunction between them. The most common coordinating conjunctions are and, but, or, nor, yet, for, and so. Examples include: "It was warm, so I left my jacket at home" and "It was warm, and I left my jacket at home."

A subordinating conjunction is one that joins a subordinate clause and an independent clause and establishes the relationship between them. An example is: "We can play a game after Steve finishes his homework." The dependent clause is "after Steve finishes his homework" because the reader immediately asks, "After Steve finishes, then what?" The independent clause is "We can play a game." The concern is not the ability to play a game, but "when?" The answer to this question is dependent on when Steve finishes his homework.

**Run-ons and comma splices**

A run-on sentence is one that tries to connect two independent clauses without the needed conjunction or punctuation and makes it hard for the reader to figure out where one sentence ends and the other starts. An example is: "Meagan is three years old she goes to pre-school." Two possible ways to fix the run-on would be: "Meagan is three years old, and she goes to pre-school" or "Meagan is three years old; however, she goes to pre-school."

A comma splice occurs when a comma is used to join two independent clauses without a proper conjunction. The comma should be replaced by a period or one of the methods for coordination or subordination should be used. An example of a comma splice is: "Meagan is three years old, she goes to pre-school."

**Fragment**

A fragment is an incomplete sentence, which is one that does not have a subject to go with the verb, or vice versa. The following are types of fragments:

Dependent clause fragments – These usually start with a subordinating conjunction. An example is: "Before you can graduate." "You can graduate" is a sentence, but the subordinating conjunction "before" makes the clause dependent, which means it needs an independent clause to go with it. An example is: "Before you can graduate, you have to meet all the course requirements."

Relative clause fragments – These often start with who, whose, which, or that. An example is: "Who is always available to the students." This is a fragment because the "who" is not identified. A complete sentence would be: "Mr. Jones is a principal who is always available to the students."

The "ing" fragment lacks a subject. The "ing" form of a verb has to have a helping verb. An example is: "Walking only three blocks to his job." A corrected sentence would be: "Walking only three blocks to his job, Taylor has no need for a car."

Prepositional phrase fragments are ones that begin with a preposition and are only a phrase, not a complete thought. An example is: "By the time we arrived." "We arrived" by itself would be a complete sentence, but the "by" makes the clause dependent and the reader asks, "By the time you arrived, what happened?" A corrected sentence would be: "By the time we arrived, all the food was gone."

Infinitive phrase fragments have the same problem as prepositional phrase ones. An example is: "To plant the seed." A corrected sentence would be: "To plant the seed, Isaac used a trowel."

**Speaking skills children should have**

Children of elementary/intermediate school age should be able to:

- Speak at an appropriate volume, tone, and pace that is understandable and appropriate to the audience
- Pronounce most words accurately
- Use complete sentences
- Make eye contact
- Use appropriate gestures with speech
- Exhibit an awareness of audience and adjust content to fit the audience (adjust word choices and style to be appropriate for peers or adults)
- Ask relevant questions
- Respond appropriately when asked questions about information or an opinion, possibly also being able to provide reasons for opinions
- Speak in turn, not interrupt, and include others in conversations
- Provide a summary or report orally
- Participate in small and large group discussions and debates
- Read orally before an audience
- Conduct short interviews

Provide directions and explanations orally, including explanations of class lessons

**Viewing skills children should have**

Children of elementary school age should be developing or have attained the ability to understand the importance of media in people's lives. They should understand that television, radio, films, and the Internet have a role in everyday life. They should also be able to use media themselves (printing out material from the Internet or making an audio or video tape, for example). They should also be aware that the purpose of advertising is to sell.

Children of intermediate school age should be developing or have attained the ability to obtain and compare information from newspapers, television, and the Internet. They should also be able to judge its reliability and accuracy to some extent. Children of this age should be able to tell the difference between fictional and non-fictional materials in media. They should also be able to use a variety of media, visuals, and sounds to make a presentation.

## Listening skills children should have

Through the elementary/intermediate school years, children should develop the following listening skills:

- Follow oral instructions consistently
- Actively listen to peers and teachers
- Avoid creating distracting behavior or being distracted by the behavior of others most of the time
- Respond to listening activities and exhibit the ability to discuss, illustrate, or write about the activity and show knowledge of the content and quality of the listening activity
- Respond to listening activities and exhibit the ability to identify themes, similarities/differences, ideas, forms, and styles of activities
- Respond to a persuasive speaker and exhibit the ability to analyze and evaluate the credibility of the speaker and form an opinion describing whether they agree or disagree with the point made

Demonstrate appropriate social behavior while part of an audience

## Teaching viewing skills

Viewing skills can be sharpened by having students look at a single image, such as a work of art or a cartoon, and simply asking students what they see. The teacher can ask what is happening in the image, and then elicit the details that clue the students in to what is happening. Of course, there may be more than one thing happening. The teacher should also question the students about the message of the image, its purpose, its point of view, and its intended audience. The teacher should ask for first impressions, and then provide some background or additional information to see if it changes the way students look at or interpret the image. The conclusion of the lesson should include questions about what students learned from the exercise about the topic, themselves, and others.

Students are exposed to multiple images every day. It is important for them to be able to effectively interpret these images. They should be able to make sense of the images and the spoken and print language that often accompany them. Learning can be enhanced with images because they allow for quicker connections to prior knowledge than verbal information. Visuals in the classroom can also be motivational, can support verbal information, and can express main points, sometimes resulting in instant recognition.

Some of the common types of images that students see every day include: bulletin boards, computer graphics, diagrams, drawings, illustrations, maps, photographs, posters, book covers, advertisements, Internet sites, multimedia presentations, puppet shows, television, videos, print cartoons, models, paintings, animation, drama or dance performances, films, and online newscasts and magazines.

Activities at school that can be used to strengthen the viewing skills of students of varying ages include:

- Picture book discussions – Students can develop an appreciation of visual text and the language that goes with it through guided discussions of picture books that focus on the style and color of the images and other details that might capture a child's attention.
- Gallery walks – Students can walk around a room or hallway viewing the posted works of other students and hear presentations about the works. They can also view a display prepared by the teacher. Students are expected to take notes as they walk around, have discussions, and perhaps do a follow-up report.

Puppet theater and drama presentations – Students can learn about plots, dialogue, situations, characters, and the craft of performance from viewing puppet or drama presentations, which also stimulate oral communication and strengthen listening skills. Discussions or written responses should follow performances to check for detail acquisition.

### Classroom viewing center

A classroom viewing center should contain magazines, CD-ROMs, books, videos, and individual pictures (photographs or drawings).

Students should have a viewing guide that explains expectations related to the viewing center (before, during, and after using the center). For younger students, the teacher can ask questions that guide them through the viewing rather than expecting them to read the guidelines and write responses.

- Before viewing, students should think about what they already know about the subject and what they want to learn from the viewing.
- During the viewing, students should make notes about whatever interests them or is new to them.
- After viewing, students could discuss or individually write down what they found to be the most interesting idea or striking image and explain why it caught their attention.

### Important questions pertaining to viewing a narrative

A teacher should make students responsible for gaining information or insight from the viewing. Setting expectations increases student attention and critical thinking. As with any viewing, the students should consider what they already know about the topic and what they hope to gain by watching the narrative before viewing it. During the viewing, the students should take notes (perhaps to answer questions provided by the teacher).
After the viewing, students should be able to answer the following questions:

- What was the time period and setting of the story?
- Who were the main characters?
- How effective was the acting?
- What was the problem or goal in the story?
- How was the problem solved or the goal achieved?
- How would you summarize the story?
- What did you learn from the story?
- What did you like or dislike about the story or its presentation?
- Would you recommend this viewing to others?

How would you rate it?

### Learning by listening difficulties

It is difficult to learn just by listening because the instruction is presented only in spoken form. Therefore, unless students take notes, there is nothing for them to review. However, an active listener will anticipate finding a message in an oral presentation and will listen for it, interpreting tone and gestures as the presentation progresses. In group discussions, students are often too busy figuring out what they will say when it is their turn to talk to concentrate on what others are saying. Therefore, they don't learn from others, but instead come away knowing only what they already knew. Students should be required to respond directly to the previous speaker before launching into their own comments. This practice will force students to listen to each other and learn that their own responses will be better because of what can be added by listening to others.

### Speaking

Volume – Voice volume should be appropriate to the room and adjusted according to whether or not a microphone is used. The speaker should not shout at the audience, mumble, or speak so softly that his or her voice is inaudible.

Pace and pronunciation – The speaker shouldn't talk so fast that his or her speech is unintelligible, nor should the speaker speak so slowly as to be boring. The speaker should enunciate words clearly.

Body language and gestures – Body language can add to or distract from the message, so annoying, repetitive gestures such as waving hands about, flipping hair, or staring at one spot should be avoided. Good posture is critical.

Word choice – The speaker should use a vocabulary level that fits the age and interest level of the audience. Vocabulary may be casual or formal depending on the audience.

Visual aids – The speaker should use whatever aids will enhance the presentation, such as props, models, media, etc., but should not use anything that will be distracting or unmanageable.

**Listening and new language**

Listening is a critical skill when learning a new language. Students spend a great deal more time listening than they do speaking, and far less time reading and writing than speaking. Two ways to encourage ESL students to listen are to:

- Talk about topics that are of interest to the ESL learner. Otherwise, students may tune out the speaker because they don't want to put in that much effort to learn about a topic they find boring.
- Talk about content or give examples that are easy to understand or are related to a topic that is familiar to ESL students. Culturally relevant materials will be more interesting to
- ESL students, will make them feel more comfortable, and will contain vocabulary that they may already be familiar with.

Listening is not a passive skill, but an active one. Therefore, a teacher needs to make the listening experience as rewarding as possible and provide as many auditory and visual clues as possible. Three ways that the teacher can make the listening experience rewarding for ESL students are:

- Avoid colloquialisms and abbreviated or slang terms that may be confusing to the ESL listener, unless there is enough time to define them and explain their use.
- Make the spoken English understandable by stopping to clarify points, repeating new or difficult words, and defining words that may not be known.

Support the spoken word with as many visuals as possible. Pictures, diagrams, gestures, facial expressions, and body language can help the ESL learner correctly interpret the spoken language more easily and also leaves an image impression that helps them remember the words.

**Top down and bottom up**

ESL students need to be given opportunities to practice both top-down and bottom-up processing. If they are old enough to understand these concepts, they should be made aware that these are two processes that affect their listening comprehension.

In top-down processing, the listener refers to background and global knowledge to figure out the meaning of a message. For example, when asking an ESL student to perform a task, the steps of the task should be explained and accompanied by a review of the vocabulary terms the student already understands so that the student feels comfortable tackling new steps and new words. The teacher should also allow students to ask questions to verify comprehension.

In bottom-down processing, the listener figures out the meaning of a message by using "data" obtained from what is said. This data includes sounds (stress, rhythm, and intonation), words, and grammatical relationships. All data can be used to make conclusions or interpretations. For example, the listener can develop bottom-up skills by learning how to detect differences in intonation between statements and questions.

**Listening lesson steps**

All students, but especially ESL students, can be taught listening through specific training. During listening lessons, the teacher should guide students through three steps:

- Pre-listening activity – This establishes the purpose of the lesson and engages students' background knowledge. This activity should ask students to think about and discuss something they already know about the topic. Alternatively, the teacher can provide background information.
- The listening activity – This requires the listener to obtain information and then immediately do something with that information. For example, the teacher can review the schedule for the day or the week. The students are being given information about a routine they already know, but need to be able to identify names, tasks, and times.

Post-listening activity – This is an evaluation process that allows students to judge how well they did with the listening task. Other language skills can be included in the activity. For example, this activity could involve asking questions about who will do what according to the classroom schedule (Who is the lunch monitor today?) and could also involve asking students to produce whole sentence replies.

**Helping ESL students by speaking**

To help ESL students better understand subject matter, the following teaching strategies using spoken English can be used:

- Read aloud from a textbook, and then ask ESL students to verbally summarize what was read. The teacher should assist by providing new words as needed to give students the opportunity to practice vocabulary and speaking skills. The teacher should then read the passage again to students to verify accuracy and details.
- The teacher could ask ESL students to explain why the subject matter is important to them and where they see it fitting into their lives. This verbalization gives them speaking practice and helps them relate to the subject.

Whenever small group activities are being conducted, ESL students can be placed with English-speaking students. It is best to keep the groups to two or three students so that the ESL student will be motivated by the need to be involved. English-speaking students should be encouraged to include ESL students in the group work.

**Helping ESL students by reading**

There are supplemental printed materials that can be used to help ESL students understand subject matter. The following strategies can be used to help ESL students develop English reading skills.

- Make sure all ESL students have a bilingual dictionary to use. A thesaurus would also be helpful.
- Try to keep content area books written in the ESL students' native languages in the classroom. Students can use them side-by-side with English texts. Textbooks in other languages can be ordered from the school library or obtained from the classroom textbook publisher.

If a student lacks confidence in his/her ability to read the textbook, the teacher can read a passage to the student and have him or her verbally summarize the passage. The teacher should take notes on what the student says and then read them back. These notes can be a substitute, short-form, in-their-own-words textbook that the student can understand.

## Helping ESL students with general strategies

Some strategies can help students develop more than one important skill. They may involve a combination of speaking, listening, and/or viewing. Others are mainly classroom management aids. General teaching strategies for ESL students include:

- Partner English-speaking students with ESL students as study buddies and ask the English-speaking students to share notes.
- Encourage ESL students to ask questions whenever they don't understand something. They should be aware that they don't have to be able to interpret every word of text to understand the concept.
- Dictate key sentences related to the content area being taught and ask ESL students to write them down. This gives them practice in listening and writing, and also helps them identify what is important.
- Alternate difficult and easy tasks so that ESL students can experience academic success.
- Ask ESL students to label objects associated with content areas, such as maps, diagrams, parts of a leaf, or parts of a sentence. This gives students writing and reading experience and helps them remember key vocabulary.

## Technological content

A curriculum that is project-based begins with explicit questions meant to stimulate the curiosity of students and serve as a basis for launching various research ideas and directions. Teachers can see that curricular units provide a valuable advantage in motivating students with regard to developing hypotheses, finding research information in many sources of data in order to confirm or argue the hypotheses, and in developing arguments which are based upon understanding certain intended concepts. The Internet can provide a wealth of information but can also provide challenges for teachers. Students with literacy challenges have difficulties finding information, identifying relevant information and then reading that which they find. These challenges may at times be linked to the inability of a student to draw conceptual parallels in content and then translate them into an Internet search.

## Culturally-relevant approaches

Teachers should develop learning environments that are reflective of their students' social, cultural and linguistic experiences. These serve as instructors, mediators, guides, consultants and advocates for students in helping them to find a way that is most effective to connect their cultural and community-based knowledge to their learning experiences in the classroom. A key criterion for teaching that is culturally relevant is nurturing and supporting competence in cultures both at school and at home. Teachers should use the student's home cultural experience as a base on which to build skills and increase knowledge. Content that is learned in this manner becomes more significant to the student and helps facilitate a transfer of school learning to real-life.

## Peer influence

Peer influence on children's behavior as well as on learning is well recognized in psychological literature. Peer influence can operate both ways, positive and negative. Teachers will try normally exploit the positive influence on peers and promote many of the learning experiences the children may have by organizing them into small groups in which they can become involved in learning. The negative aspects of peer influence are obvious when parents of children expect him and her to show interest in school work and spend time on homework but many of the children's peers do not have the same goals on their agendas. It is under such circumstances that it might become necessary to have the child discontinue his or her association with those peers who are negative influences.

**Terms**

Phonological awareness
A conscious sensitivity to the structure of language by sound. It includes the ability to distinguish between parts of speech such as syllables and phonemes.

Phonemic awareness
A part of phonological awareness in which listeners may understand and distinguish between phonemes.

Alphabetic principle
An assumption which underlies systems of alphabetic writing, in that each speech sound or phoneme of a particular language requires its own distinctive representation graphically.

Decoding
Willingness and ability to sound out words through generation of sounds into recognizable words, known as a phonological recording.

Sight vocabulary
That stable of words a reader can automatically identify.

Phonics - a methodical approach to reading and spelling which emphasizes the basic relationships between symbols and sounds; often used with beginning readers or with people who are new to a language.

Grapheme - a letter or combination of letters in the written language which represents a meaningful sound (phoneme) in the spoken language.

Syntax – the rules which govern the grammatical relationship between words and other units within a sentence.

Grammar – rules for syntax, inflection and word formation which govern how sentences are formed.

Semantics – the study of linguistic meaning in a language, including words, phrases, and sentences.

Dialect – a language variation occurring in a certain region or social class; differs from the standard language in pronunciation, grammar or vocabulary.

**Systems of language**

Before a child enters school, he has already developed language at home. Language is defined as a system of expressing and taking in information in a meaningful way. Speech is the verbal expression of language. Four language systems have been identified:

1. Phonological (sound) system – refers to the meaningful sounds of a language (phonemes) and their corresponding letters of the alphabet.
2. Syntactic (structural) system – refers to the structural organization (grammar) of a language which dictates how words are combined into sentences; components of syntax include word order, capitalization, punctuation, and morphemes.
3. Semantic (meaning) system – refers to vocabulary, including synonyms, antonyms, and idioms.
4. Pragmatic (social & cultural) system – refers to the social and cultural aspects of usage, such as how language varies among different social classes, ethnic groups, and geographic areas.

**Literacy differences across content areas**

Studies have shown that it is impossible to separate practices in the classroom such as strategies for activating prior knowledge from the larger cultural and social contexts in which the practices exist. Researchers say that a need exists for adolescent literacy that includes the adolescent's literacy practices beyond the confines of the classroom setting, their expanded conceptions of text such as the Internet, and the relationship that exists between the development of identity and literacy. However, the need for additional research in the teaching and learning of context in secondary schools still exists. For instance, more study is needed on the interactions between student and teacher, and between student and student; also on how students perceive themselves as readers, what their interests are at a particular time, and how institutional configurations affect the daily events occurring both in and out of school.

**Teaching Vocabulary**

Teaching specific words
Here is an example of how to teach specific words in class. A teacher might have his class read a novel. The novel may have a concept that is important to the plot so the teacher might try several ways to ensure the students understand what that concept means. For instance, the teacher might have students discuss the concept and read a sentence from the book that contains the concept. He might then ask students to use context and prior knowledge to try and determine what the concept means. The teacher might ask students to use the concept word in their own sentences to help deepen the understanding of the word. Students must develop word-learning strategies such as using dictionaries or using knowledge about word parts to determine what a word in text means.

Extended and active engagement
Extended and active instruction can be used to better learn words. For example, a first-grade teacher wants their student to understand the concept of work. Over time, the teacher has the students do exercises in which they repeatedly use the meaning of the concept of work. The students have many opportunities to see and use the word in different contexts that will reinforce its meaning. The teacher will ask them what they already know about work and have them give example of the type of work their parents perform. The class could have a discussion about the work that is done at school. The teacher can find a simple book about work that introduces ideas about specific work that should be done. The teacher can ask students to make up sentences describing the work their parents do.

Repeated exposure to words
Repeated exposure to words can be taught in a manner such as this: A second-grade class is reading about George Washington. The story talks about his role as a farmer. The teacher wants to ensure that the students understand the meaning of "farm" and "farmer," not only because these words are an important part of the book, but also because they are words that students need to know in school and in their everyday lives. The teacher calls the students' attention to the words farm and farmer when mentioned in textbooks and reading selections. The teacher has students use the word in their own writing. The teacher asks the students to find the words in print in newspapers. Upon reading the book, the teacher discusses George Washington's role as a farmer and how farms were different from today.

Using word parts
Knowing common prefixes and suffixes along with base and root words can help students learn the meanings of many words. Just learning the most common English prefixes (un-, re-, in-, dis-) gives students clues to more than half of all the English words with prefixes. Prefixes are relatively easy to learn because their meanings are clear. For instance, un- means "not" and re- means "again." They are usually spelled similarly

from word to word and they are always at the word's beginning. Suffixes can be more challenging to learn because their meanings are more abstract than prefixes. For instance, -ness means "the quality or state of" something. Other suffixes are easier to figure out such as -less which means "without." Teachers should teach word roots as they occur in texts as well as teaching those root words that are most likely to be encountered.

Using dictionaries and other reference aids
Here is an example of how dictionaries and other reference material can be used to teach vocabulary. A second-grade teacher finds that many of his students do not know the word "might" as it is used in the sentence, "The children moved the rock with all their might." The teacher shows them how to find the word "might" in the classroom dictionary and shows that there are five definitions for the word "might." The teacher reads each definition and discusses with the class whether each definition would fit in the sentence's context. The students eliminate the definitions of might that do not work in the sentence. The teacher then has students substitute the most likely definition for "might" into the original sentence to ensure that it makes sense.

Using context clues
Here is an example of how to use context clues to determine the meaning of a vocabulary word. A student reads the sentence, "The birds were chirping loudly and the cat was quickly tiring of the racket. The cat quickly became unhappy with the birds. The cat finally solved the problem when it accidentally stuck its head into a bowl and was not able to hear a thing." The teacher tells the students that the context of the paragraph helps to determine what racket means. There is chirping and it is loud. The cat was unhappy. When the cat got its head stuck in a bowl, it could no longer hear the chirping. These are all clues that the birds are being noisy and that racket means loud noise.

**Reading disorder**

Students who have a reading disorder have problems with their reading skills. Their skills are significantly below that which is normal for the student's age, intelligence, and education. The poor reading skills can cause problems with the student's academic success and in other areas of life. Signs associated with reading disorders include poor word recognition in reading, very slow reading, or making many mistakes. They may also show poor comprehension. Students who suffer from reading disorders normally have low self-esteem, social problems, and a higher drop-out rate in school. Reading disorders may be associated with conduct disorder, attention deficit disorder, depression, or other learning disorders. Reading disorders are usually brought to the attention of a child's parents in kindergarten or the first grade, when reading instruction becomes a very important facet of teaching.

**Bias in selecting tests**

When selecting tests, care should be taken to ensure the test is not biased or offensive with regard to race, sex, native language, geographic region, or ethnic origin, as well as other factors. Those who develop tests are expected to show sensitivity to the test-takers' demographic. Steps can be taken during test development and documentation to minimize the influence of cultural factors on the test scores. These may include evaluating the items for offensiveness and cultural dependency, and using statistics to identify differential item difficulty. Questions to ask include: "Were the tests analyzed statistically for bias?" "What method was used?" "How were the items selected for the final version?" "Should the test be used with non-native English speakers?"

**"Scaffolding" in reading-writing**

As proposed by Lev Vygotsky as part of his Social Cultural learning model, scaffolding is the process in which an adult/teacher provides help to a child, then decreases the level of assistance as the child masters the skill or topic. Scaffolding ties in with what Vygotsky termed the Zone of Proximal Development (ZPD), which is the gap between what an individual knows about a topic and what he does not. In children, ZPD refers to the range of tasks a child can do with help from a parent or teacher but which he cannot accomplish on his own. A teacher can use scaffolding and awareness of ZPD in planning lessons involving reading, writing, speaking, and listening. Specifically, a teacher reading out loud provides students with an opportunity to model that behavior, and then to write and read further about the topic, perhaps through the utilization of a KWL chart.

## Literacy

<u>Social class and family background variables</u>
The social class and family background variables are prominent in emergent literacy research. Numerous studies have addressed links between parental occupation, income, and children's achievements. One finding is that there are wide variations in children's achievements, regardless of social class in relation to a child's early literacy experiences. Specific factors in family environments such as parental interest, positive attitudes, and modeling have been identified as major predictors of academic success despite social class or educational levels. There is considerable variation among family environments in the status and value given to books, the presence of materials for writing, and the time that is spent reading and writing. Studies have shown that early readers tend to come from homes with more pencils, paper, and books, and that have mothers who read more often.

<u>Sociocultural theory and the genetic analysis aspect</u>
Sociocultural approaches to literacy developed out of more general sociocultural theory which came from the theories of Soviet psychologist L.S. Vygotsky. The three central planks of sociocultural theory that have contributed to a new interpretation of literacy are the concepts of genetic analysis, social learning, and mediation. Genetic or developmental analysis suggests that it is possible to understand mental functional aspects by understanding their origin and transitions. From genetic analysis it is understood the futility of seeing literacy as something that is isolated. Rather, a proper understanding of the emergence of literacy has to take into account the broad cultural, social and historic factors that relate to the significance of reading and writing for human communication and cognition.

<u>Social learning and mediation aspects</u>
Along with genetic analysis, social learning and mediation are the three major components of a sociocultural approach to literacy. Social learning refers to the social origin of mental functioning. Vygotsky said that every function in the child's cultural development appears first on the social level and later on the individual level. The first development is between people and the second is inside the child. Vygotsky also believed the development occurred through such means as apprenticeship learning, or interaction with teachers and peers. This view looks at learning not as an isolated act of cognition but rather a process of gaining entry to a discourse of practitioners. Mediation is the notion that all human activity is mediated through signs or tools. It is not so much the tools, such as computers or writing, by themselves as it is how they transform human action in a fundamental way.

## African-Americans and "acting white"

Dr. John Ogbu has argued for years that the blacks have developed an oppositional cultural identity because of discrimination developed by their own culture. This stems in part from the times when blacks were asked to have the same behavior and speech as whites, such as after emancipation. With the Black Power Movement of the 1960s, an oppositional cultural identity was in place where racial pride was expressed. Regardless, Ogbu believed that blacks still try to enter white culture. A resulting behavior, derided by some, especially younger blacks, called "acting white" can be stressful for blacks. They are accused of being an Uncle Tom or being disloyal to the black community. Speech, in particular, is one activity in which blacks may be labeled as acting white.

### Concept of multiliteracies

A great deal of interest has risen around the world in the future of literacy teaching through so-called "multiliteracies." The multiliteracies argument is that our personal, public, and working lives are currently changing in some very significant ways and that these changes have the effect of transforming cultures and the ways in which we communicate. The ramification of this is that the way literacy is now taught will become obsolete and what counts for literacy must also change. Multiliteracies has at its heart two major and closely related changes. First is the growing significance of cultural and linguistic diversity. This is reinforced every day by modern media. Each day, both globally and in our local communities, we have to negotiate differences that are interconnected with our working and community lives. As this happens, English is becoming a world language. The second major shift is the influence of new communications technologies.

### Home vs. school literacy experience

Studies have shown that a positive relationship exists between children's literacy experiences at home and their ease in transitioning to school. Family literacy environments do differ in some aspects. While the development of print awareness appears to be common across cultures, major differences occur in the quantity of exposure children have had to the written language, storybooks in particular. There also is a difference in the perception of the roles that parents have in their children's literacy experiences. Studies have found that such family characteristics relating to reading achievement include parental aspirations for the child, academic guidance, attitude toward education, and having reading materials in the home.

### Advantages of literacy starting at home

Children's school readiness is influenced by their parents' educational levels. The higher the parents' education, the more likely the child will succeed in school. Children who are raised in literate homes are likely to enter first grade with several thousand hours of 1-to-1 pre-reading experience. Children have a better chance of becoming fully literate adults if they are encouraged to read at home. Studies have shown that improving parents' skills positively affects their children's language development. Without parental support, the cycle of under-education will continue in families from generation to generation. With support from family literacy programs, children who may have otherwise been educationally and developmentally behind their peers came into school on par with their peers.

### Places literacy is learned

Literacy does not just come from going to school. It is learned everywhere, from reading bus stop signs and cereal boxes to listening to family stories in the language of the home. Caregivers as well as parents have a profound impact on their children's readiness upon entering school. Each year, the influence grows and changes form. The positive influence of the family continues to be important as the children develop through elementary, junior high, and high school. It can be enhanced through meaningful involvement in ways such as engaging parents, having parents and children participate in literacy activities together, and helping parents through adult education. Likewise, peers and community members will all play a significant part in mutually developing literacy.

**Metacognition process**

In the simplest terms, metacognition is the process of thinking about thinking. The concept is most often associated with John Flavell, a developmental psychologist at Stanford University. As applied to reading and writing, students can use metacognition to develop specific plans of action to enable a better understanding of the material. The three key elements of this process are: 1) designing the plan of action; 2) monitoring it; and 3) assessing its effectiveness. The process can be facilitated by encouraging students to ask a series of questions. For instance, when developing the plan, a student should ask questions such as "Why am I reading this?" and "How much time do I have?" Questions for the monitoring phase include "What information is most important?" and "What should I do if I don't understand?" Finally, the assessment phase prompts questions such as "How did I do?" and "What could I have done differently?"

**Reading-writing connection**

Reading and writing are generally viewed as two sides of the same coin. Reading leads to writing and vice-versa. When a child reads, he learns structure, punctuation, and vocabulary, all of which can make him a better writer and a better reader. To help make the connection, a teacher may require a student to keep a journal in which he writes about what he reads. The process of writing will help the student analyze and question what he has read. Therefore, a journal can also be a vital tool for enhancing metacognition. For older students, a classroom debate would require students to read pertinent material and write position papers. Another metacognitive approach to making the reading-writing connection is the KWL chart. Before reading new material, students will be asked to write down what they Know about the topic and what they Want to know. Afterwards, they will write down what they Learned.

**Phonemic awareness**

Different levels of phonemic awareness in terms of abilities include:

1. Hearing rhymes and alliteration as measured by knowing nursery rhymes.
2. Doing tasks such as comparing and contrasting the sounds of words for rhyme and alliteration, also known as oddity tasks.
3. Blending and splitting syllables.
4. Performing phonemic segmenting such as counting out the number of phonemes contained in a word.
5. Performing tasks of phoneme manipulation such as adding or deleting a particular phoneme.

Instruction in phonemic awareness might include:

1. Engaging preschool children in activities that direct their attention to sounds in words, such as rhyming games.
2. Teaching segmentation and blending.
3. Combining letter-sound relationship instruction with segmentation and blending.
4. Sequencing examples systematically when teaching blending and segmentation.

<u>Phonological recoding</u>
Phonological recoding refers to the use of systematic relationships between letters and phonemes in order to produce the pronunciation of a printed string that is unknown or to spell words. Phonological recoding includes regular word reading, irregular word reading, and advanced word analysis. Regular word reading includes beginning recoding such as the ability to read from left to right words that are regular and unfamiliar, generation of sounds for letters, and blending sounds into recognizable words.

Beginning spelling is translating speech to print through phonemic awareness. Irregular word reading is reading those words that cannot be decoded because either the letter sounds are unique to the word or a few words or the letter-sound correspondences in the word have not yet been learned. Advanced word analysis is knowing those words needed for fluency.

Important phonemic awareness skills

Children of kindergarten age require development of phonemic awareness by hearing, identifying, and manipulating phonemes or individual sounds within spoken words. Once children acquire knowledge of letters, they can be taught to perform activities to isolate phonemes and achieve phoneme segmentation by pointing to or manipulating letters along with sounds. Blending and segmentation in phonemic awareness is important because they provide a foundation for skills such as spelling. Studies have shown that phonemic awareness can be acquired with as little as 20 hours of instruction, although some children might require more instruction in order to accurately segment words. The individual students should be assessed to verify that the instruction was successful. More instruction might be required for some children than others.

Sing-songs and phonemic awareness

Rhyme is a prominent feature of many songs. Listening to and singing songs helps make children aware of the phonemic nature of spoken language. Songs that help children to manipulate sounds in words are most effective in having children pay attention to a language's sound structure. Manipulating sounds in words can be challenging for those children in the early stages of phonemic awareness development, so children should be given many opportunities to learn the songs before they start trying to manipulate the sounds. One way this can be done is to play tapes of such songs during transitional activities such as snack time or clean-up time in order to help children become more familiar with sound play.

**Onset-rime blending**

Children can be encouraged to think about words as sounds when someone is able to break the words down into smaller parts. One particular way in which a syllable can be broken down is into onset and rime. Onset is everything that comes before the vowel, while rime refers to the vowel and everything that comes after it. For instance, truck could be broken down into /tr/ and /uck/. Rhyming is blending a new onset onto an old rime. Children must have a great amount of experience recognizing rhymes before they are able to produce rhymes. Among the daily activities that help early childhood classes gain these skills are by listening to rhyming stories, reciting poetry that rhymes, and singing rhyming songs.

**Orthographic analogies**

Orthographic analogies are word families that can be generated from knowing onsets and rimes. Using orthographic analogies can help students rapidly build their reading and writing vocabularies. For instance, if a child knows the word "man," they could use a rime analogy to read or write any word that rhymes such as "tan," "fan," "can," etc. There have been studies that question the effectiveness of using orthographic analogies for young children. These studies indicate that children do not see the orthographic similarities but rather hear a word from an adult that functions as a clue. The studies indicate that using analogies in teaching reading may not always be helpful if an adult is required to be there to give the word clue to a child.

**Body-coda blending**

Vowels are the loudest parts of syllables, or the peak if you will. One may always stretch the vowel and say it out loud. Children can break syllables on either side of the loud vowel, with relative ease. For example, they might break "ship" into "sh-ip" or "shi-p." In discussing the body of a syllable, the reference is to all of the phonemes within the vowel. Those consonants that are found after the vowel are called codas. For instance, in the word dream, /dre/ is the body of the syllable and the coda is /m/. The reward for body-coda blending is that it is easier than onset-rime blending because some distortion frequently occurs during onset-rime blending.

## Understanding alphabetic principle

Sound analysis training
Children can understand that the letters in printed words represent the sounds in words that are spoken. Children can change single consonants at the start or end of one-syllable words upon a teacher's request, such as changing "cat" to "rat." Sound analysis alone has been found to be effective in developing alphabetic principle skills. But teaching sound analysis along with the relationships between sounds and letters that give practice in using these letter-sound relationships in reading and writing provides the greatest benefit. Alphabetic mapping is also useful. When children know sounds of four or five consonants, they can start to develop an understanding of how the alphabetic principle works. Using movable letters to show switched letters can help highlight different sound combinations.

Word families
Knowing that words containing the same sound pattern will often share spelling patterns is important for a child to know. When a child learns that a number of frequently occurring patterns of spelling occur and has learned that these spelling patterns can be generalized, the child will be able to analyze and identify unfamiliar words more efficiently. The major value of word families, also known as phonograms, in kindergarten is that they give the student the opportunity to practice decoding the beginning letters in a word. It should not be expected that the children will learn to use the word families in generative ways. In other words, they are not expected to learn word families as a means of independently decoding new words. Word families give children more practice with the application of the alphabetic principle.

## Constructivist theory and learning

A major portion of constructivist theory is the idea that learning is an active process in which those who learn build new ideas or concepts based upon their current and past knowledge. Those who learn select and transform information, build a hypothesis, and make decisions that rely on a cognitive structure in order to make it work. Cognitive structures such as mental models or schema provide meaning and organization to experiences. This lets the individual go beyond the information that is given there. In constructivist theory, instruction should address:

1. A predisposition towards learning,
2. The different ways knowledge can be built so that the learner most readily grasps it,
3. The most effective sequences in which material can be presented, and
4. The nature as well as pacing of rewards and punishments.

## Increasing prior knowledge

Accretion is one form of increasing prior knowledge. Each time something new is taught or referred to in a class, there are traces of it that are left in a student's memory. Tuning happens when students modify and reshape information they receive until it fits their needs. Reconstruction occurs when students learn something that goes against what they previously thought was true. Students can build on what they already know when they can expand on terms and information they understand. Increased background information on more in-depth ideas about a topic also helps the student better understand what is being read.

Students can also provide real-life experiences to help with understanding.

### Schemas and stages of reading

Prior knowledge and experience are common to the various stages of reading transactions. Readers build meaning before, during, and after a reading transaction based upon their interest in and prior knowledge about:

1. Facts relating to a particular topic
2. Concepts and vocabulary that is related to those concepts and
3. The underlying principles and generalizations.

Readers have schemas, or organized networks of prior knowledge and experiences, about certain topics which foster expectation whenever they read about those topics. When students are reading, they add to or adjust their schemas as they boost their comprehension of what is being read.

### Reading aloud to children

Storybook reading at home is a key component of early reading acquisition, according to several studies. Studies have documented the relationship between reading to children and their later success on reading readiness tasks. Children who are read to have also been found to acquire concepts about the function of written language in books. Findings show that most successful early readers have had contact at home with written material. When poor readers enter school they have had much less experience with books and reading than those who become better at reading. In short, children learn how to attend to language and apply that knowledge to literacy situations by interacting with others who model functions of language.

### Social constructivism

Social constructivism is a variant of cognitive constructivism that puts an emphasis on the collaborative nature of learning. This theory was developed by Soviet psychologist Lev Vygotsky. He was a cognitivist but he rejected postulations by other cognitivists such as Piaget and Perry which said that separating learning from its social context was possible. Vygotsky theorized that all cognitive functions originate and must be explained as products of social interactions and that learning was not simply the accommodation and assimilation of new knowledge attained by those learning. Instead, he felt it was the process by which learners were integrated into a community of knowledge. Vygotsky believed that the cultural development of children appears first on the social level and only later inside the child. This applies equally in voluntary attention to logical memories and forming concepts. Higher functions come from actual relationships between people, Vygotsky postulated.

### Cultural constructivism

Cultural constructivism is a theory asserting that knowledge and reality are products of their cultural context. This means that two independent cultures will likely form different methodologies of observation. Western cultures usually utilize objects for making scientific descriptions, while Native American cultures use events to describe phenomena. Beyond social environments for learning are wider cultural influences such as custom, language, religion, biology, and tools. The tools such as language and symbols that people use can have an effect on the way they think, according to this theory. There are some schools of thought which hold that tools redistribute the cognitive load of some task between the people and the tools being used. For instance, a telephone can change a conversation's nature.

### Culturally responsive teaching

One goal of effective teaching is to make learning a meaningful endeavor for children. In order to fully comprehend their experience, children must see connections between what they know and what they experience in schools and other settings. Increasing the congruence and continuity between children's home and school environments is a crucial aspect in achievement for children who come from diverse cultures and varied social classes. Recognizing and fostering the cultural knowledge of children from culturally and linguistically diverse backgrounds can help bridge the gap between home and school. Creating a culturally responsive learning situation takes a lot of work. This includes effective partnerships between schools and families where each is treated as a full partner in attaining a successful outcome.

## Sapir-Whorf hypothesis

The Sapir-Whorf hypothesis says that a systematic relationship exists between grammatical categories of the language a person speaks and how the person thinks and behaves in it. The hypothesis was actually an axiom developed by anthropologist Edward Sapir and his student and colleague Benjamin Whorf. The hypothesis is also known as the principle of linguistic relativity. There are arguments to the version of this idea that thought is constrained by language. One argument is that all people have occasional problems expressing themselves due to the language being inadequate for what they are meaning to say. Thus, thought is not a set of words because a concept can be understood without it being expressed in words. Arguments also exist for the extreme opposite—that language does not at all influence thought.

## Fluency

Fluency is key to becoming competent as a reader. It involves getting words right as well as phrasing and proper intonation. Children who are younger readers engage in stop and start reading. These children are spending most of their time decoding text. But studies have shown that the more time children give to text decoding, the less they will comprehend the text. Studies also show that higher-order skills such as synthesizing, analyzing, and summarizing require fluency in reading. A lack of comprehension in reading affects all content areas. Because students cannot read fluently, their time is spent decoding the words rather than taking in the text from which they should be learning.

### Fluency and development of meaning

Fluency and reading comprehension are closely related. By learning to read accurately, children are able to comprehend text. Also, research shows that students who score low on fluency tests also tend to score low on reading comprehension assessments. Fluency is not the same as automaticity which refers to a reader's ability to recognize words automatically, accurately, and rapidly. Fluency involves reading connected passages with little effort and with expression. Automatic word recognition is important, but is insufficient as a skill for developing fluency. Fluent readers are able to read grade-level text with 90 percent accuracy and a rate of about 90 words per minute. They are also able to demonstrate comprehension of text when they read aloud.

### Developing fluency in reading

Developing fluency requires extensive practice and exposure to reading. Research indicates that repeated oral reading is particularly effective for readers who are both beginning and struggling. This practice can help improve accuracy, word recognition, speed, and fluency. It may also lead to an increased reading comprehension. Students benefit from reading the same story aloud several times until they are fluent enough to read the passage independently. The number of required repetitions is often three or four, but varies depending on the student. Practicing by reading aloud sight words from lists is not sufficient in improving fluency. This is because the student may be able to recognize a sight word in isolation but still be unable to read it.

## Stages of reading for young children

Children gain literacy through emergent, beginning, and fluent stages. The emergent stage is marked by children noticing environmental print, showing interest in books, pretending to read, and using picture cues and predictable patterns in books in order to retell a story. They also can identify some letters, reread books with patterns that are predictable, and recognize up to 10 familiar words. The beginning stage will show the child identifying letter names and sounds; matching written and spoken words; using the beginning, middle, and ending sounds to decode words; recognizing as many as 100 high-frequency words; reading slowly, word by word; and self-correcting while they are reading. The fluent stage features automatic identification with most words, reading with expression, reading at about 100 words per minute or more, preferring to read silently, recognizing up to 300 high-frequency words, and often reading independently making inferences.

## Reading proficiency at a young age

There is strong evidence that young people who are not fluent readers and writers by the end of the third grade may never catch up with their peers. One study found that first graders who were not on grade level by the end of the year stood a 1-in-10 chance of never having proficiency at grade level in reading. A governor of Indiana indicated that the determination of how many new prison beds to build was based, in part, on the number of second graders who do not read at second grade level. The number of future prison beds in California depends on numbers of children who do not go past the fourth grade reading level.

## Orthography

The orthography of a language refers to the set of rules of how to write correctly in the writing system of a language. The term comes from the Greek ortho-, meaning correct, and graphos meaning "that writes." In the modern sense of the word this includes spelling and punctuation, as well as the rest of the writing system of a language. For instance, English has 26 letters in an alphabet for both consonants and vowels, but no glyph or specific symbols that represent a semantic or phonetic unit of definitive value for emphasis. But each letter in the English alphabet may represent more than one sound and each sound may be written by more than one letter, as demonstrated by "f" and "ph." Orthography entails certain rules on how letters are used such as "i before e except after c."

## Inflection and word formation

It is possible to distinguish between two kinds of morphological rules. Some rules relate different forms of the same lexeme. Other rules relate two lexemes that are different. Rules that relate to the different forms of lexeme are called inflectional rules. Those rules relating to multiple lexemes are word formation rules. The plural for dog, dogs, is an inflectional rule. Compounds such as cowboy or firefighter are examples of word formation rules. Word formation informally forms new words while inflection provides more forms of the same word. A distinction also exists between two kinds of word formation, derivation and compounding. Compounding involves combining complete word forms into compounds. Derivation involves prefixes or suffixes that are not independent words.

## Allomorphy and morphophonology

The one-to-one correspondence between meaning and form hardly ever holds in language and this is one of the largest sources of complexity in morphology. There are words in English such as deer/deer, goose/geese where the differences between singular and plural forms are signaled differently from a regular pattern or are not at all signaled. Even the cases considered normal are not that simple. For example, consider that the -s in cats and the -s in dogs are not pronounced the same way. In plural like dishes there is another vowel before the -s. The cases where the same distinction is affected by different changes of form for different lexemes are known as allomorphy. The study of allomorphy resulting from the interaction of morphology and phonology is called morphophonology.

**Morphology**

Morphology - a sub-discipline of linguistics, or the study of word structure. Words are accepted as being the smallest syntactical units, but in most languages words can be related to other words by rules. Those who speak English recognize that these relationships can be formulated as rules applying to many other pairs of words. For example, fire is to firefighter, as cow is to cowboy. Morphology is the linguistic branch that studies such rules across and within languages.

Morpheme-based morphology
There are three primary approaches to morphology that attempt to capture the distinctions in different ways. They are morpheme-based morphology, lexeme-based morphology, and word-based morphology. Morpheme-based morphology is where word forms are analyzed as sequences of morphemes, or the minimal meaningful unit of language. Words such as independently have in-, depend, -ent, and -ly as morphemes, with the root word being depend. The other morphemes are derivational affixes, or morphemes that attach to words. In words such as cats, cat is the root and -s is an inflectional morpheme. Analyzing word forms as if they were composed of morphemes that are put after one another like a string of pearls is called "item and arrangement morphology."

Lexeme-based morphology
There are three primary approaches to morphology that attempt to capture the distinctions in different ways. They are morpheme-based morphology, lexeme-based morphology, and word-based morphology. Lexeme-based morphology normally follows an "item and process" approach. Rather than analyzing word forms as sets of morphemes that are arranged in sequence, the word form is a result of applying rules that alter word forms or stems in order to produce new ones. An inflectional rule takes a stem, makes changes to it, and outputs a word form. Unlike the item and arrangement process, one may take a word such as geese and not consider it a zero-morph. Instead, while the plural of cat is made by adding -s to the end of the word, the plural of goose is made by changing the vowel stem.

Word-based morphology
There are three primary approaches to morphology that attempt to capture the distinctions in different ways. They are morpheme-based morphology, lexeme-based morphology, and word-based morphology. Word-based morphology is considered a "word and paradigm" approach to morphology. This theory takes paradigms as a central notion. Rather than stating rules to combine morphemes into word forms, or generate word forms from stems, word-based morphology has generalizations that hold between inflectional paradigm forms. A main point behind this approach is that many generalizations are hard to state with either morpheme-based or lexeme-based morphology. An example is where a piece of a word is given. In a morpheme-based theory it would be called an inflectional morpheme and correspond to a combination of grammatical categories. A word and paradigm approach treats these as whole words related to one another through analogy rules.

**Lexical affixes**

Lexical affixes, also known as semantic affixes, are bound elements that appear as affixes, but function as incorporated nouns within verbs and as elements of compound nouns. In other words, they are similar to word roots or stems in function, but are similar to affixes in form. Although they are similar to incorporated nouns, lexical affixes differ in that they never occur in freestanding nouns. They always appear as affixes. Such affixes are relatively rare. Lexical suffixes often bear little or no resemblance to free nouns with similar meaning. When used, lexical suffixes usually have more general meanings. For instance, a language may have a lexical suffix that means water in a general sense, but not have a noun equivalent referring to water in general. Instead it may have several nouns with more specific meanings, such as saltwater or groundwater.

**Form function of oral language**

The form function of oral language consists of phonology, morphology, and syntax. Phonology is the system of phonemes or sounds in language. Morphology is the system of rules governing word structure and organization. Many sounds have no meaning by themselves; these are phonemes. Every morpheme, however, has meaning on its own, as a root word, or attached to a root word as a prefix, suffix, or word ending. In English, the normal sentence is structured as subject + verb + object. Syntax refers to the way in which words are combined into sentences. Students with an understanding of syntax can comprehend how the various parts of a sentence relate to one another other.

**Ausubel's theory**

The major idea in Ausubel's theory of meaningful learning is the hierarchical organization of knowledge, or the idea that new information is meaningful only in that it can be related to that which is already known. Consequently, the theory stresses a hierarchical type of learning rather than rote learning or memorization, as well as emphasizing received knowledge instead of discovery learning. Ausubel postulated four processes which are environments for meaningful learning. Derivative subsumption describes a situation in which new information learned is an example of something one has already learned. Correlative subsumption is a process by which new information may be accomodated, such as a when one is accustomed to seeing blue skies, but instead encounters gray. Superordinate learning classifies information such as learning different types of clouds. Finally, combinatorial learning describes a process in which a new idea stems from another idea but has neither a higher nor lower hierarchy.

**Areas that help boost readers**

Specific instruction in writing for different reasons and audiences as well as instruction in strategies to help clarify and enrich language expression is crucial. Language mechanical skills such as usage, capitalization, and grammar can be taught and integrated into the students' own writing through the process of editing. For instance, students might study the use of adjectives and adverbs, and then write descriptive compositions. Cooperative learning can be a very effective upper elementary reading and writing instruction if used properly. Students should generally work in groups of four or five members that stay together for six-to-eight weeks. Each group might be presented a lesson on main idea and the students can work in groups to practice such a skill.

**Group reporting student assessment**

Group reporting is a fun way for students to show the teacher and their peers what they have learned. In this assessment method, students interact with one another in small groups. The students are able to learn from one another and practice social skills. Groups that work together consistently may create a portfolio of the group work. This could include self-assessments in which the students can comment on what they have learned while creating the portfolio. A group skit is a creative way to demonstrate almost anything the students have learned. A mini-fair is another activity where, after a small group project, the students can share their learning, using booths in a location where other class members can see it.

**Word identification approach**

The identification or recognition of words is the ability of students to develop an automaticity when reading isolated words. Automaticity refers to the speed and accuracy with which students are able to read these isolated words. Automatic words recognition is an important part of literacy because the level of students' abilities to recognize known words and decode or determine unfamiliar words can affect how fluently the students may read, and fluency is essential for comprehension. It should be remembered that building meaning is the goal of any literacy endeavor. Developing strong word recognition skills is also critical for students who, for whatever reason, did not develop strong phonological awareness in early childhood. These students may need to rely more heavily on their vocabularies and less on decoding skills.

**Critical questioning vs. critical thinking**

Critical thinking requires a systematic monitoring of thought. Ideas must not be accepted at face value, but should be analyzed for accuracy, clarity, breadth, logicalness, and depth. Critical thinking also requires that reasoning occur within various points of view and frames of reference, that it stem from goals and objectives, and that it have an informational base. When data are used for reasoning, it is vital to remember that the data are interpreted and that the interpretation involves concepts containing assumptions, all of which may have implication. The result of critical thought is that the basic questions of Socrates can be more focally framed and used, leading to questions regarding:

1. ends and objectives,
2. wording of questions,
3. sources of information and fact,
4. method and quality of information collected,
5. assumptions that are behind the concepts being used.

**Role of the newspaper**

Students learn when they are motivated and the topics they study hold interest and relevance to their lives. Many classrooms are using newspapers as a source for motivational and timely resources. It is a concept that dates back to 1795 when the Portland Eastern Herald in Maine published an editorial that put forth the role that newspapers can play in helping to deliver, extend, and enrich the curriculum. Classrooms around the world are using newspapers to complement text books and other relevant resources for a variety of disciplines. Newspapers featuring articles, editorials, and advertising help students apply literacy and numeracy skills as well as appreciate the importance of studying history and current affairs. Studies have shown that students who use newspapers score higher on reading comprehension tests and develop stronger critical thinking skills.

**First grade reading comprehension**

The process of learning to read is not a linear one. Students need not learn decoding before they learn to comprehend. Both skills should be taught at the same time, beginning at the earliest stages of instruction for reading. Comprehension strategies can be taught using both material that is read to children and material that they read for themselves. Before reading, teachers can delineate the reason for the reading: reviewing vocabulary, encouraging children to predict what stories are about, or activating background knowledge. Teachers can direct children's attention to subtle or difficult portions of the text during reading, point out difficult words and ideas and ask children to find problems and solutions. After reading, children can be taught particular metacognitive strategies such as asking themselves regularly whether what is being read makes sense.

## Reciprocal teaching

In many ways, reciprocal teaching is the aggregation of four separate comprehension strategies: summarizing, questioning, clarifying, and predicting. Summarizing presents the ability to identify and integrate the information that is most important in a text. Text can be summarized across sentences and paragraphs, and also across passages. When students start the reciprocal teaching procedures they are usually focused on sentences and paragraphs. Questioning reinforces the strategy of summarizing. When students identify questions, they identify a kind of information that is important enough to provide substance for a question, then post the information in question form. Clarifying is important for students with comprehension difficulty. They are taught to be alert to the effects of comprehension impediments and to take the necessary measures to restore meaning. Predicting is when students predict what the author will discuss next in the text.

Rationale behind reciprocal teaching

What is most important in reading education is turning out readers who can understand the meaning in texts. Reciprocal teaching is a scaffolded discussion technique for instilling some of the methods that good readers can use to comprehend text through questioning, clarifying, summarizing, and predicting. Teaching students the four strategies gives them the tools that great readers use in meeting their text-reading goals. Thus, it is the four strategies that are taught rather than reading skills. These multiple strategies help students to read by giving them a choice of strategies to be used in reading. The scaffolding gives support to help the students connect what they know and can do with what they need to do in order to be successful at learning a particular lesson. This also gives the students a chance to support each other and foster a sense of community among classmates.

Goals of reciprocal teaching

The word "reciprocal" in reciprocal teaching is somewhat misleading in that it does not entail students doing the teaching. But the students use a set of four strategies—summarizing, clarifying, predicting, and questioning—to improve reading comprehension. That improvement is the ultimate goal. Other aspects of the method include:

1. The teacher scaffolds instruction of the strategy by guiding, modeling, and applying the strategies.
2. It guides students to become metacognitive and reflective in the use of strategies.
3. It helps students monitor their comprehension of reading.
4. It uses the social nature of learning in order to improve and scaffold the comprehension of reading.
5. The instruction is presented through different classroom settings including whole group, guided reading groups, and literature circles.

How reciprocal teaching works

The order of the four stages of reciprocal teaching is not of great importance. A teacher will want to try out various ways to employ the strategy in order to see which particular sequence best fits a teaching style and the students' learning style. The teacher should also carefully choose text selections so that they all fit in with the four stages of reciprocal teaching. In order to successfully implement reciprocal teaching, the students must be taught the four strategies and have ample opportunities to use them. One approach could be having students work from a chart with four columns. Each column will be headed by the different comprehension activity that is involved. The students could then be placed in groups of four and each given one of the four roles: summarizer, questioner, clarifier, and predictor.

How reciprocal teaching exercise operates

The students would have their defined role on a note card. The students could then read several paragraphs of the assigned text passage. They should be encouraged to use note-taking strategies such as selective underlining or sticky notes in helping for their role in the discourse. At a given stopping point, the summarizer will give the key ideas up to this particular point in the text. The questioner will then ask questions about the text such as unclear parts, puzzling information, connections to concepts that have already been learned, or motivations of the characters or actors. The clarifier will try to clear up the confusing parts and answer questions that were asked. The predictor may then make guesses about what the author might tell next. The roles would then rotate one person to the right as another selection is read.

**Two-column note taking strategy**

Two-column note taking will find a student drawing a lengthwise line down the middle of a piece of paper. As the student reads or listens, the major concepts or headings are noted in the left-hand space and the supporting details are recorded in the right column. Only one side of the paper is used. When it is time to study, the paper is folded down the center so that either the main ideas or the details can be seen, but not both. This helps a student studying for an essay test recall details while looking at main ideas. For multiple choice tests, the student tries to recall main ideas while looking at the details. The notes are a memory device that is more efficient than either recalling from memory or rereading.

Challenges of student note-taking

Reading for certain information and then taking notes are perhaps the most challenging steps in the process of solving information problems. Students in grades 3-8 require many developmentally-appropriate chances to locate information before the techniques are mastered. Note-taking consists of identifying keywords and related words, skimming and scanning, and extracting needed information. These steps begin after students define and narrow the task, construct researchable questions, and find the right sources. After students build researchable questions from the information needed to finish a task or solve an information problem, the questions can be transferred to graphic organizers or data charts. This can allow them to focus on the key words. Skimming and scanning will help them make use of the text with less time and effort. Information may be extracted and recorded with different forms of note-taking, including citation, summary, quotation, and paraphrasing.

**Test-taking strategy**

A reason for test anxiety and poor performance on tests is often a lack of preparation. Children often know about a test in advance. Some teachers also tell parents when tests will be given. Knowing when the test is scheduled and what will be covered can help give the child a study schedule to prepare for the test. One schedule is for the student to study nightly for several nights before the test. Teachers may encourage parents to determine how long the child can be expected to concentrate at a given sitting. The parent should also be encouraged by the teacher to ask the child what material might be on the test and to go over questions at the end of chapters and sections. Maps, charts, and diagrams should receive special attention. A sample test can be developed from this information, which can even make studying fun.

**Intermediate school student pre-test strategy**

Before a test students should:

Begin to study the material a few days before the test and take study breaks every 20-30 minutes.

1. Take time to do some kind of physical activity that will help reduce tension and stress.
2. Eat a good breakfast the morning of the test and get a good night's sleep the night before the test.
3. Skim the material and determine which parts are best understood and which ones are still difficult.
4. Read a sentence or two and reread what they don't understand.
5. Pick out main ideas or key terms and think up possible test questions by themselves.
6. Read aloud and study with a partner or parent. While reading, the students should listen to themselves.
7. Think about what important points the teacher talked about during class.
8. Remain motivated and positive.

**Elementary school student pre-test strategy**

Students should follow directions carefully. Have the student listen and read the directions to the test so they understand what is expected of them. Teachers need to make sure the students understand vocabulary words and concepts in the directions. Words appearing in the test directions that are common should be introduced to students as part of the process of test preparation. Ensure that the students understand what they are to do. If students have questions, they should be encouraged to ask the teacher before the test starts. Listening and reading activities that will provide practice for following directions can be incorporated into the classroom. Students must know how to budget their time for the test. They should work fast but comfortably. Students can practice this.

**"High interest, low vocabulary" books**

Books that have a high interest and low vocabulary are materials with controlled vocabulary and reading difficulty levels, but which also contain plot and topics appropriate to older students. These give an older student, such as a young teen, the opportunity to read without having to read something that might be embarrassing for the teen because it is intended for much smaller children. These high interest and low vocabulary books must also provide supports for those with reading problems, just as the early picture books do. This includes illustrations that support text, vocabulary that is carefully chosen, an appropriate vocabulary load, simple sentences, characters that interest the reader, and compelling stories.

**Reading apprenticeship model**

The reading apprenticeship model was developed from the reconceptualization of content reading. This instructional platform is centered on the dual ideas of literacy as complex social and cognitive processes and of teaching as a cognitive apprenticeship. For adolescents to move from beginners to experts in certain content area practices, the subject matter teacher, as the expert practitioner, must guide, make explicit, model, and support the apprentice in his or her development. Because ways of thinking, speaking, reading, and writing differ from subject matter to subject matter, some believe the most appropriate source for students to learn these specific practices is teachers who already have expertise in these fields. A reading apprenticeship involves student and teacher as partners of a collaboration that inquires into reading and reading processes as content area texts are engaged.

**Exploring dimensions of classroom life**

There are four integrated dimensions of classroom life that are explored together by student and teacher in a reading apprenticeship: social, personal, cognitive, and knowledge building. The social dimension is based on constructing a community of readers using literacy as a way to connect with their interests, each other, and the social world that they are learning about. The personal dimension involves building students' awareness of themselves as readers, of why they are reading, and of what they hope to accomplish. The cognitive dimension is part of the structure that includes instruction in and use of strategies for comprehension, monitoring tools, and reading flexibility. Knowledge-building is centered on areas such as building schemata, or content knowledge, the vocabulary of the subject matters, and the structures of text and language.

## Literacy in content areas

Attention should be paid to literacy in content areas for several reasons. The 2003 National Assessment of Educational Progress Reading Report shows that general test scores have improved over recent years, but very few young people in the United States can read at proficient or advanced levels. Most can decode and answer simple comprehension questions, but few can synthesize ideas, interpret the information they receive, or critique the ideas they read about, especially when they work with expository texts. Also, literacy in content areas has consequences that go beyond the ability to understand a subject-matter text. Advanced or specialized literacy forms are tools that signify success, both academically and socially, and can be important for economic, social, and political success beyond school.

## Background knowledge

In order for students to ask the right questions about a subject, they need background knowledge. Activating prior knowledge and then building upon that knowledge is a big concern for teachers. Teachers can use language arts strategies to help students find ways to know what they know and what they should know, and to help them visualize content. With such a perspective, teachers can connect the focus on content in the curriculum in order to gain more general literacy strategies that students experience elsewhere. Teachers are also concerned with a lack of comprehension. Students often show a lack of deep conceptual understanding. One challenge is to design ways to help students become more skillful in what they do not know, so that understanding can be used in supporting learning.

## Cubing

Cubing is a literacy strategy in which students are able to explore topics from six separate dimensions or viewpoints. The student can:

1. Provide a description of the particular topic.
2. Compare the topic to a different topic.
3. Associate the topic with something else and provide specific reasons for the choice.
4. Analyze the topic and tell how the topic came about.
5. Give an explanation of what the topic comprises after analysis.
6. Provide an argument for or against the topic.

The teacher chooses a topic related to the thematic unit and students are divided into six groups. Students brainstorm about their dimension ideas and then use a quick write or quick draw. These are shared with the class and are attached to the sides of a cube box. This strategy can be applicable to subjects such as social studies.

## History frames/story map

A history frames/story map strategy is used in helping a student think on the major points of a history story by:

1. Identifying the important individuals who are a part of the story.
2. Succinctly summarizing the story by highlighting its main events.
3. Putting the story into context and realizing the problem that was to be overcome or the goal to be achieved.
4. Explaining the outcome.
5. Relating the story to history, to themselves, and to the world.

Four graphic organizers are used: the history frame, the story map, the story pyramid, and the framed character. The history frame can be used by students who choose main events from a chapter and fill in varying sections for participants, goals, summary, and resolution. The story map can be used for individual articles, for excerpts from oral histories and biographies, or to help understand motives of key historical players.

**Writing prompts**

Such a strategy could include a four-step process to help students in decision-making on their writing. It helps the students consider:

1. The writer's role or voice.
2. The audience to whom the piece is written.
3. The format used for writing the piece.
4. The topic to be written about. The teacher can give examples for subjects such as social studies.

The students look over the four questions and consider the topic; then individually, and in small groups, they use the process to plan their writing. Students can have various roles, formats, and audiences. For a unit on World War II, a role might be offered for an American, German, or Japanese soldier, or a French resistance fighter. An audience might be self, community, government, or home. Format could include letters, diary, speeches, news articles, or editorials.

**Debate strategy**

Debate practices oral language skills and higher order thinking skills through a structured argument, while discussing knowledge of content. The teacher must choose a topic represented by a single question that can be answered with a yes or no. Alternatively, the topic may be stated as a resolution. The teacher may also choose one of several debate formats. They may be in the Webster-Hayne format in which students are divided into two teams of unlimited size with each side taking turns to speak. The Lincoln-Douglas, Kennedy-Nixon, and academic debate formats are more formal, allowing two speakers each, a specific time period, a designated order, and a time limit for speaking. Students are given a side to argue and they must research material to support their side.

**Technical vocabular**

A strategy for technical vocabulary and language development is a word category exercise requiring thinking on an interpretive level. A teacher will establish sets of four words in which three of the words are related. Students circle the word that is not related. On a line at the top of the set, they write a word or phrase that defines the relationship of the three remaining words. This is a way to comprehend historical terms in a manner other than memorization of definitions and facts, and it forces the student to employ higher-level thinking. It can help to review and show a vocabulary understanding, as well as knowing information from a chapter or unit. It may also be used to mark periods with sets of historical people, places, ideas, and events.

**Value box reading**

Value boxes help students change from thinking to writing with graphic organizers that prepare them to build written arguments. It categorizes and notes values that are associated with an idea in three areas: positive, negative, and interesting. Partners or small groups can meet to discuss ideas and add to lists which are then used to formulate writing. This strategy can be used to help answer higher level thinking questions that need reflection on historical decisions or the impact of historical events. After writing positive, negative, or interesting, students would then write an expository essay with a thesis that evaluates the impact and argues points written in the value boxes.

### Four-way sharing group

A four-way sharing group may be used for any content area. It encourages students to listen to and generate oral language. The four-way sharing helps provide equal access to all students and helps to manage the talk in the classroom, especially after a charged issue. Four students sit on the floor facing each other from the positions of the cardinal directions. The teacher directs the "North" to speak for a full five minutes and the rest of the group will listen. Each of the other directions also get five minutes. It might be helpful to start with a much shorter time period until the students are comfortable doing the circuits. Teachers can find out how effective students use speaking and listening time in this strategy as well.

### Charts

A student can use charts to help develop a thesis when writing about history papers using charts that list the key events during a particular time period. The student would imagine how the story would seem in a movie and list scenes and locations that are crucial to the plot. He would then work with others to develop a list of key events in those locations and of the moments and factors that contribute to how characters or situations evolve. This also may be displayed, compared, and discussed as a continuing aid for understanding the story. The students will generate different hypotheses about the information found on the charts. All of the hypotheses are listed and students pick one or two that might help them in writing. Students also share ideas in peer feedback groups.

### Comic books

Children have been reading comic books since before the middle of the 20th century. Researchers investigated using comic books in stimulating students in language arts classes because of their popularity. One pair of researchers, Wright and Sherman, suggested that teachers should use comic strips in language arts classes for three reasons.

1. Their students showed a high level of interest in the particular genre.
2. The wide circulation of comic strips makes them a very viable source of material economically.
3. Most comic strips have readability levels that are low, with words and sentences that are linguistically apt for readers of elementary and middle school levels.

Comics, TV, drama, and other multimedia formats may provide a way to reach even more language arts students and keep them engaged in the study of literacy skills.

### Media literacy

Media literacy includes both reading (or decoding) and writing (or encoding) media messages. It is a communication that is a basic for the traditional idea of literacy. The skills or competencies involved in media literacy also enter many content areas and can be integrated across the curriculum in the same manner that writing and reading are required skills beyond language arts and English curricula. Some state educational curricula have begun to incorporate media literacy, requiring students in some states to understand the selection of all media in news coverage, draw conclusions about the media's reports and the public's response, and recognize propaganda. While misuses of television and videotape have taken place in some classrooms, there is a much better recognition of the value of media literacy.

### Multimedia literacy

Multimedia literacy is an aspect of literacy that is being recognized as technology expands how people communicate with each other. Literacy, as a concept, emerged as a measure of how one can read or write. It means today that someone reads or writes at a level that is adequate to communicate.

Multimedia calls for a more fundamental meaning of literacy when looked upon at a societal level. Multimedia is the use of several different media to send or receive information. These include text, audio, graphics, animation, virtual reality, computer programming, and robotics. The basic literacy of reading and writing is often handled by computer these days and provides a foundation for more advanced levels of multimedia literacy.

**Film and television**

Television and film can help students explore cultural context and are easily integrated into the curriculum. They are entertaining media and allow for a great deal of flexibility in techniques of teaching and material. Surveys indicate that more teachers than ever are integrating television and videotapes into their curricula. Teachers are seeking quality programming with the appropriate structure and length, as well as advance information that allows them to preview the programming. Also found in the surveys was that both teachers and students are becoming more media savvy as they use camcorders and other video production equipment with increased frequency. That effect is likely to grow even further with such mobile video platforms as digital cameras and cell phones.

Television news and documentaries have long been used in secondary and postsecondary classrooms for writing instruction. There have been suggestions that the structure and content of news presentations mirror the writing of essays and can help in serving as effective writing instruction. A selected TV program can be viewed in one class period with time for students to ask questions and give comments. Student can also produce outlines for the news report, to be collected at the end of the class period. Advertising images, magazines, and television series may also help promote critical thinking during the writing process.

**Trade books**

Language arts can be infused into content areas such as mathematics and science by using trade books. This includes picture books, fiction, and nonfiction books other than text books. Studies have shown that trade books appeal to a student's imagination and curiosity even more than text books. They also help students understand concepts by showing them in language that is familiar. Literature can help students make personal connections to ideas in math and science by putting these subjects into contexts that are meaningful and familiar. Some of these trade books may not be specifically about math or science, but they may show characters who engage in activities involving math and science. Such strategies help students gain confidence in such subjects and develop perseverance in solving problems.

**Electronic textbooks**

Technology is commonly used in learning situations, such as elementary science students watching a video of an experiment being performed, middle school students manipulating commercial software that helps them prepare for a rapidly-changing technological workplace, and high school students playing interactive chemistry games on the Internet that score their manipulations of chemical equations and formulas such as those used to solve problems in real life. Technology can help a child who is blind to hear audible descriptions that allow him or her to understand procedures and participate in a particular portion of class. Students who are physically impaired can complete computer activities with commercial software that has adaptive devices to permit the student to independently complete a task. Students who are hearing impaired can use CD-ROM or Internet video with captions.

**Lifelong learning**

Lifelong learning is important in the lives of people in general, and specifically in the lives of teachers. The rapid change in the social, technological, and economic world have required people to prepare for a second or even third career and to keep themselves abreast of new developments that impact their goals, both personally and socially. Lifelong learners keep their senses active and think of new ideas. Much of the learning is self-directed. Skill for lifelong learning include the ability to ask questions, form hypotheses, use the right resources to answer questions, read with comprehension, and take in and evaluate information. Preparing students to be lifelong learners will require that the teacher possess the skills to continually seek knowledge as well.

**Mediating children's literature**

The model of mediation is a general and dynamic framework that is meant to guide problem solving for teachers. It does not serve as a guide to analyze particular tasks or a list of steps. It is dynamic because it both evolves and guides through the social interaction that takes place in learning. When the teacher is interacting with a student, he or she must continually analyze how the student thinks and examine the strategies the student uses in problem solving. The analysis tells the teacher both what type of support to provide and how much should be given. The goal of instructional mediation is to help learners develop their own self-directed system of mediation, to become self-directed and independent readers. The decision-making process for the teacher looks at the purpose, the strategies, and the reflection.

**Multicultural literature**

There are a number of considerations in selecting multicultural literature for children. They include:

1. Accuracy. Books should have current and accurate information. Stories should acknowledge events that are recent.
2. Stereotypes. Books should reflect the lives of individual people rather than giving general behaviors or personality traits to an entire group of people.
3. Setting. The settings in books should be accurate and, again, avoid stereotypes.
4. Language. Be careful in selecting books that might separate characters into groups of those who speak standard English and those who do not.
5. Epithets. Some books may contain racial or ethnic epithets.
6. Illustrations. The illustrations should show that those in ethnic groups look different from one another.

**Adolescent literature**

A number of reasons exist why adolescent literature is important. These reasons include:

1. It helps adolescents understand various concerns and issues.
2. It is a safe place to read real-world experiences. Reading in a medium that is open-ended and not threatening allows students to empathize with others, as well as to consider and understand a wide variety of circumstances and the consequences of what takes place.
3. It helps students discover their place in the world and helps them to discover themselves.
4. It provides models that assist them in dealing with the problems that they may face every day. Adolescents with troubles may identify with the characters and the literature may help them in solving the problems that they have.

**Computers**

There is a potential for students to engage in behavior with computers that is not intended, such as "surfing the 'net." Many schools have written guidelines for the use of computers in school and also have teachers sign statements acknowledging the rules for using the computers. Teachers should adopt management schemes that limit problems and ensure that the computers are used appropriately. These are some possible considerations that teachers may opt for when using computers in class:

1. There is zero tolerance for misusing laptops.
2. A "lids down" or "think time" should be designated to ensure that the students' attention is directed at the teacher.
3. Planning should be done ahead for recharging batteries.
4. Identical software packages should be installed.
5. Software shortcuts should be set up.
6. Students should save files to specific directories.

A classroom which is equipped with computers for all students might resemble a computer lab to some students, so teachers should make attendance rules well known to get the class off to a better beginning. A routine may also need to be established for students who are put off by the non-traditional roles that computer technology has them assume. Pacing is also a concern in a classroom with computers. Fewer activities exist for students to work on at their own pace than those that are carefully-timed activities during class periods. Teachers who set goals and activities for a class at the beginning of the class and then let students work at their own pace are usually more comfortable with computers in the classroom.

**One-computer classroom**

It can be a challenge to have multimedia activities with only one computer in class but it can be done using strategies to get the most student access. The computer can accordingly be used as a presentation platform for both teacher and student, such as through the use of Power Point-style programs. A single computer may also function as a learning or research center or as a small-group development station. A projection unit or TV converter can be used to turn the computer into a presentation platform. The teacher can demonstrate, provide, and use teaching techniques that are technologically-enhanced. Students can also show their projects to the class. As a learning or research center, computers can be set up where students can find multimedia encyclopedias, the Internet, and various application software such as word processors.

**Making use of technology**

Various lessons can be enriched by the use of technology. This includes:

1. Digital presentations. Students can show their learning in a digital presentation. They might create a Web site or create a stand-alone presentation. Students should cite their sources of information as with any research project. They should also be taught the importance of seeking permission for copyrighted matter.
2. Have students read books online. Thousands of books are available online at Web sites such as Online Books Page.
3. Have Web quests. This is an activity that is good for language arts and exploration of literature. The quests list sets of questions and tasks on which students can perform Internet research.
4. Word processing. Word processing programs are good for projects that would require having multiple drafts.

Technology can be used in lessons for a host of content areas. Some examples include:

1. Language arts. The Internet can be used to look at photos described in novels and can provide information about the social fabric of the community, helping students to learn the context.
2. Mathematics. Spreadsheets can be used to calculate distance, speed, and

travel time between two cities. The data can be exposed in several forms to help foster the understanding of variables.

3. Science. The Internet can be used to view topographic and satellite maps to help determine an area's rock formations.
4. Physical education. The Internet can be used to watch basketball techniques in slow motion to help improve shooting form.

**Benefitting from technology**

Even young children can benefit from using technology. Technology can be a resource for teachers, students, and parents. Research has shown that students using technology have higher achievement levels and enhance their basic skills in reading, writing, and math if they can practice those skills with the use of technology. Students are engaged for longer time periods with the use of technology. It intensifies their basic tasks in learning. Technology can motivate students to learn which helps increase their desire to go to school and continue on to college. It can give students a chance to explore other lands through the internet. Instruction can be enhanced through the use of visual aids and lessons on the internet to boost comprehension.

**Reporting the news**

Students are told to be reporters and report the news for their school. They are told that they will need to report on local news, world news, national news, sports, entertainment, and weather. The reporter should visit various news websites to gather information for the stories. The stories must be accurate, informative, and interesting. The audience is the students' fifth grade class so it must be in language they can understand. The teacher functions as the editor. In this exercise, the student learns the parts of the newspaper: the headline, the lead, quotes, body, and ending. There should be pre-writing planning and collection of information. The student gets a "beat" to cover, finds a story, and writes about it.

**Composing texts**

The framework for composing texts includes invention, drafting, revision, and editing. Many recursive strategies lie inside these components. Invention refers to the ways in which a writer might think about what he or she wants to do and how it could be done. It involves using outlines, seeking other opinions and perspectives, and research. It is recursive in that writers invent throughout the act of writing, planning, revising, and editing. Drafting refers to the different versions of a text before closure. Writers discover as a result of writing a draft, and then draft some more. Some view revision as a way to see the text from different perspectives. Revision is also rethinking ideas and how they may be conveyed. Editing refers to decisions that writers make to produce writing in which the words and punctuation are correct, along with flowing sentence structure and diction.

**Developmental stages of writing**

Writing develops in stages from being dependent to becoming independent. The first stage is a novice who has little, if any, individual style. He or she is dependent on the teacher and seeks approval from the teacher. Stage 2 is a transitional writer. The writer needs support and coaching in order to develop. is the writer learns from modeled behaviors. Stage 3 is the willing writer, who is able to collaborate with others and can learn from criticism. This writer enjoys practicing the craft and develops an appreciation for the audience. Stage 4 is the independent writer. This writer is autonomous, has developed a sophisticated personal style, has developed a writer's voice, is self-aware, and is self-motivating.

## Supporting the writing process

Students who are at an intermediate writing level respond well to a classroom structure that is predictable while offering some choice and flexibility. It is important to develop an environment in which students are encouraged to feel safe in taking risks in order to develop a community of writers, sharing with and supporting each other. The teacher is part of the community. The teachers should let students help to set rules and guidelines. Desks can be arranged in groups and tables can be used for several students. Resources can be provided on a specified shelf. These resources include dictionaries, language texts, literature for models, and samples of writing by class members. Information on the writing process can be displayed on bulletin boards. The teacher can designate certain classroom areas for specific activities connected with writing.

## Class publications

There are several ways of creating publications for students within their classes including the use of the Internet along with developing hard-copy publications. This includes:

1. Dividing classes into groups to produce a newsletter or similar publication. Newsletters are relatively simple to produce using the templates that come with many word processing programs.
2. Assigning and electing an editorial board to be responsible for publishing.
3. The teacher can be the editor who selects what will be published. Students submit their work to the teacher which he or she can organize to reflect goals of the class or topics that are covered.

The copies of these publications can make the student proud.

## Vocabulary

A vocabulary is a set of words that a person or other entity knows that are a part of language. A person's vocabulary is defined either as the set of all words that person understands or the set of all words the person is likely to use when constructing new sentences. The richness of a person's vocabulary is most times thought of as a reflection of intelligence or level of education. Increasing the size of one's vocabulary, or vocabulary building, is an important part of learning and improving one's skill in a language. Students in school are taught new words as part of a particular lesson. Many adults find vocabulary building enjoyable. Words help derive meaning from a text, which is the main goal in reading. Reading comprehension is needed for all subjects that a person learns. A deep vocabulary helps all readers better understand what is read.

### Language expansion

Language expansion is the process of taking a verbalization used by a child and adding to it. Language modeling is the process of talking to children and narrating what occurs in their immediate environment. This involves the pairing of actions or objects with simple words in order to explain the purpose of those words. Language modeling and expansion give the child an opportunity to hear and learn language by allowing the child to hear the appropriate articulation and attempt to imitate sounds and combinations of sounds. Modeling and expansion involves the use of simple words or basic sentences that are easy to understand and have complex structures that are reduced. Most words are learned during everyday experiences with language. Interactions between children and adults are the best way for children to expand their vocabularies.

### Direct instruction of vocabulary

While much vocabulary is learned indirectly, some vocabulary needs to be directly taught. Direct instruction helps student learn words that are difficult such as those words representing concepts that are not part of the everyday experience of a student. The direct instruction of vocabulary in the case of a text leads to better comprehension. Direct instruction includes giving students specific word instruction and teaching students strategies for learning words. Specific word instruction can help expand a student's knowledge of word meanings. A deeper knowledge can help students understand what it is they are writing or speaking. Before having students read a text, the teacher should teach them specific words that will appear in the text.

Extended instruction

Extended instruction promotes active interaction with vocabulary which improves learning words. Children learn words best when instruction is provided over an extended time period and when the instruction has them working actively with the words. The more that the students use those new words, the more they will be used in different contexts which leads to the students being more likely to learn the words. Repeated exposure to vocabulary in many contexts helps word learning. Students learn new words better when they see them often and in different contexts. The more that children hear, see, and work with specific words, the better they can learn them. Students are given repeated exposure to new words when extended instruction is provided.

Indirect instruction

Indirect instruction of vocabulary can be encouraged in two major ways. First, students should be read to, no matter what grade level. Students of all ages can learn words from hearing texts being read to them. Reading aloud is most efficient as a means of indirect teaching when the teacher discusses the selection with the class before, during, and after the selection is read. The teacher should talk with students about the new vocabulary words and concepts, and help them relate the words to their prior experiences and knowledge. Another way to indirectly teach vocabulary words is to encourage students to read expansively on their own. The students should be encouraged to read on their own during independent work sessions.

Word selection

A teacher will most likely have the ability to teach perhaps eight to ten new words per week, so the words that are to be taught must be chosen carefully. The focus should be on teaching:

1. Important words. When words are taught before students read a text, the words that are important to understanding concepts in the text should be taught directly. The students may not know several other words in the selection, but there will not be time to teach them all.
2. Useful words. Words that the student will likely see and use many times should be taught.
3. Difficult words. Some instruction should be given on words that are difficult for the students. Particular challenges include words with multiple meanings depending on the context in which they are used.
4. According to need. Plan and implement instruction addressing strengths and needs.

Three levels of word knowledge

Knowledge of words by a student is not simply a matter of them knowing or not knowing those words. Instead, the words are known to certain degrees. They may not have seen or heard a word before. They may have heard it or seen it but only vaguely know what that word might mean. Or they may be very familiar with a word meaning and be able to accurately use it in speech and writing. The three levels of word knowledge are known as unknown, acquainted, and established. At the unknown level, the word is completely unfamiliar and the meaning is not known. At acquainted, the word is somewhat familiar and there is some idea of meaning. At the established level, the word is very familiar, can be easily recognized, and can be used correctly.

Four types of word learning

There are four different types of word learning that have been identified: learning a new meaning for a known word; learning the meaning of a new word that represents a known concept; learning the meaning of a new word that represents an unknown concept; and clarifying and enriching the meaning of a known word. These different kinds of word learning have varied levels of difficulty. Perhaps one of the most common and most challenging is learning the meaning of a new word that represents an unknown concept. This type of word learning is necessary for learning in content areas. Learning words and concepts in mathematics, social studies, and science can be particularly challenging because each concept is often associated with other concepts.

Dictionary game

A dictionary game is a team activity that can help students build their vocabularies and improve their dictionary skills. In the game, the student teams first compete against one another to find word definitions in the dictionary. The team that is the fastest reads the word definition, tells what part of speech the word is, and correctly uses the word in a sentence. Other teams can challenge the team's response. Points are given for correct answers or challenges. The value of this game is in demonstrating the difference between the primary definition of a word and its specific use in the context of a particular content area or in reading. Students should quickly learn that the primary definition of a word is not necessarily going to be its meaning in all contexts.

Word analogies

Word analogies can be used to let students connect familiar words and concepts with new ideas and prior experiences with new information. In such a strategy, the student is confronted by two words which are related and is then challenged to explain the nature of their relationship. Next, the students apply the same relationship to other pairs of words. The form for a word analogy exercise is typically: "Term A is to Term B as Term C is to what word?" Students display critical thinking on two levels using this exercise. First, they describe the relationships between the first pair of words and then suggest new word pairs with similar relationships.

## Student appreciation

Assignments that make learning personal are often very effective in helping students appreciate studying and completing those assignments. Such work often lets students look into their family, community, and cultural experiences and gain a better appreciation of both their own and their peers' backgrounds. Family tree projects in social studies classes are an example because of the great diversity of most American schools. These projects or others such as historical ones in which family members are sought out may often bring out values that the students might not otherwise appreciate and can also foster closer family relationships. Making assignments personal and valuable gives students a great incentive to appreciate studying about a subject and to find learning as a quest.

## Immigrant students

American schools have been a major agent for helping those children and youth who recently arrived in this country with adapting to the civic and social demands of their new homes. Classroom lessons and socialization on the school yard take place. But sometimes the home culture teachings and expectations are contrasted with those of American schools. This can lead to labeling children as disabled when no disability actually exists. These students do have issues with psychosocial stress as they attempt to adapt. A transition that is successful to one's new country requires a secure cross-cultural identity. How much of each culture forms this identity depends on the person's needs, skills, experience, education, and support. Recognition of these transitioning needs and support are among the strategic help that can be given to these children.

## Culture capsule

A culture capsule is a biliteracy activity that is usually prepared outside class by students, but presented during class for about five or 10 minutes. It consists of a paragraph or two and explains one minimal difference between an American custom and that of another culture's custom. It also includes several photos and other information that is relevant. These capsules can be used in addition to role playing. Students may act out a part of another culture. Essentially the capsule is a brief description of some aspect of the target culture followed by contrasting information from the students' native language culture. These are done orally with teachers giving a brief talk on the chosen cultural point and then leading a discussion on cultures.

## Teaching culture

A framework for teaching and learning culture includes:

- Knowing about getting information. The nature of content and getting information. Facts about the United States and important facets of its culture.
- Learning objectives—demonstrating a mastery of information.
- Techniques and activities—cultural readings, films, videotapes, cultural artifacts, and personal anecdotes.
- Knowing how culture is traditionally taught. Are students given information and asked to show that they know it.
- Knowing how to develop behaviors—knowing about what facts you learned and acting upon them.
- Learning objectives—demonstrating ability, fluency, expertise, confidence, and ease.
- Techniques—dialogs, role playing, simulations, and field experiences.
- Knowing where communicative competence in the language occurs. Students know both what to say and how to say it in an appropriate manner.

## Goals for teaching culture

The following are goals that should be attained in teaching culture:

- Interest. The student shows a curio
- sity about the target culture and also shows empathy toward its people.
- Who. The student understands that effective communication requires the discovery of the culturally conditioned images that are seen in the minds of people when they think, act, and react to the world that is around them.
- When and where. The student recognizes that situational variables and convention mold behavior significantly. He or she should know how people in the target culture act in both normal situations and crisis situations.
- Why. The student knows that people generally act the way they do because they are using options for satisfying basic physical and psychological needs and that cultural patterns are interrelated and tend to mutually support the satisfactions of needs.

## Attitudes over foreign cultures

Ways to measure the change in attitudes about foreign cultures include:

- Social distance scales. This is to measure the degree to which one separates oneself socially from members of another culture. For instance: Would you marry, have as a close friend, have as an acquaintance, or work with someone from another culture?

- Semantic differential scales. This is to judge the defined culture group in terms of a number of traits that are bipolar. For instance, are people from this culture clean? Are they dirty? Are they good? Are they bad?
- Statements. This is to put a check in front of statements the student agrees with. Is the person you know envious of others? Self-indulgent? Quick to understand? Tactless?
- Self-esteem change. This is to measure self-esteem changes in the primary grades. For instance, am I happy with myself?

**Importance of learning various cultures**

Students may display behaviors in their cultures that are different from those in the American mainstream; thus, they are at risk for being labeled by uninformed educators as having behaviors that are "wrong." Teachers should familiarize themselves with a student's home culture's values and practices. There should be an awareness of differences that promotes understanding, tolerance, acceptance, and celebration of others and their ways. Information on other cultures can be found in many textbooks and travel books, and on various Web sites. Another way to develop familiarity with a student's cultural background is the use of a "cultural informant." This is someone who might be familiar with the group and their ways, such as teachers or other successful members of that cultural group.

**Actions of immigrant students**

Immigrant students are often under a great deal of anxiety and stress as they learn English and cope with new surroundings. The pressure can result in feelings of being overwhelmed, confused, or frustrated. If this is the case, support services such as counselors or social workers may be needed to help relieve this stress. At times, the way a student responds to a perplexing situation may be misinterpreted by educators. Humans tend to use behaviors that have worked for them before and students are likely to use behaviors reinforced by their home and home culture. These misunderstandings have sometimes resulted in immigrant children being labeled as emotionally disturbed and being placed in special programs.

**Relationships with immigrant stundents**

Students need to feel welcomed and valued by their teacher. A direct verbal communication may not be feasible, but there are other methods of showing acceptance and personal warmth toward students. This will help relieve anxiety and can promote an enthusiasm to learn academics and American patterns of behavior. Smiles are a good way to reach different cultural, ethnic, and linguistic groups. Also, teachers should take time to talk with the youngsters, even through an interpreter. Having students talk about their prior life will help the teacher become more familiar with their concerns and enable the teacher to emotionally support the new students. The teacher may also answer questions about schools and what is needed to live here in America. The teacher may also discuss how he or she can help make the transition easier.

**Learning culture**

Students learning culture should be taught to react appropriately in social situations. They should be able to describe a pattern in the culture and recognize a pattern when it is illustrated. Additionally, they should be able to explain these patterns and predict how a pattern is likely to apply in a given situation. Students learning culture should describe or manifest an attitude that is important for making oneself acceptable in a foreign society. They should evaluate the form of a statement concerning a culture pattern and describe or demonstrate defensible methods of analyzing a sociocultural whole. They should identify basic human responses which signify that that which is being taught is understood.

### High expectations for immigrant students

It is common for some teachers to become frustrated upon seeing that they are unable to reach one or more of their students. Becoming more culturally informed can help enhance the teaching repertoire. This information can also help teachers realize that these students may have trouble under the teaching of any skilled instructor. But the belief that is expressed in a student helps to create persistence and motivation on their part. Linguistic as well as academic achievements in the United States are often only realized because of the patience, tolerance and encouragement which American teachers display. Effort is promoted by teachers who are supportive and who create a valuing, welcoming and accepting educational setting.

### Support services for immigrant students

Schools can help recent immigrants feel welcome and supported while developing positive identities that are cross-cultural. Schools have many ways to assist their students in learning the curriculum and adapting to American culture and habits. For example, a recent arrival can be partnered with another student who speaks his or her language or dialect, even if they are not necessarily of the same nationality or heritage. Cross-age tutoring is also an option that might be considered. Candidates include someone from the student's culture or region, other recent immigrants, or an accepting and helpful American youngster. Hiring paraprofessionals who speak the student's language can also be helpful.

### Becoming acquainted with strengths and needs

An important part of planning and organizing for instruction is acquiring an understanding of the students. It is useful, early in the school year, to learn as much as possible about the students, what their interests, learning abilities, and learning styles are. As a teacher talks directly with each student, information is provided about how that student perceives himself or herself as a learner. Also useful is:

- Give oral or written diagnostic questionnaires or surveys to assess the students' current abilities, interests, and attitudes.
- Consult other personnel, student portfolios, and the students' records from previous years.
- Consider the potential for using previously successful adaptations with each student, and plan other adaptations to address the specific needs for learning.

### Inventory of learning styles

A teacher wants to know what types of learning styles a student has as well as answers to other questions. These are the answers teachers must use to determine how instruction may be personalized for the students. This can also be surprising information for the students as well. An inventory of student learning styles can build self-esteem by helping the student to discover his or her strengths, learn about the areas in which more effort is required, and appreciate the differences among fellow students. A number of published inventories are available to help students determine their learning strengths. Inventories may also be found for free on the Internet.

### Terms

Research
Tends to support within-class ability grouping, grouping those with like abilities, as helping most students learn. It is generally flexible and not as stigmatizing as other groups. If such groups are considered, teachers might want only two such groups to make management of the grouping process easier.

Cooperative learning
an instructional strategy in which students are put into heterogeneous groups. It is perhaps one of the best researched innovations in recent times and can have dramatic student achievement effects when implemented properly.

Individualized instruction
The best way to deal with individual student difference, but it is very difficult to accomplish. Computer-assisted instruction may change that.

**Grouping formats**

Small group reading instruction has been shown in a number of studies to be more effective than instruction of the class as a whole. Most of these studies did not include students who were disabled. Having teacher-led groups of three to 10 students helps the students learn much more than when they are taught using instruction of the whole class. Smaller groups of three to four are usually more efficient than larger groups in terms of time, peer interaction, and improved skills. Combinations of formats also produce reading benefits that are measurable, especially for those children with disabilities. For instance, students who work in pairs for two days and in small groups for two days can be combined with whole-class instruction for a part of a period.

**Nongraded or ungraded grouping**

Nongraded and ungraded grouping usually refers to grouping children in classes without designation of grade levels and with age spans of more than one year. The original rationale was to increase the heterogeneity of class compositions and liberate children and teachers from rigid achievement expectations that are based on the age of a student. But research later found that implementing these classes tended to result in homogeneous grouping of children based on ability and achievement level, despite age. In many instances of nongraded groups, children in classes are put in regular or temporary groups for specific instruction, regardless of age. In such approaches, the main goal is to increase homogeneity of ability of groups rather than interaction across ability group lines.

**Progress with respect to class groupings**

Continuous progress generally means that children remain with their classroom peers in an age cohort, despite having met or surpassed specific grade-level achievement expectations. This term is usually associated with an emphasis on the individualized curriculum, so that teaching and learning tasks are responsive to previous experience, and on the rate of progress of the child despite age. This practice is sometimes referred to as social promotion. The main reason for this practice is that there might be a stigmatizing effect on children if removed from their age cohort. Like ungraded approaches, the programs that are focused on continuous progress are not aimed at maximizing the educational benefits of children of different abilities and ages being together. Instead their goal is to let the children progress without being made to meet expectations of achievement.

**Age grouping schemes**

Grouping practices might seem to have slight distinctions but there are significant implications in practice. Ungraded or nongraded approaches indicate that age is not a good indicator of what children are ready to learn. It emphasizes regrouping children for class based on perceived readiness to acquire skills and knowledge instead of age. Its main goal is of homogenizing children for instruction based on achievement rather than age. Combined grade groupings and continuous progress practices do not intend to increase a sense of family within class or to encourage children to share knowledge and experience, but mixed-age grouping does take advantage of heterogeneity of experience and skills in a group of children.

### Valuing correct answers

One of the most effective ways to establish a safe learning environment for students is to help them learn that errors are friends rather than faults. Students often apologize for not knowing something. They can be reassured that no one knows everything and that everyone has something to learn. Teachers can teach them to value their correct answers rather than dwelling on their errors. Students have learned to count errors, but they can be taught to instead count the number they got right, thus offering positive reinforcement. Even if a student gets one item correct and the remainder incorrect, the student can be told that they have already learned something. Patterns of errors can be pointed out as well.

### Conflict resolution

The numerous, well-publicized instances of violence in schools, and in society as well, have prompted many schools to consider making violence prevention and conflict resolution a part of the curriculum. These programs rely on instruction that is ongoing and discussion that helps change the perceptions, skills, and attitudes of children. A number of these curricula have been available since the 1980s. These include conflict resolution, violence prevention, and curricula for solving social problems. These curricular approaches are typically integrated into a broader program that has other components such as peer mediation, cooperative learning, and programs that address school wide behavior management and anger management.

### Safe learning environment

Most incidents of school violence or serious disruption begin as less serious behavior that has escalated to the point of requiring attention. Many aggressive or disruptive behaviors that spiraled out of control could have been prevented by early and appropriate classroom responses. A well-documented knowledge base exists on how to prevent misbehavior escalation in the classrooms. A number of those programs that integrate those findings into classroom management packages have become available. Most rely on principles of effectively managing the classroom including:

- Multiple options that rely on various strategies and responses for maintaining an effective learning environment.
- Emphasizing the positive.
- Teaching responsibility.
- Decelerating emotional conflict.
- Consistently communicating appropriate behavior.
- Early responses that let the student know what the school and classroom rules are and that they will be enforced.

### Bullying prevention

Many of those involved as perpetrators in the well-publicized school shootings in recent years had been picked on or persecuted by their peers. This highlights why addressing bullying in school is essential. Studies show that almost one-third of elementary students are bullied. About 10 percent of secondary school students have reported being bullied. But studies have also shown that school personnel persistently underestimate the extent of bullying that takes place in their school. Students also worry that no action will be taken. A whole-school approach may be needed to combat bullying rather than individual interventions. This could include awareness programs for teachers, parents, and students. Also, a strict enforcement of school and classroom policies helps to send a clear message that there is no tolerance for bullying.

## Preventing school violence

There are three assumptions underlying most of the methods schools use to reduce the risk that minor incidents and disruptions will turn into life-threatening violence. These assumptions are:

- Violence is preventable. Serious violent incidents seem unpredictable, but prevention programs can make a difference. No guarantee exists that schools with comprehensive programs will be violence free, but schools that implement violence prevention components do see fewer incidents of disruption, which can lower the chance of serious violence.
- There is no one quick fix. Many schools have begun using metal detectors in the wake of school shootings or have instituted no tolerance suspensions and expulsion, but no data exists to show the effectiveness of these measures.
- Prevention requires continuous planning and commitment. Effective school safety must have ongoing planning, commitment, and partnerships among the school staff, parents, and community.

## Intrinsic and extrinsic motivation

Intrinsic motivation can be seen when people take part in an activity for its own sake, without some obvious external incentive present. An example is a hobby. Extrinsic motivation is the desire to perform a behavior based on the potential external rewards that the activity might bring. It was once thought that both intrinsic and extrinsic behavior were additive and could not be combined to form higher motivation levels. Some scholars believe that students are more likely to experience intrinsic motivation if they:

- Attribute their educational results to internal factors that they can control.
- Believe that they can be effective agents in reaching their goals.
- Are motivated by the deep mastery of a topic rather than rote learning just to get a grade.

## Reading due to motivation

Motivated readers are those who generate their own literacy learning opportunities, and thus, determine their own literacy learning destiny. This places motivation in part of an engagement process. An engaged reader reads for different purposes, participates in meaningful social interactions focused around reading, and scaffolds knowledge that helps construct new learning. Motivation can take place at any time with any young reader. Teachers can suggest to parents ways to motivate children to read at home, even when the parent is busy and cannot drop what they are doing. One way to get the child another reading audience is to suggest that the child read to a few dolls or stuffed animals. This kind of activity can help both prereaders and beginning readers.

## Book clubs

Student-organized and student-driven book clubs help to build a community in the classroom and to encourage students to read independently. They are in effect taking responsibility for their learning of literacy. Book clubs let students choose what they want to read, where they read, how they read, and with whom they read. The choice is valued by students. Students must work together to negotiate places and times to meet, along with the pacing and discussion of their books in order to have successful book clubs. They learn to value one another as readers and learners. Teachers can allow book clubs to meet in small-group times during reading in order to give the students freedom in operating their own club.

## Building activities for book clubs

Activities in which school book clubs can grow together as a group include:

- Letting the group name themselves. Let them decide on a club mascot.
- Allowing each club to keep a group reading notebook or journal where they track their readings. Perhaps they might decorate the journal if they so wish.
- Allowing groups to decide upon projects that are inquiry-based. For example, a group might decide to explore something of specific interest to them and search for the information. After these steps are taken, teachers should explain the process and allow some class time so that students may discuss the activities and establish their first groups. Those students who are not interested in this voluntary activity can read on their own.

## Learning development problems

Some primary organic conditions are associated with developing learning problems as secondary symptoms. The child's reading and more general learning are thought to result from cognitive or sensory limitation that follow from the diagnosis. These include:

- Cognitive deficiencies. Children with severe cognitive deficiencies usually develop very low, if any, reading achievement. Factors associated with this include very low birth weight, fetal alcohol syndrome, lead poisoning, or nutritional deficiency.
- Hearing impairment. Hearing impairment is another condition associated with reading difficulty. This may be caused by chronic ear infections that lead to hearing loss.
- Early language impairment. Some children are so clearly behind by age 3 that it arouses concerns of parents, neighbors, preschool teachers, or others. Delayed language development is often the first indication of a broader primary condition, including developmental disability, autism, or hearing impairment.
- Attention deficits. Those with reading problems often have attention deficits.

## Nature of reading difficulties

The foundations of good reading for children are all the same. All readers need to develop fluency, comprehension, and motivation to read in order to become successful readers. This is true regardless of the reader's age, aptitude, or gender. Children who have reading difficulties are no different. They must also develop the basic foundations for reading and they also require the same type of learning experiences in order for that to happen. Most young children with reading difficulties have problems with development of fluency. The rate at which they read is slow, their word identification is hesitant, and they rely too much on contextual clues. Since most of their mental or cognitive effort is spent trying to identify words, their comprehension falters.

## Biologically related reading disability

A reading disorder is often presumed to be a dysfunction of the central nervous system, or a biological defect. But the actual role of biology is much more complex than such an assumption implies. Biological differences can play some role with reading disabilities and in learning to read as they do for a variety of cognitive abilities in humans. But little evidence exists that most children identified in school as reading disabled actually have a biologically-based problem. Evidence that factors such as genetics actually keep children from learning to read is also lacking. However, evidence does exist that labeling children as poor readers and assuming they have an intrinsic disorder caused by biology may create lower teacher expectations.

### Unexpected reading failure

Reading disorders have historically been looked at as unexpected or unexplained reading failures in contrast to failures from low intelligence, poor listening comprehension, poverty, or sensory impairment. Such a concept came about at a time when significantly less was known about the cognitive processes used in learning to read. It is now known that learning to read uses many different abilities and not all correlate to IQ. Someone may have serious problems with word decoding, yet still score high in IQ testing. Reading problems are not unexpected for children if there is monitoring of their cognitive abilities such as phonological awareness. The idea of unexpected failure is no longer useful in conceptualizing problems with reading.

### Symptoms of dyslexia

Typical symptoms of dyslexia include the terms "dysphonetic" and "dyseidetic." A person who is dysphonetic has problems connecting sounds to symbols and may have difficulty sounding out words. Spelling mistakes would show a very poor phonics understanding. This is also sometimes known as "auditory dyslexia" because of its relation to the way a person processes language sounds. On the other hand, a dyseidetic person usually understands phonics concepts but has great problems with word recognition and spelling. This is also known as "surface dyslexia" or "visual dyslexia." Words are usually spelled in a way that can easily be deciphered phonetically, but may be far from correct. One might also see transpositions and reversals in spelling, but the letters that correspond to the right sounds are there. Most remedial programs use phonics.

### Language disorders

- Stuttering is an interruption in the rhythm or flow of speech that is characterized by hesitations, repetitions, or prolongation of sounds, syllables, words, or phrases.
- Articulation disorders are difficulties with the way sounds are formed and put together. They are usually characterized by substituting one sound for another (wabbit for rabbit), omitting a sound (han for hand), or distorting sounds.
- Voice disorders are characterized by pitches that are inappropriate, such as being too high, too low, never changing or breaking, excessive or inadequate volume, or vocal qualities such as harsh, hoarse, nasal, or breathy.
- Aphasia is the loss of speech and language abilities as a result of a head injury or stroke.
- Delayed language is characterized by a marked slowness in grammar and vocabulary development that is needed to express and understand ideas and thoughts.

### Manifestations of dyslexia

Dyslexia involves a brain difference that is not a defect but does make it excessively hard to learn language. A child with dyslexia will have problems from the very beginning in learning to understand speech and being understood. The child might need to describe what he or she wants, might have trouble sequencing words, or may speak words in an incorrect order. A child may have problems positioning letters when he or she enters school. Dyslexia is difficult to recognize because many of its manifestations are part of the natural maturing process of young children. When children get stuck in these stages and it lasts for an abnormally long period, parents and teachers should recognize this as a possible problem. But a dyslexic mind may have exceptional ability for singing or playing a musical instrument at an early age.

### Traumatic brain injury

Traumatic brain injury may be of the following types:

1) Closed head injury, or bruising. This is common at the point of impact and on the opposite side of the brain. It is also common where the brain is adjacent to the rough and bony surfaces of the skull.
2) Shearing. This is commonly seen in the brain stem from severe head injury and is commonly in the frontal and temporal lobes where the brain surface rubs against bony skull ridges.
3) Hematoma, or bleeding. This occurs in areas that receive the brunt of the injury. These injuries are associated with specific deficits that are related to a particular brain area.
4) Frontal lobe damage. Deficits in regulating behavior including social and cognitive behavior.

### Results of traumatic brain injury

Traumatic brain injury causes the following results:

- Difficulty concentrating
- Weak orientation to task and difficulty in shifting from task to task
- Relatively slow performance
- Difficulty organizing tasks or information
- Difficulty with abstract thinking
- Difficulty thinking strategically
- Difficulty remembering new information or assignments
- Lower academic performance than before the injury
- Poor awareness of cognitive limitations
- Impulsive or inappropriate behavior in class
- Conflicts with teachers or peers
- Excessive moodiness
- Exaggerated responses to stress
- Excessive tiredness
- Depression and withdrawal
- Limited safety judgment
- Anxiety
- Anger and acting out
- Apathy
- Difficulty starting tasks without being prompted to do so

### Student assessment systems

Assessment system types include norm-referenced, criterion-referenced, and individual or alternative assessments. Criterion-referenced systems are those in which an individual's performance is compared to a certain learning objective of performance standard rather than the performance of other students. Norm-referenced systems are those in which student performance is compared to a "norm group," which may be a national sample that represents a diverse cross-section of students. These tests usually sort students and measure achievement based on some performance criterion. An individual assessment is one focusing on the individual student, such as a portfolio assessment. This is a portfolio of the student's classroom work. Alternative assessments are those requiring students to respond to a question rather than a set of responses.

### Wide-Range Achievement Test

The Wide-Range Achievement Test is one of a number of standardized achievement assessments to determine a child's cognitive ability. It is designed for individuals ages 5-75. It contains scoring for reading, spelling, and math. It provides up to 30 minutes for each of the three forms. The test uses a single-level format as well as alternative forms. These alternative forms may be used individually or with one another in order to provide a more qualitative assessment of academic skills. The reading subtest includes letter naming and word pronunciation out of context. The spelling subtest asks the student to write his or her own name, and then write words as they are directed. The mathematical portion includes counting, reading problems, number symbols, and written computation.

**Informal reading inventory**

The informal reading inventory is an individually administered survey that is designed to help determine a student's needs in reading. The student's performance on the informal reading inventory will help to determine the instructional level and the amount and type of support the student is likely to need. Specifically, using the informal reading inventory will help teachers assess a student's strengths and needs in the areas of word recognition, word meaning, reading strategies, and comprehension. While an informal reading inventory is a suitable tool for determining a student's reading ability and needs, it is not infallible. An educator should use information from the inventory along with other tests and information to make decisions about instructional plans.

**Student reading inventory**

To administer a student reading inventory certain materials would be needed such as a stop watch to time the student, a copy of all readings for both the student and the teacher, and comprehension questions for scoring purposes. Steps to be taken when administering the inventory include:

1. Explain to students that this is not a test. Tell them that this inventory is really to tell how the teacher can teach them better.
2. Set the timer.
3. Begin the timer as the student reads the first excerpt aloud.
4. Score errors on the teacher's copy.
5. Stop the timer when the student stops and record the total time. 6) Give the comprehension questions and record the answers.

**On-demand, direct writing assessment**

An on-demand writing assessment for a ninth-grader might embed stages of the writing process into defined time periods. Students write about events from their past. The prompt focuses on some aspect of the social or intellectual development of the students. The topic is meant to encourage ninth grade students to be reflective. An example topic might be when the student got into a new interest, or a book or TV show that had a particularly strong effect on what they did or thought. The assessment includes the task introduction, a short reading selection that serves as a model, some discussion questions, one or more planning suggestions, a prompt, and a checklist of revision and editing questions.

**Formative assessment**

A formative assessment is a diagnostic use of assessment to provide feedback to teachers and students over the course of instruction. That is in contrast to a summative assessment, which usually happens after a period of instruction and requires making judgments about the learning that has occurred, such as with a test score or paper. Assessments in general include teacher observation, classroom instruction, or an analysis of student work, including homework and tests. Assessments are formative when the information is used to adapt teaching and learning to meet the needs of the students. When teachers know how students are progressing and where they are having difficulties, they can use this information to make needed instructional adjustments, such as reteaching, alternative instruction approaches, or offering more practice opportunities.

The goal of formative assessment is to gain an understanding of what students know or don't know in order to make responsive changes in teaching and learning. So techniques such as teacher observation and classroom discussion have an important place along with analyzing tests and homework. Questioning and classroom discussion is a good way to increase the students' knowledge and improve understanding. The teacher does need to make sure to ask thoughtful, reflective questions instead of simple factual ones and give students sufficient time to respond. Students might be invited to discuss their thinking about a question in small groups. Several possible answers could be provided and students allowed to vote on them. Or students could be asked to write down an answer, with the teacher then reading a selected few out loud.

**Rubric**

A rubric is a set of assessment criteria that specifies characteristics, knowledge, and competencies that indicate a student's level of achievement. It is basically a list of characteristics that are used to assess a learning product's quality. Rubrics identify traits and components that indicate the extent to which a learning outcome has been achieved. Rubrics are often used to attach authentic meaning to both letter and number grades. Rubrics also offer advantages such as:

- Rubrics allow students to document the grade they earned rather than the grade given or assigned.
- Tests and research papers may not offer a valid reflection of learning outcomes while rubrics are tied to learning outcomes.
- Grades alone offer limited reflections of a student's learning.

**Informal assessment**

Although there are no uniformly accepted definitions for formal and informal assessments, informal can mean techniques that are easily put into classroom routines, and learning activities to measure a student's learning outcome. Informal assessment can be used without interfering with instructional time. The results can be an indicator of the skills or subjects that interest a student, but they do not provide comparison to a broader group like standardized tests. Informal tests require clear understanding of the levels of a student's abilities. Informal assessments seek identification of a student's strengths and weaknesses without a regard to norms or grades. Such assessments may be done in structured or unstructured manners. Structured ones include checklists or observations. Unstructured assessments are those such as student work samples or journals.

**Questioning techniques**

Key questions should be planned to give direction and structure to the lesson. Spontaneous questions that come up are fine, but the overall direction of the discussion should have been mostly planned. Here are some simple guidelines to asking questions that will help teacher's questioning skills:

- Be sure the question is clear. Think about what it is required from the student before asking the question.
- Frame the question without calling on a particular student. Other students are free to ignore the question when a student is called upon before the question is asked.
- After framing the question, pause to give the students a chance to think of an answer before calling on a student to respond. This pause, called wait time, is an important questioning skill. The wait time between a question and asking for response should be 2-4 seconds.

**Use of performance assessments**

Performance assessments can be used to document and evaluate the work done by students during a fixed time period. These assessments tend to take the form of lengthy, multidisciplinary problem-solving activities. Teaching and learning with performance assessments should be documented and assessed with tools based on performance of real tasks. Students should have the opportunity to exhibit their expertise before family and community. Performance assessments may be short-answer or extended response. They include oral questions, traditional quizzes, open-ended prompts, and tests.

**Authentic assessment**

Authentic assessment asks students to apply their skills and knowledge the same way that they would be used in real-world situations. It is a performance-based assessment that requires each student to exhibit his or her in-depth knowledge and understanding through a mastery demonstration. It is an assessment of authentic learning, which is the type of learning in which activities and materials are framed in real-life contexts. The underlying assumption of such an approach is that the material is meaningful to students, and thus more motivating and deeply processed. Some of the terms or concepts that are related to authentic learning include contextual learning and theme-based curriculum.

**Multiple assessment methods**

Multiple assessment methods give a comprehensive view of how well students are achieving the learning outcomes that a program identifies. A quantitative assessment lets educators provide numerical evidence of student learning, while qualitative measures show descriptive evidence of what the student has learned. Selection of the appropriate assessment method is dependent upon the desired outcomes of student learning. For instance, if students completing a program should have knowledge of the discipline, the knowledge would be best measured by a carefully constructed quantitative assessment. But if students are expected to use multiple perspectives when solving a problem, the evidence might be better provided in some written form, and examined in a qualitative manner by using scoring rubrics.

**Constructed-response tests**

Constructed-response tests are a type of non-multiple choice exam that requires some type of written or oral response. Selected-response tests consist of questions to be answered from a predetermined list of answers, with formats that include multiple choice, true/false, matching, or fill in the blanks. Each type of test has its benefits. Selected-response formats allow more questions to be asked in shorter time periods. Scoring is faster and it is easy to create comparable test forms. Since selected-response tests can normally be answered quickly, more items that covers several content areas can be administered in a short period of time. They can also be machine-scorable tests that allow quicker and more objective scoring. Constructed-response tests have the potential for gathering deeper information about a student's knowledge and understanding of a content area. Constructed-response items are more time consuming and allow fewer items to be covered.

**Portfolio assessments**

A portfolio can be thought of as a scrapbook or photo album that records the progress and activities of the program and those who participate in it. It showcases them to interested parties both inside and outside of the program. Portfolios can be used to examine and measure progress by documenting the learning as it takes place. They extend beyond test scores to include a substantive picture of what a student is doing and experiencing. Portfolios are useful in documenting progress in higher-order goals such as applying skills and synthesizing experience beyond what standardized or norm-based tests can do. The portfolio contents are sometimes known as "evidence" or "artifacts." They can include drawings, writing, photos, video, audio tapes, computer discs, and copies of program-specific or standardized tests.

### Using portfolio assessment s

Portfolio assessment is best used for the following:

- Evaluating programs with flexible or individualized outcomes or goals.
- Allowing individuals and programs in the community to be involved in their own change and decisions to change.
- Giving information that provides a meaningful insight into behavioral change.
- Providing tools to ensure communications and accountability to a wide range of audiences. These participants, such as families or community members, may not be sophisticated in interpreting statistical data and can better appreciate more visual or experiential evidence of success being achieved.
- Assessing some of the more important and complex aspects of many constructs.

### Advantages of portfolio assessments

The advantages of using portfolio assessments include:

- Allows evaluators to see the student or group individually, with unique characteristics, needs, and strengths.
- Provides for future analysis and planning by showing a total pattern of an individual's strengths, weaknesses, or barriers to success.
- Serves as a concrete communication vehicle and provides ongoing communication or information exchange for those involved.
- Promotes ownership. Participants and groups can take an active role in where they have been and where they would like to go.
- Offers the possibility of addressing the limitations of traditional assessments. It offers the possibility of assessing more complex and important facets of a topic or area.
- Covers a broad scope of information and knowledge, from different people who know the program or person in different contexts.

### Process and product portfolios

Many portfolio assessments exist, but most fall into two types: process and product portfolios. Process portfolios document growth over time toward a goal. This documentation includes statements of end goals, criteria, and future plans. Also included should be baseline information or items used to describe a participant's performance or mastery at the beginning of the program. Other items may be selected at different interim points to demonstrate the steps toward mastery. Product portfolios include examples of the best efforts of a group or participant. These include final evidence, or items which demonstrate that end goals are achieved. They can encourage reflection about learning or change. They can help to show a sense of strength and ownership and to showcase or communicate a person's accomplishments.

### Characteristics of developing portfolios

Portfolios used for assessment have certain essential characteristics including:

- Having multiple data sources including both people and artifacts. People can be teachers, participants, or community members. Artifacts can be test scores, drawings, writings, videotapes, or audiotapes.
- Having authentic evidence that is related to program activities.
- Being dynamic and capturing change and growth. Portfolios should include different stages of mastery which will

allow a much deeper understanding of the change process.
- Being explicit in that participants should know what is expected of them.
- Being integrated, meaning having the evidence to establish a connection between program activities and life experiences.
- Being based on ownership, or having the participant help to determine what evidence to include to show that the goals are being met.
- Being multipurposed, or allowing for assessment of the effectiveness of the program while also assessing the performance of the participant.

**Miscue analysis**

A miscue analysis is an assessment in which a child reads a story aloud and the teacher checks for errors in the recognition and comprehension of words. Such an analysis might be performed in the following manner:

- The teacher instructs the student that they will read a passage aloud without the teacher's help.
- A videotape or audiotape should be made for analysis after the session.
- After reading the teacher marks all miscues, including insertions, mispronunciations, omissions, and corrections by the student.
- The teacher records the miscues by writing what the text said in one column and what the reader said in another.
- The miscues are analyzed using criteria, including whether the miscue went with the preceding context and whether it was corrected.
- Percentages are calculated based on the total number of miscues.

**Self-evaluations**

Self-evaluations let students synthesize their past work over a given time period and do reflective writing. Self-evaluations are occasions for reflection and feedback. The goal is not right or wrong answers but thoughtful, tentative responses to questions. There are different types of self-evaluations, including those which ask students to look back and assess their own work, those which ask students to make connections over the entire term, and those which ask students to look ahead to future tasks. Self-evaluations can be a series of final entries in their journals as well as short or more extensive assignments that are both in and out of class.

**Samples of student work for assessment**

Teachers can construct an assessment rubric by collecting a range of student work samples that all respond to the same skill and performance assessment. The teacher begins constructing the rubric by collecting a small range of work samples that do not necessarily respond to the same performance and skill assessment. The teacher then decides the assessment criteria for the rubric. The teacher will then group together related words or phrases to define each stack of work samples. The teacher clearly defines the terms and goals of the assessment in the rubric. The students are actively involved in developing the assessment measurements for the rubric with the teacher. The teacher makes known the expectations for the rubric. The teacher considers the forms of assessment used to evaluate student work.

**Journals and reflective thought**

Journals let students write an ongoing record of thoughts, ideas, experiences, and reflections on a given topic. They go beyond the demands of usual written assignments as they promote integration of personal thoughts and expression with materials for a class. Journals provide a systematic means of collecting evidence and documenting learning for self-evaluation and reflections. Journals can be structured or free-form. Structured journals are when students are given specific questions, a set of guidelines, or a target on which to base their writing. Free-form lets students record thoughts and feelings with little direction. Whatever the form, journals are valuable in assessing a student's ability to observe, challenge, doubt, question, explore, and solve problems.

### Journals in assessments

Using journals for assessments require setting certain guidelines. Such guidelines that are helpful include:

- Designing journals to reflect specific learning objectives or goals of the course.
- Providing adequate instructions to students so they are aware of expectations. To promote effective writing, students should be given specific exercises or guiding questions.
- Explicitly discussing policies about privacy and confidentiality of the information. If journals are to be read or shared with others this should be highlighted. A teacher must disclose and report information that indicates a potential danger or harm.
- Periodically reviewing journals and providing feedback. Feedback would include constructive remarks, suggestions, questions, or encouragement.

### Types of journals

Journals can take on many forms. This all depends on the course, class objectives, topic, and instructor. The following are ideas that might stimulate instructors in developing their journal assignments based on class needs:

- Observational journal. An observational journal is used to increase a student's awareness of the relationship between events in the real world and class material. A teacher might want to assign students a specific location for a certain amount of time and have them record their observations.
- Personal experience journal. A personal experience journal lets students reflect upon their experiences in the context of a specific theory or idea. These journals promote active critical processing of course material and active encoding.
- Reading journal. A reading journal is to encourage reading assignment processing. The journals may target relationships between what students read and what they experience.

Journals for classes may take on many different forms. Some types of journals that might help stimulate a teacher's own journal assignment include:

- Minute reflection journal. These journals can be used in class to promote critical thinking that is related to particular presentations, activities, or discussions. Teachers may pose questions, then require students to take two or three minutes and record initial thoughts and reactions.
- Listening journals. These journals reflect on a presentation to clarify misconceptions or confusion. Listening journals are best suited for more difficult subjects. After information is presented, the teacher requires the student to paraphrase and explain what they heard. This can be used to monitor understanding and to clarify any confusion over concepts.
- Expansion journals. These are used to encourage a deep analysis of a particular concept or topic. After instruction, students select a single topic and expand on the information.

There are different forms of journals for classes. Here are some that might give teachers ideas for their class use:

- Daily reflection journals. These are used to encourage expression of thoughts, insights, and ideas in writing on a habitual basis. These can include emotional and personal thoughts. This can enhance personal insight as well as showing a grasp of writing strategies.
- Learning log journal. These journals promote reflection on the learning process and aid in self-assessment of strengths and weaknesses.
- Exchange journal. These journals are used in interactions between two or more peers, utilizing questions and answers.
- Academic journals. These are curriculum-oriented writings that promote reflection on material, both before and after instruction. These journals can help teachers focus on issues relevant to student concerns.

## Test validity and reliability

A test is valid when it measures what it is supposed to measure. The validity of a test depends on the purpose for which it is to be used. For instance, a thermometer might measure temperature, but it cannot measure barometric pressure. A test is reliable when it yields results that are consistent. A test may be reliable and valid, valid and unreliable, reliable and invalid, or neither valid nor reliable. A test must be reliable for it to measure validity and the validity of a test is constrained by its reliability. If a test does not consistently measure a construct or domain, then it may not be expected to have a high degree of validity.

## Types of test validity

Types of test validity include:

- Face validity. This asks the question: Does the test measure what should be measured?
- Content validity. This asks: Is the full content of the concept being defined included in the measure? It must include a broad sample of what is tested, emphasize material that is important and, require skills that are appropriate.
- Criterion validity. This asks: Is the measure consistent with what is already known and expected? There are two subcategories, which are predictive and concurrent.
- Predictive validity predicts a known association between the construct being measured and something else.
- Concurrent validity is associated with indicators that pre-exist or with something that already measures the same concept.
- Construct validity. This shows the measure that relates to a number of other measures that are specified.
- Discriminant validity. This type does not associate with unrelated constructs.

## Terms regarding consistency

Tests are reliable if they yield consistent results. The types of reliability include:

- Inter-observer. This requires consistent results among testers who are rating the same information.
- Test-retest. This requires the same results from testing at two different times with no treatment in between.
- Parallel-forms. This requires that two tests with different forms, supposedly testing the same material, yield the same results.
- Split-half reliability. This requires that items which are divided in half, such as odd versus even questions, provide the same results. For all forms of reliability, a quantitative measurement of reliability can be used.

**Threats to test internal validity**

Factors affecting how valid a test is by itself include:

- History. Outside events that happen during the course of what is being studied may influence the results. It does not make the test less accurate.
- Maturation. Change due to aging or development between or within groups may affect validity.
- Instrumentation. The reliability is questioned because of a calibration change in a measuring device or changes in human ability to measure difference, such as fatigue or experience.
- Testing. Test-taking experience affects results. This refers to either physical or mental changes, such as changes in the attitude or physiological response of a participant after repeated measures.
- Statistical regression. This is the tendency to regress towards the mean, making some scores higher or lower.

If a measure is not reliable, some variation will occur between repeated measures.

**Additional threats totest internal validity**

A test may have the following threats to its internal validity:

- Selection. Participants in a group may be alike in certain ways, but will respond differently to the independent variable.
- Mortality. Participants drop out of a test, making the group unequal. Who drops out and why can be a factor.
- Interaction. Two or more threats can interact, such as selection-maturation when there is a difference between age groups causing groups to change at different ages.
- Contamination. This is when a comparison group in some way impacts another group, causing an increase of efforts. This is also called "compensatory rivalry."

**Test reliability**

Views in recent decades on test reliability include:

- Temporal stability. This refers to implementing the same form of testing on two or more separate occasions to the same group of students. This is not practical as repeated measurements are likely to result in higher scores on later tests after students become familiar with the format.
- Form equivalence. This is relative to two different test forms based on the same content, administered once to the same group of students.
- Internal consistency. This relates to the coefficient of test scores obtained from a single test. When no pattern is found in the student responses, the test is probably too difficult and the students resorted to randomly guessing at the answers.
- Reliability is a necessary but insufficient condition for a test to be valid. The test might reflect consistent measurement but it may not be especially valid.

**Additional views of test validity**

Some conventional views on test validity in recent years include:

- Face validity. This means that a test is valid at face value. As a check on face validity, psychometricians traditionally sent test items to teachers for modification. This was abandoned for a long time because of its vagueness and subjectivity. But face validity returned in the 1990s in another form, with validity defined as making common sense, being persuasive, and appearing right to the reader.

- Content validity. This draws inferences from test scores to a large domain of items that are similar to those on a test. The concern with content validity is a sample-population representation, meaning that the knowledge and skills covered by the test should be representative of the larger knowledge and skill domain.

## Regression analysis

Regression analysis can be used to establish validity of the criteria of a test. An independent variable may be used as a predictor of the dependent variable, which is the criterion variable. The correlation coefficient between them is known as the validity coefficient. For instance, test scores are the criterion variable. It is hypothesized that if the student passes the test, he or she would meet the criteria of knowing all the specific subject matter. Criterion validity values prediction over explanation. Prediction is concerned with mathematical or non-casual dependence, whereas explanation pertains to casual or logical dependence. For instance, one can predict the weather based on the mercury height in a thermometer. The mercury could satisfy the criterion validity as a predictor. Yet one cannot say why the weather changes because of the mercury's height.

## Sources of test invalidity

Two particular threats to test validity are known as "construct underrepresentation" and "construct-irrelevant variance." The first term indicates that the task being measured in the assessment fails to include important discussions or facets of the construct. So the test results will indicate a student's abilities within only a portion of the construct intended to be measured by the test. The second term means that a test measures too many variables. Many of these variables are irrelevant to the interpreted construct. This can take two forms. "Construct-irrelevant easiness" occurs when outside clues in format permit some individuals to respond correctly or appropriately in ways which are irrelevant to the assessed construct. "Construct-irrelevant difficulty" occurs when outside aspects make it more difficult for individuals to respond correctly.

## Assessing student reading strengths

A number of tests are available on the Internet for assessing comprehension levels, as well as paper and pencil charts for assessing fluency orally. Likewise, there are tests that determine the understanding of affixes, prefixes, suffixes, compounds, and contractions to name a few. The biggest problem is deciding which test to use in obtaining a snapshot of the child's ability to read and comprehend. The reading specialist and classroom teacher can work together to administer these tests and develop a plan of action to help at-risk students. These tests may be formal or standardized. They may either be norm-referenced or criterion-referenced. Good classroom teachers and reading specialists will blend the results of these tests to come up with an instructional model for the student.

## Communicating reading evaluation with parents

Parents of children who have been assessed as having problems with reading should be told the various steps that are necessary for an accurate and fair determination. The first step is using what is already known. A group of people, most often the reading specialist and teacher, evaluates the child with information that is already available. If more information is needed, the second step is collecting more information. The school will ask the parent for permission to evaluate the child. The school then collects more information. The third step is deciding whether the child is eligible for special education or related services. Those who are doing the evaluation then come to the parents